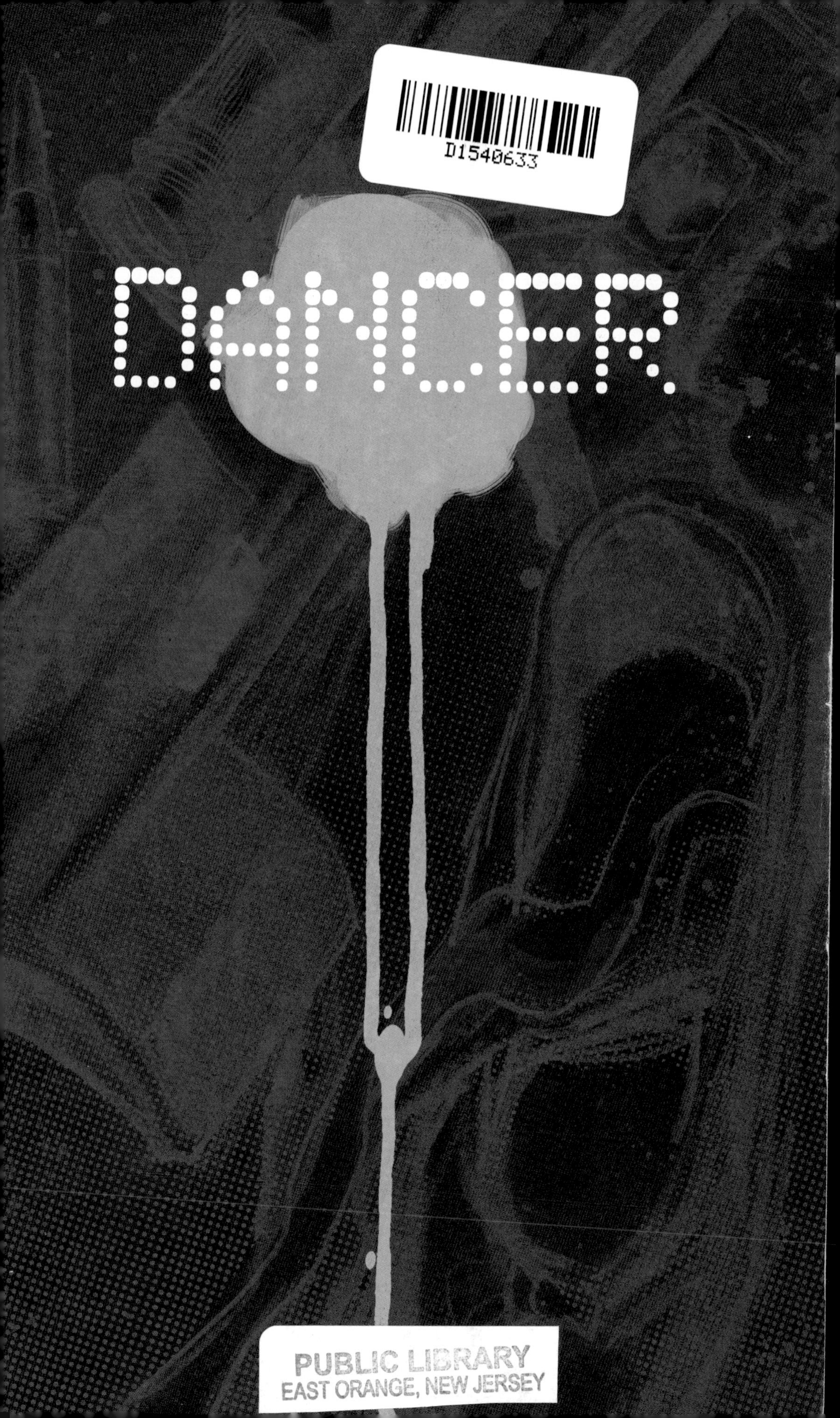
DANCER.

Y
DAN

$16.99
10|3|13
MJ

IMAGE COMICS, INC.

Robert Kirkman - chief operating officer
Erik Larsen - chief financial officer
Todd McFarlane - president
Marc Silvestri - chief executive officer
Jim Valentino - vice-president

Eric Stephenson - publisher
Todd Martinez - sales & licensing coordinator
Jennifer de Guzman - pr & marketing director
Branwyn Bigglestone - accounts manager
Emily Miller - administrative assistant
Jamie Parreno - marketing assistant
Sarah deLaine - events coordinator
Kevin Yuen - digital rights coordinator
Jonathan Chan - production manager
Drew Gill - art director
Monica Garcia - production artist
Vincent Kukua - production artist
Jana Cook - production artist

www.imagecomics.com

DANCER Trade Paperback
ISBN: 978-1-60706-627-9
First Printing

i13953977

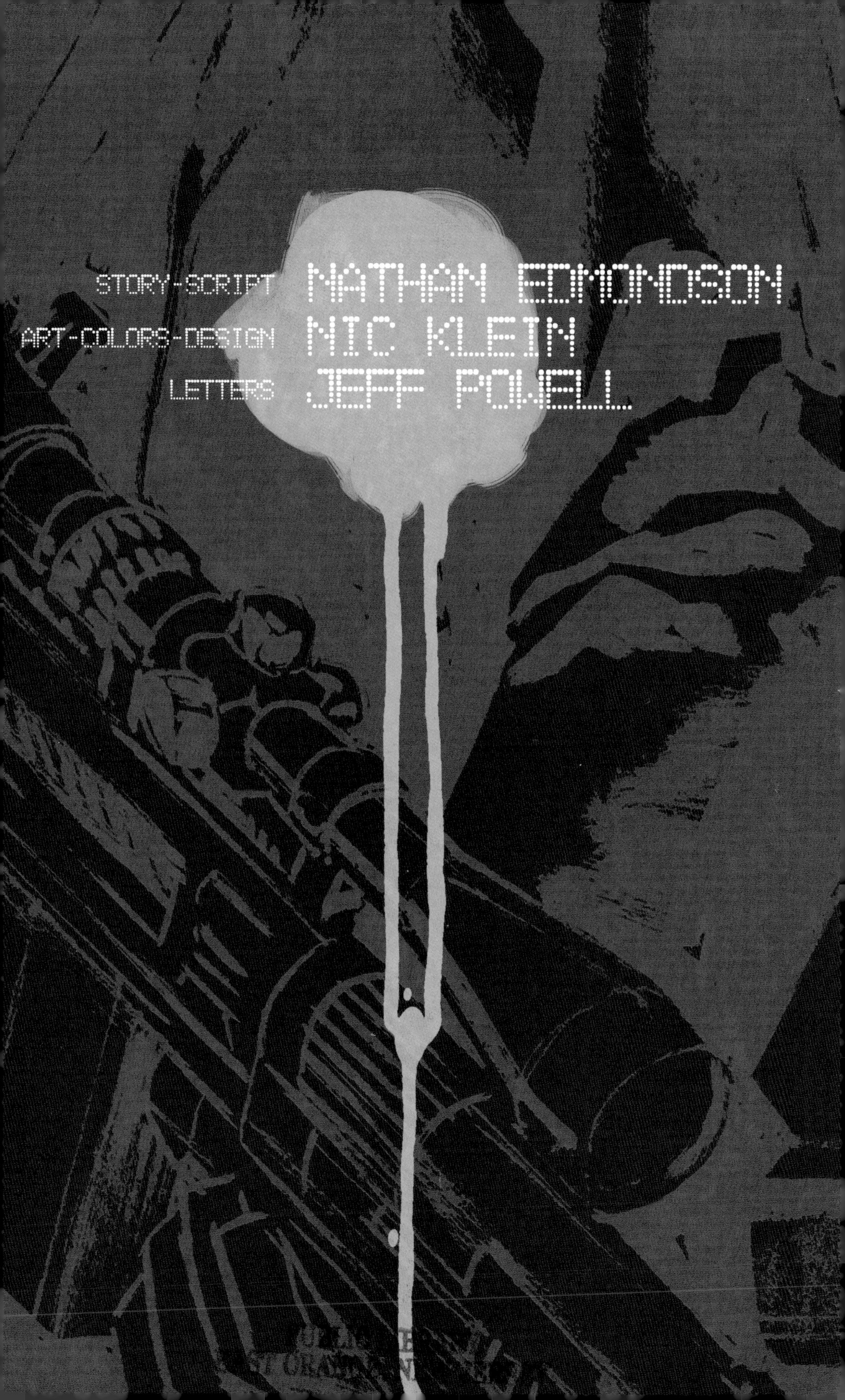

STORY-SCRIPT NATHAN EDMONDSON
ART-COLORS-DESIGN NIC KLEIN
LETTERS JEFF POWELL

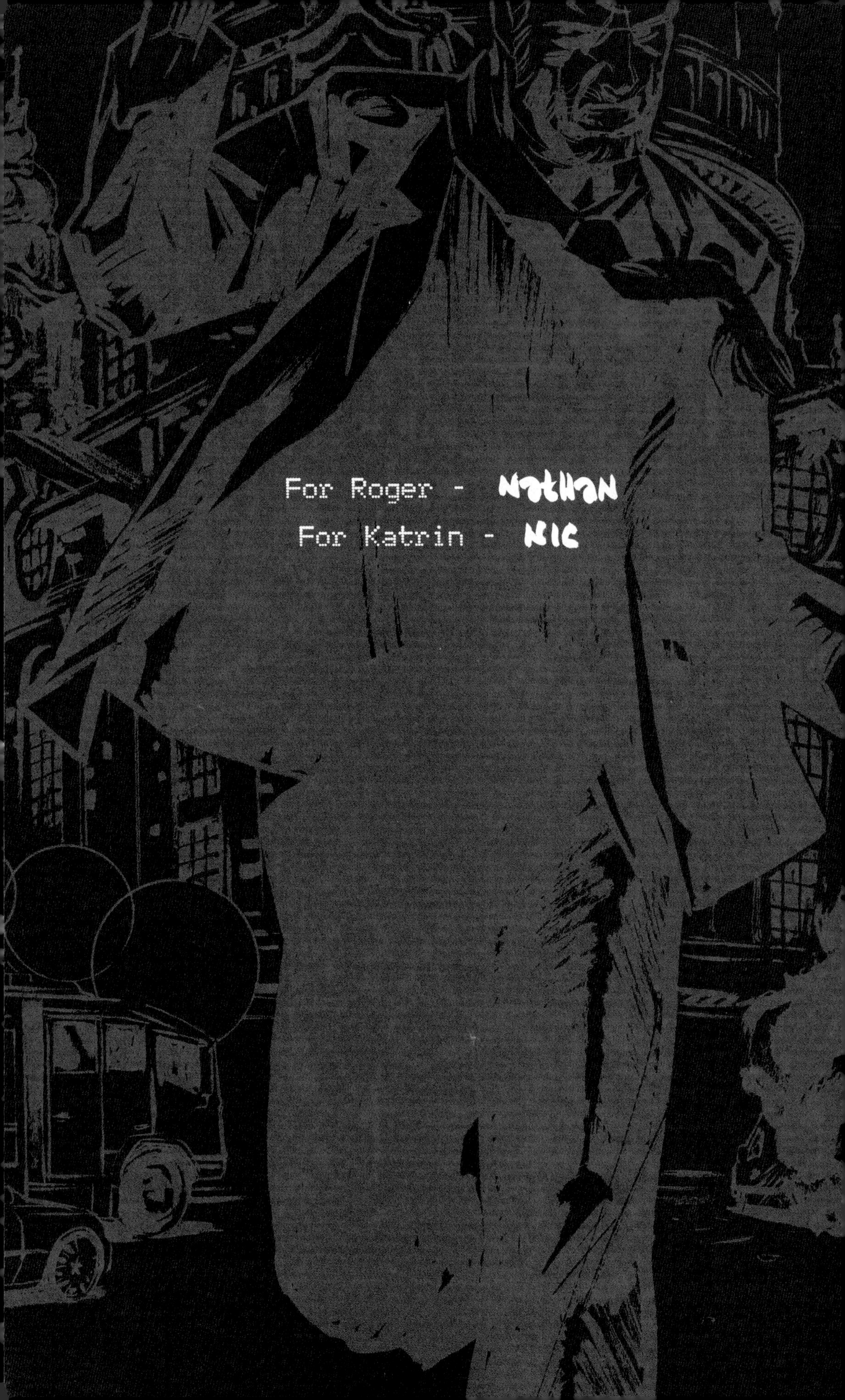

For Roger - Nathan

For Katrin - Nic

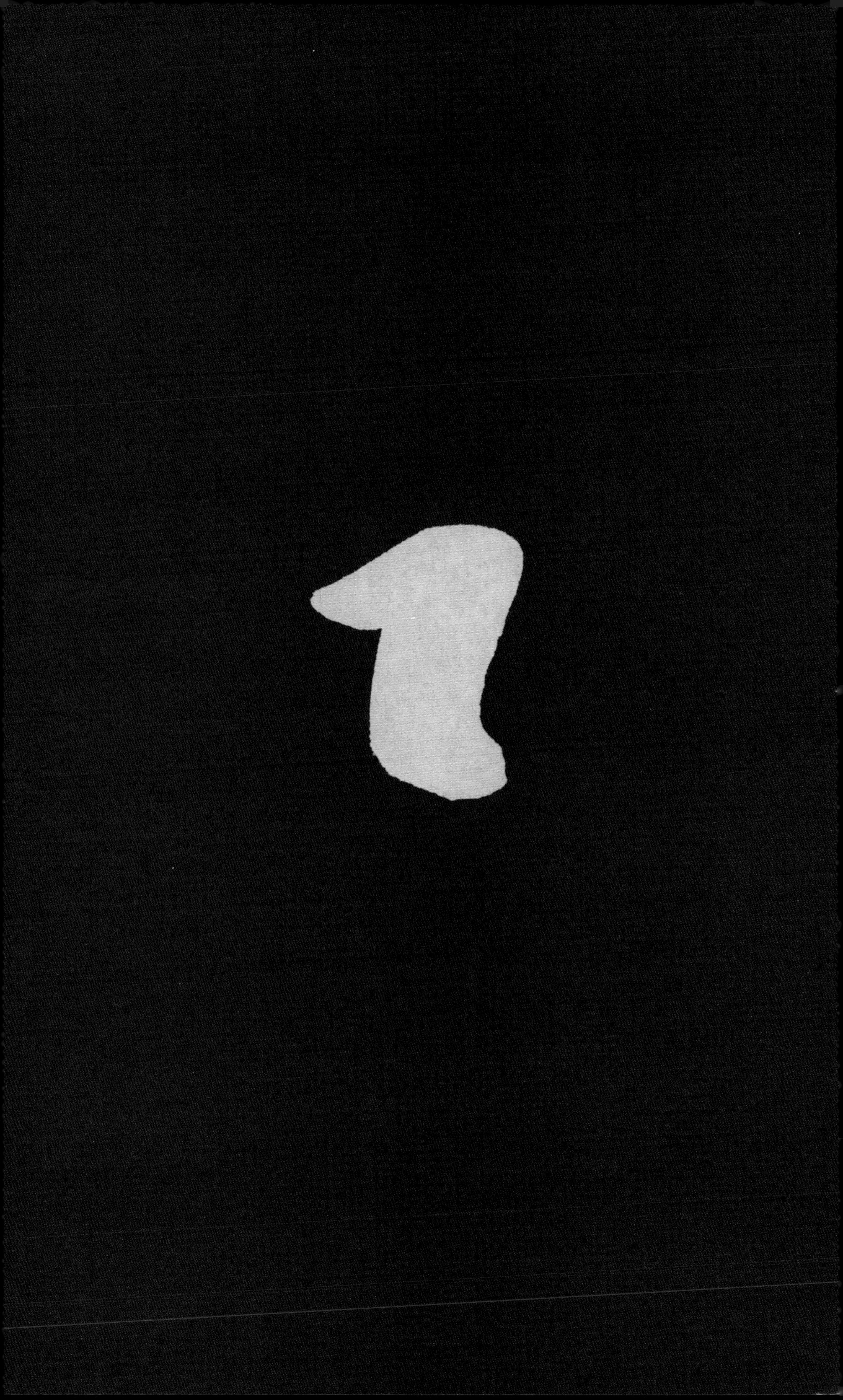

OUVERTURE

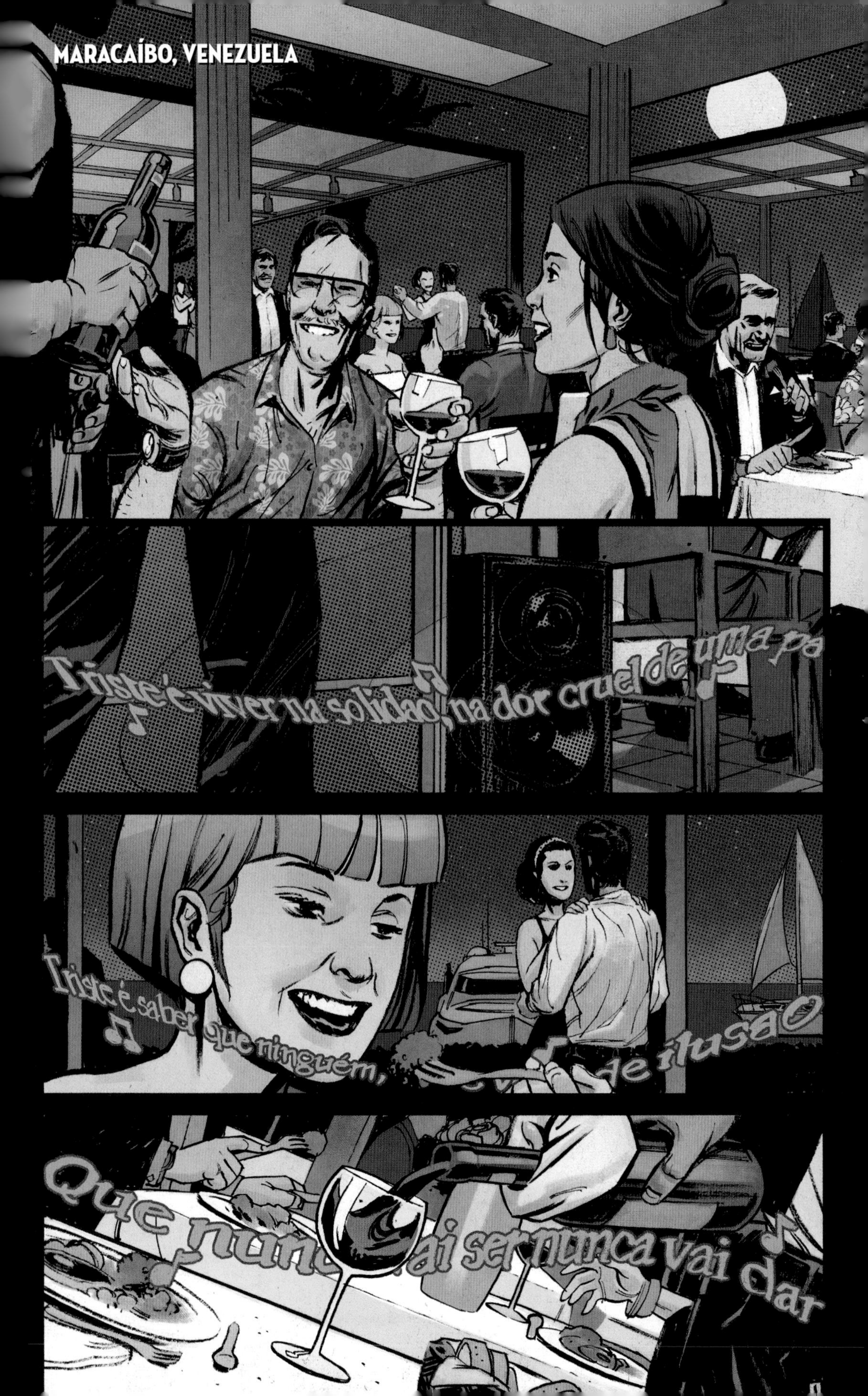
MARACAÍBO, VENEZUELA
Triste é viver na solidão, na dor cruel de uma pa
Triste é saber que ninguém, de ilusão
Que nunc ai ser nunca vai dar

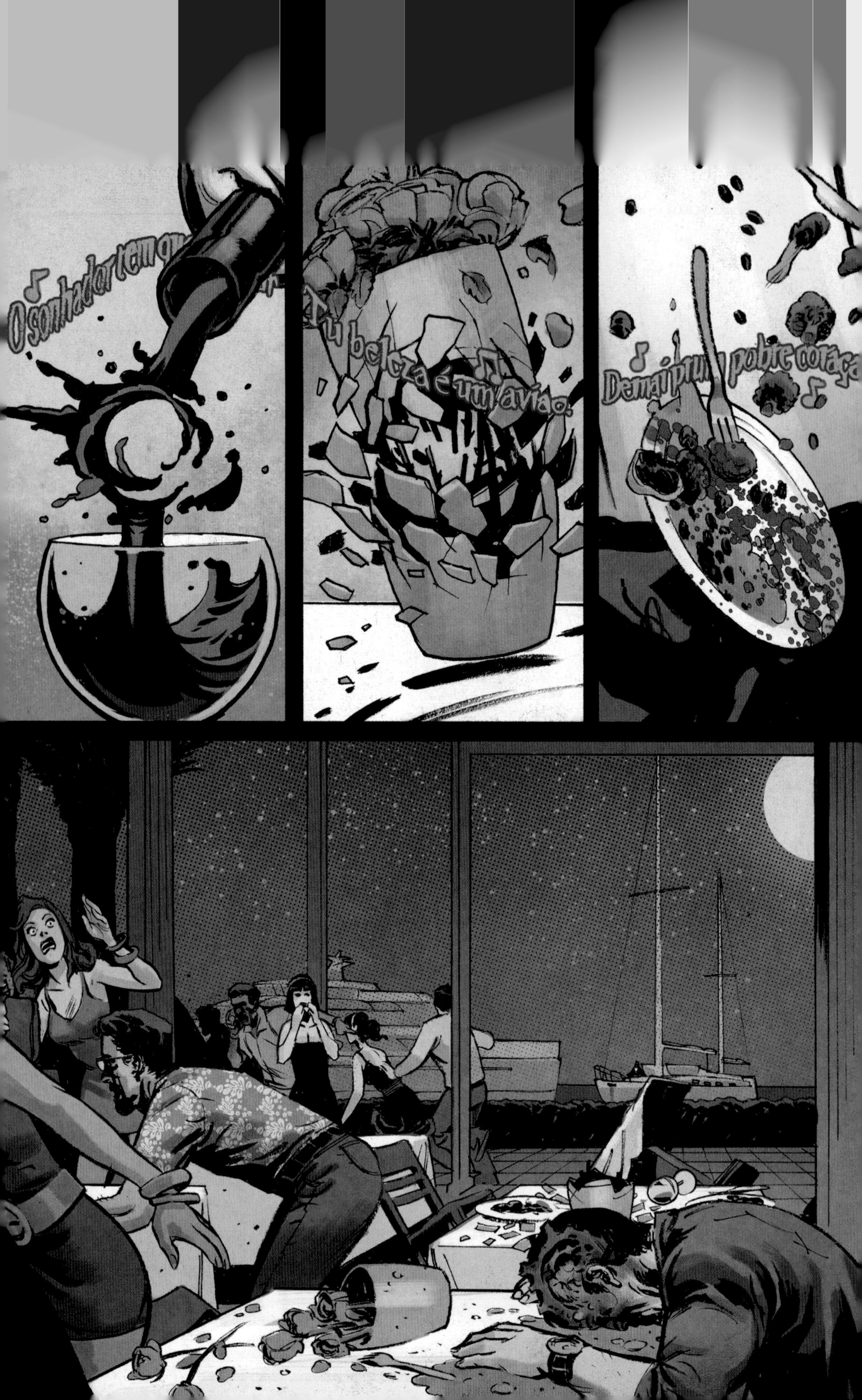
♪ O sonhador tem qu
Tu beleza é um avião. ♫
♪ Demai pr pobre coraçã ♪

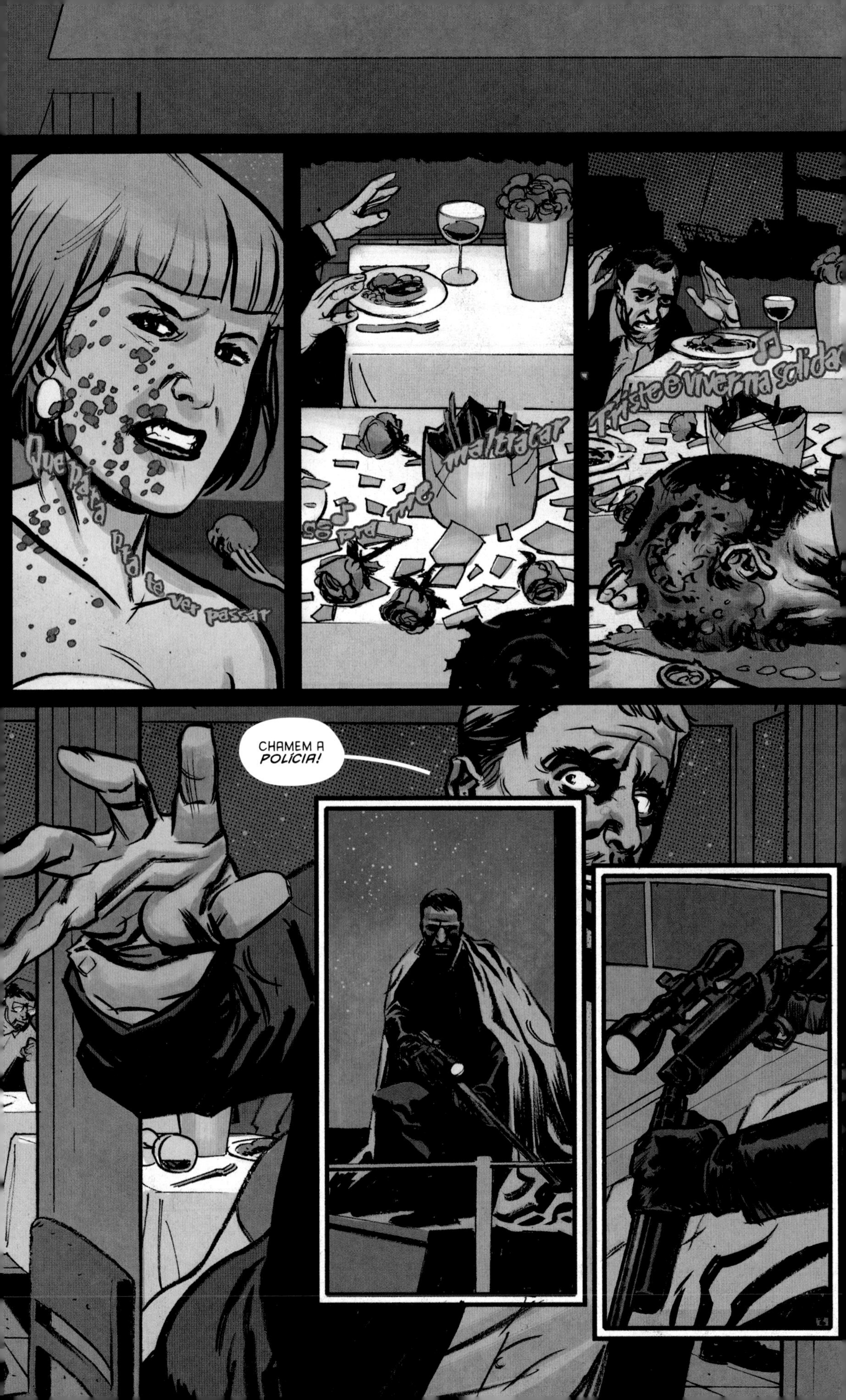
Que pára pra te ver passar
só pra me maltratar
Triste é viver na solida
CHAMEM A *POLÍCIA!*

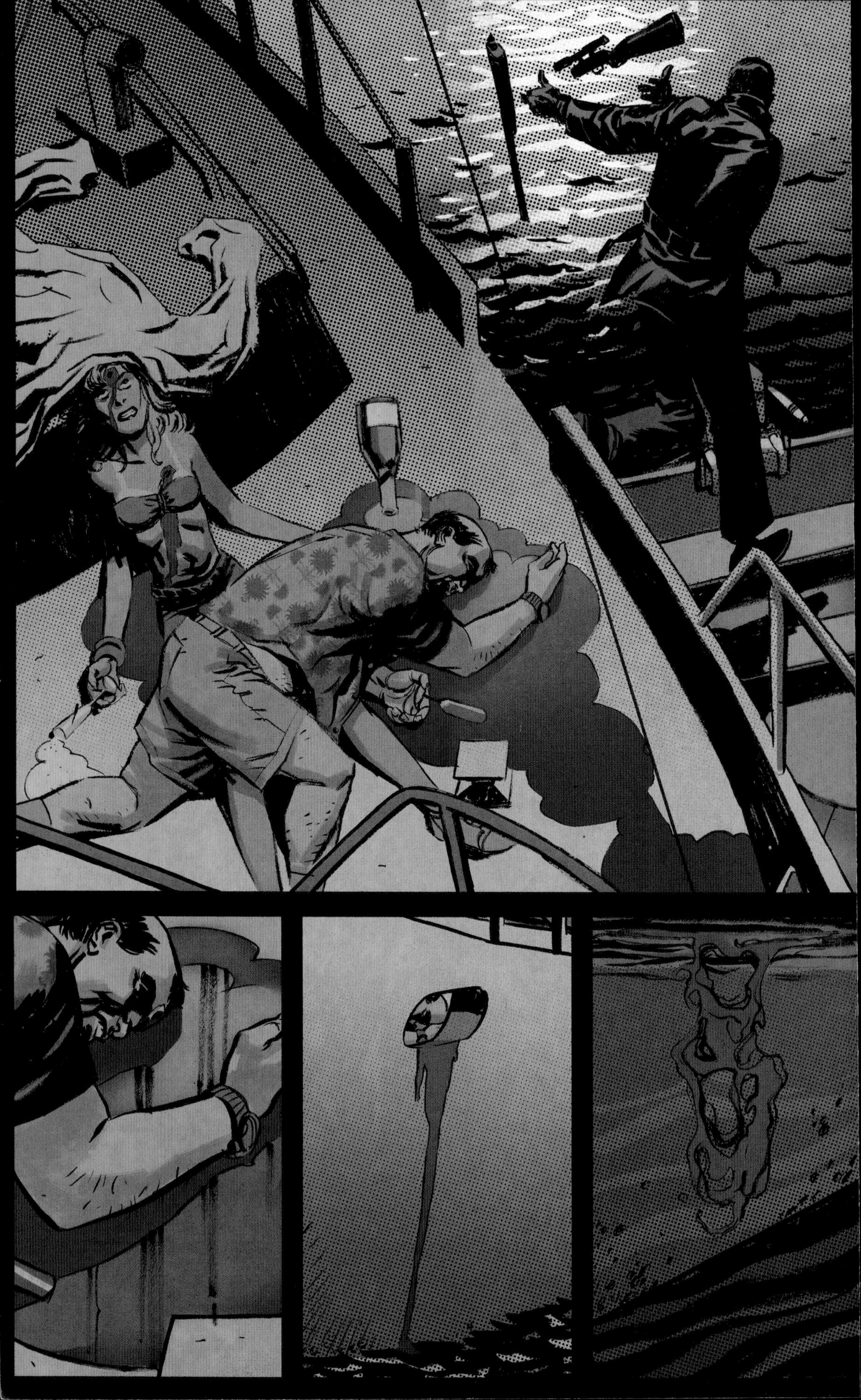

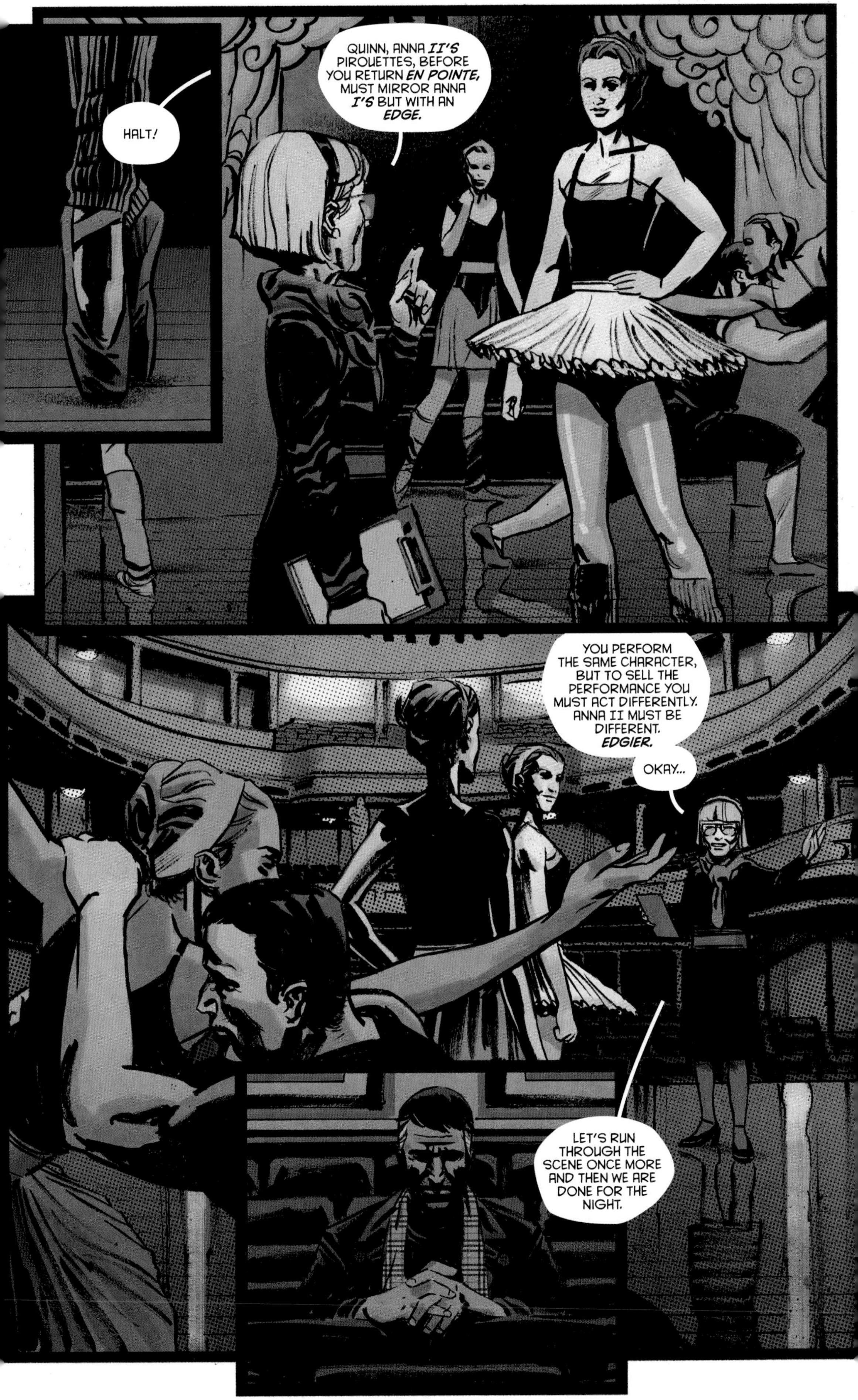
HALT!
QUINN, ANNA *II'S* PIROUETTES, BEFORE YOU RETURN *EN POINTE*, MUST MIRROR ANNA *I'S* BUT WITH AN *EDGE.*
YOU PERFORM THE SAME CHARACTER, BUT TO SELL THE PERFORMANCE YOU MUST ACT DIFFERENTLY. ANNA II MUST BE DIFFERENT. *EDGIER.*
OKAY...
LET'S RUN THROUGH THE SCENE ONCE MORE AND THEN WE ARE DONE FOR THE NIGHT.

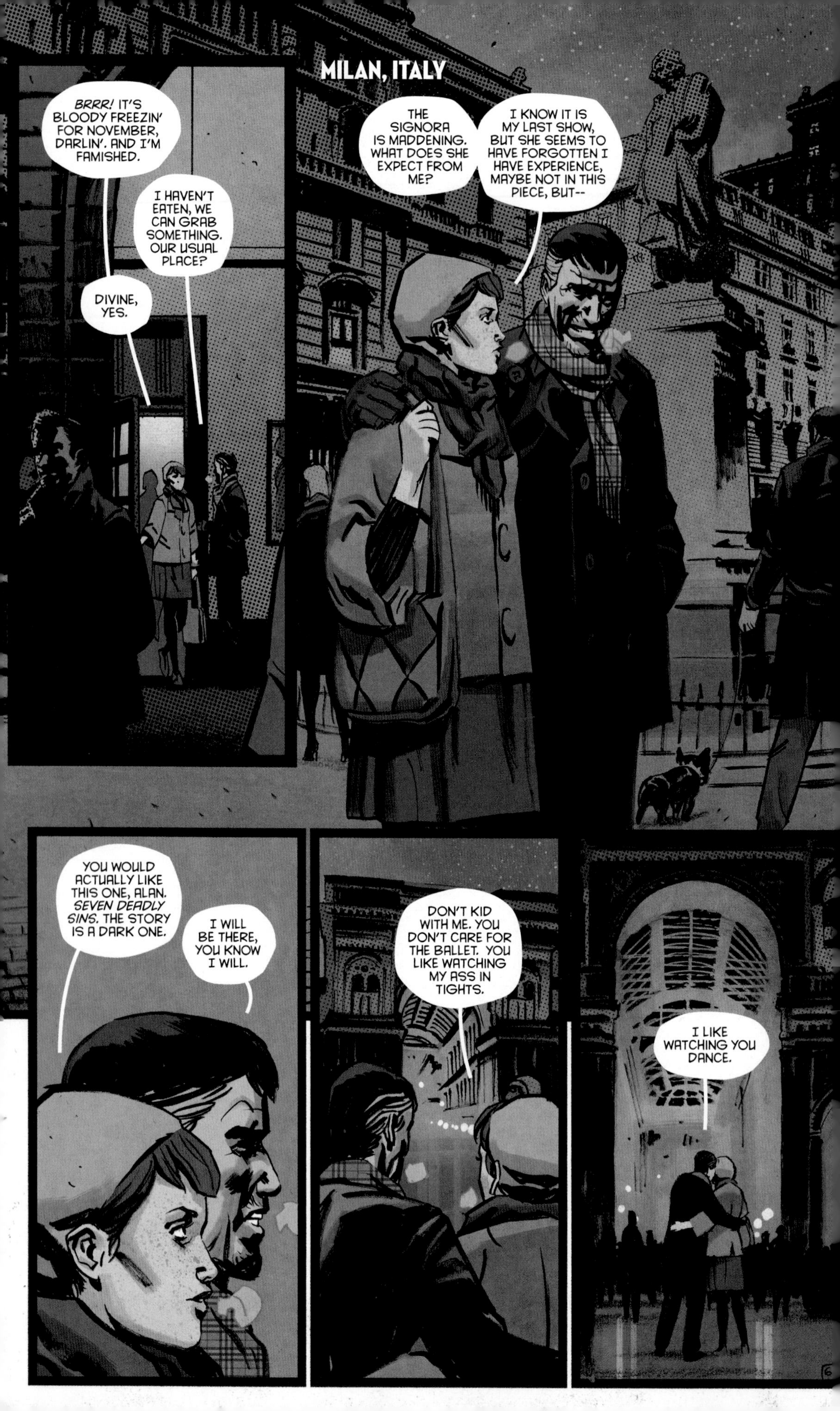
MILAN, ITALY
BRRR! IT'S BLOODY FREEZIN' FOR NOVEMBER, DARLIN'. AND I'M FAMISHED.
I HAVEN'T EATEN, WE CAN GRAB SOMETHING. OUR USUAL PLACE?
DIVINE, YES.
THE SIGNORA IS MADDENING. WHAT DOES SHE EXPECT FROM ME?
I KNOW IT IS MY LAST SHOW, BUT SHE SEEMS TO HAVE FORGOTTEN I HAVE EXPERIENCE, MAYBE NOT IN THIS PIECE, BUT--
YOU WOULD ACTUALLY LIKE THIS ONE, ALAN. SEVEN DEADLY SINS. THE STORY IS A DARK ONE.
I WILL BE THERE, YOU KNOW I WILL.
DON'T KID WITH ME. YOU DON'T CARE FOR THE BALLET. YOU LIKE WATCHING MY ASS IN TIGHTS.
I LIKE WATCHING YOU DANCE.
6

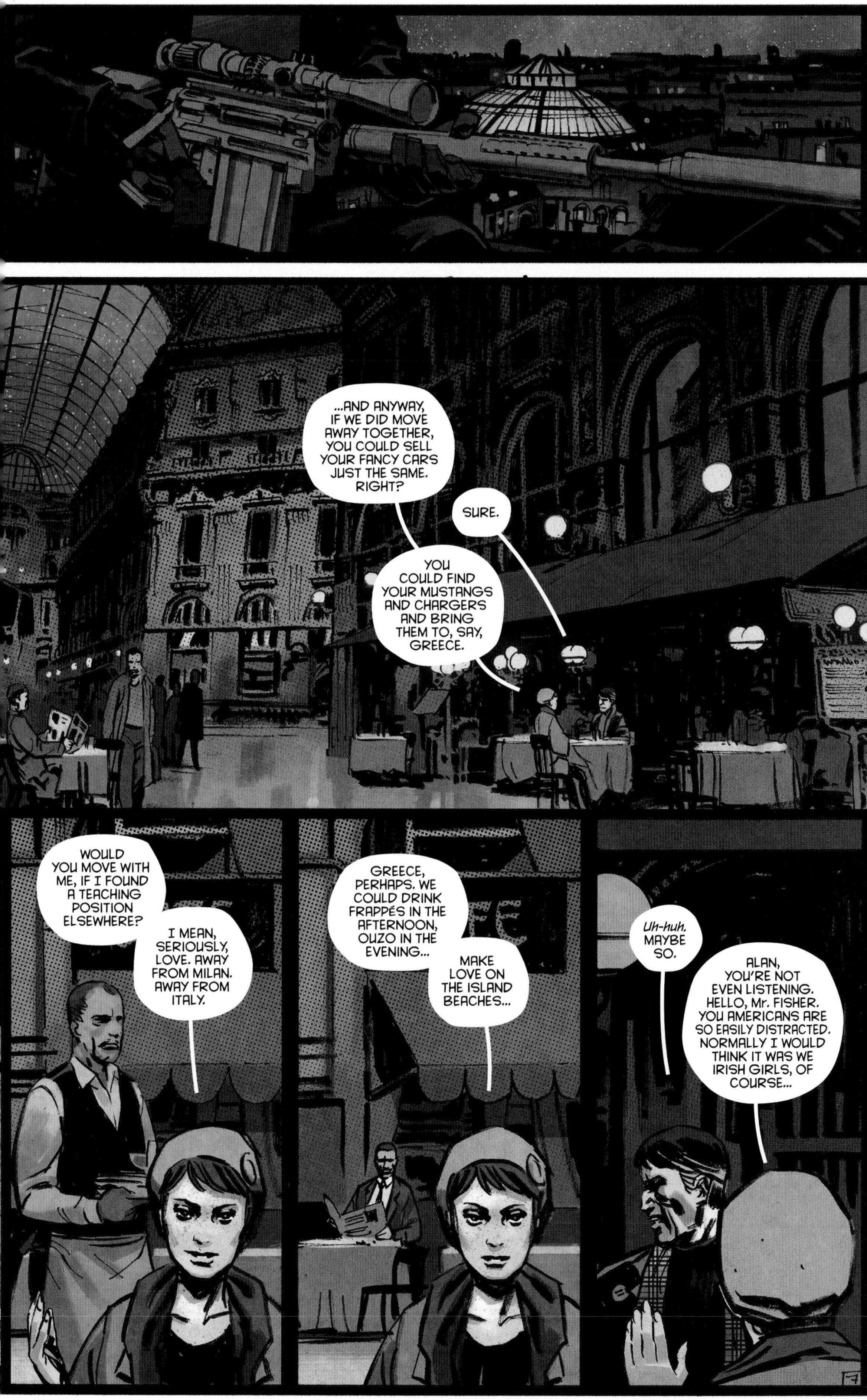
...AND ANYWAY, IF WE DID MOVE AWAY TOGETHER, YOU COULD SELL YOUR FANCY CARS JUST THE SAME. RIGHT?
SURE.
YOU COULD FIND YOUR MUSTANGS AND CHARGERS AND BRING THEM TO, SAY, GREECE.
WOULD YOU MOVE WITH ME, IF I FOUND A TEACHING POSITION ELSEWHERE?
I MEAN, SERIOUSLY, LOVE. AWAY FROM MILAN. AWAY FROM ITALY.
GREECE, PERHAPS. WE COULD DRINK FRAPPÉS IN THE AFTERNOON, OUZO IN THE EVENING...
MAKE LOVE ON THE ISLAND BEACHES...
Uh-huh. MAYBE SO.
ALAN, YOU'RE NOT EVEN LISTENING. HELLO, Mr. FISHER. YOU AMERICANS ARE SO EASILY DISTRACTED. NORMALLY I WOULD THINK IT WAS WE IRISH GIRLS, OF COURSE...

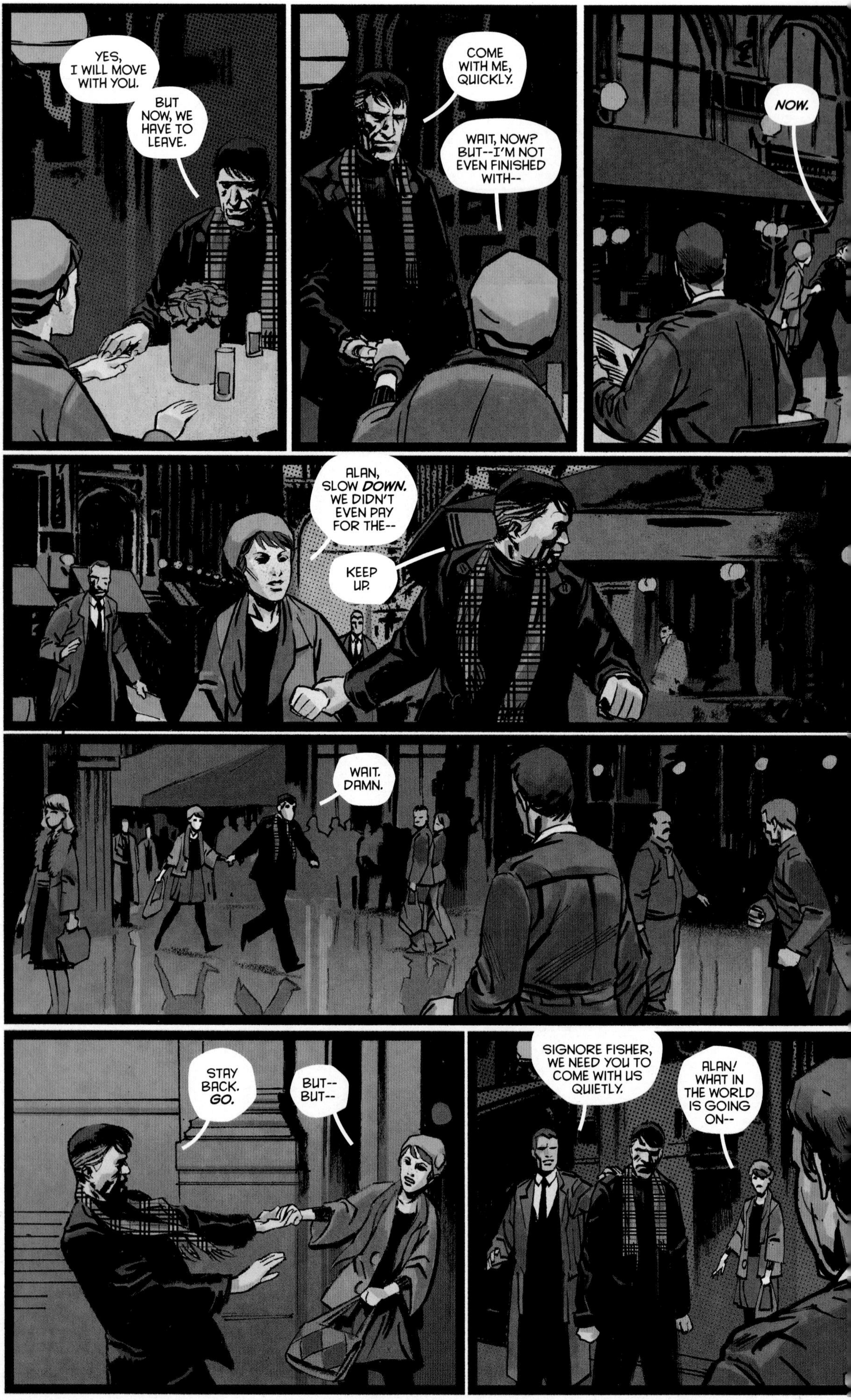
YES, I WILL MOVE WITH YOU.
BUT NOW, WE HAVE TO LEAVE.
COME WITH ME, QUICKLY.
WAIT, NOW? BUT--I'M NOT EVEN FINISHED WITH--
NOW.
ALAN, SLOW DOWN. WE DIDN'T EVEN PAY FOR THE--
KEEP UP.
WAIT. DAMN.
STAY BACK. GO.
BUT-- BUT--
SIGNORE FISHER, WE NEED YOU TO COME WITH US QUIETLY.
ALAN! WHAT IN THE WORLD IS GOING ON--

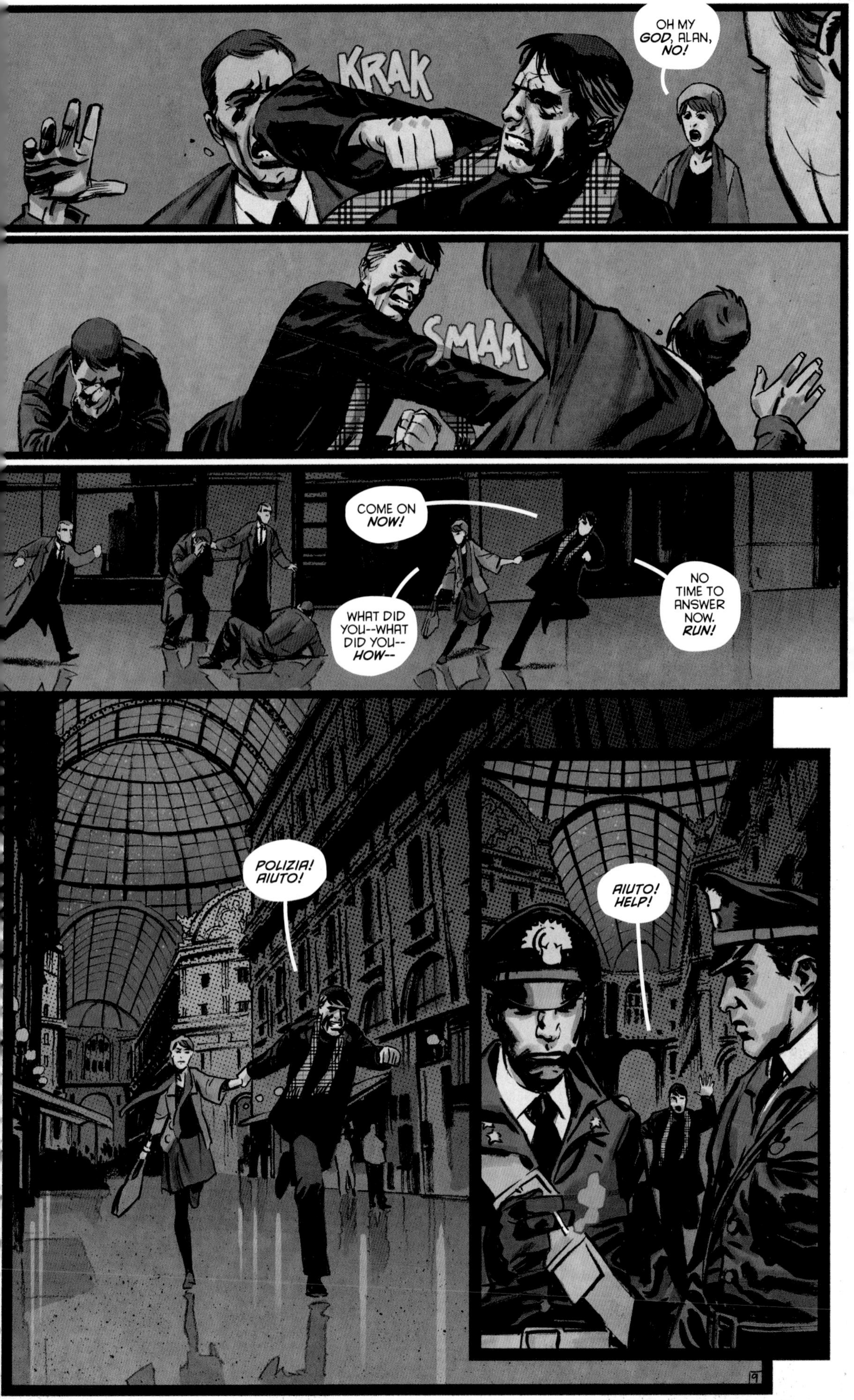
KRAK
OH MY GOD, ALAN, NO!
SMAK
COME ON NOW!
WHAT DID YOU--WHAT DID YOU-- HOW--
NO TIME TO ANSWER NOW. RUN!
POLIZIA! AIUTO!
AIUTO! HELP!
9

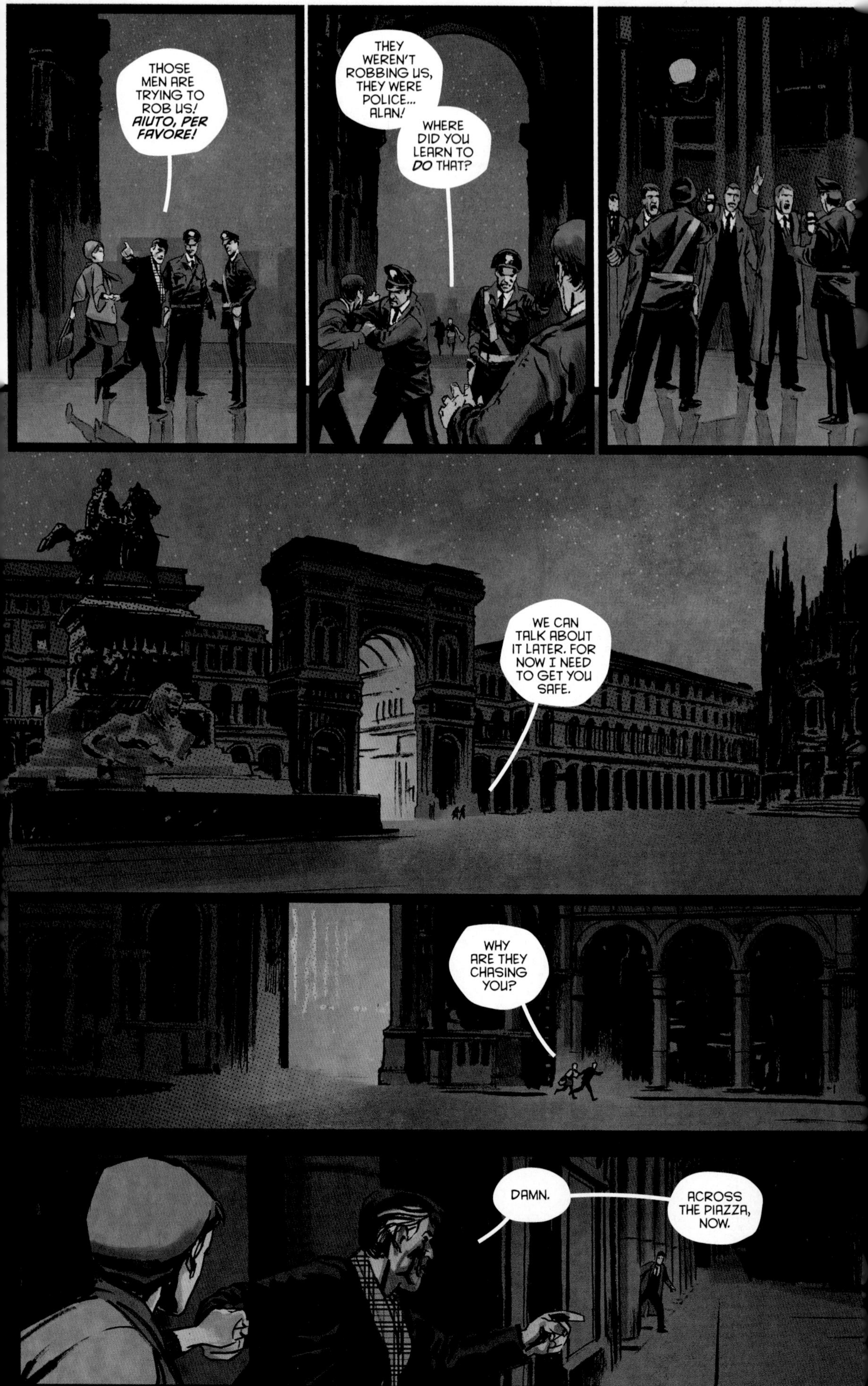
THOSE MEN ARE TRYING TO ROB US! *AIUTO, PER FAVORE!*
THEY WEREN'T ROBBING US, THEY WERE POLICE... ALAN!
WHERE DID YOU LEARN TO *DO* THAT?
WE CAN TALK ABOUT IT LATER. FOR NOW I NEED TO GET YOU SAFE.
WHY ARE THEY CHASING YOU?
DAMN.
ACROSS THE PIAZZA, NOW.

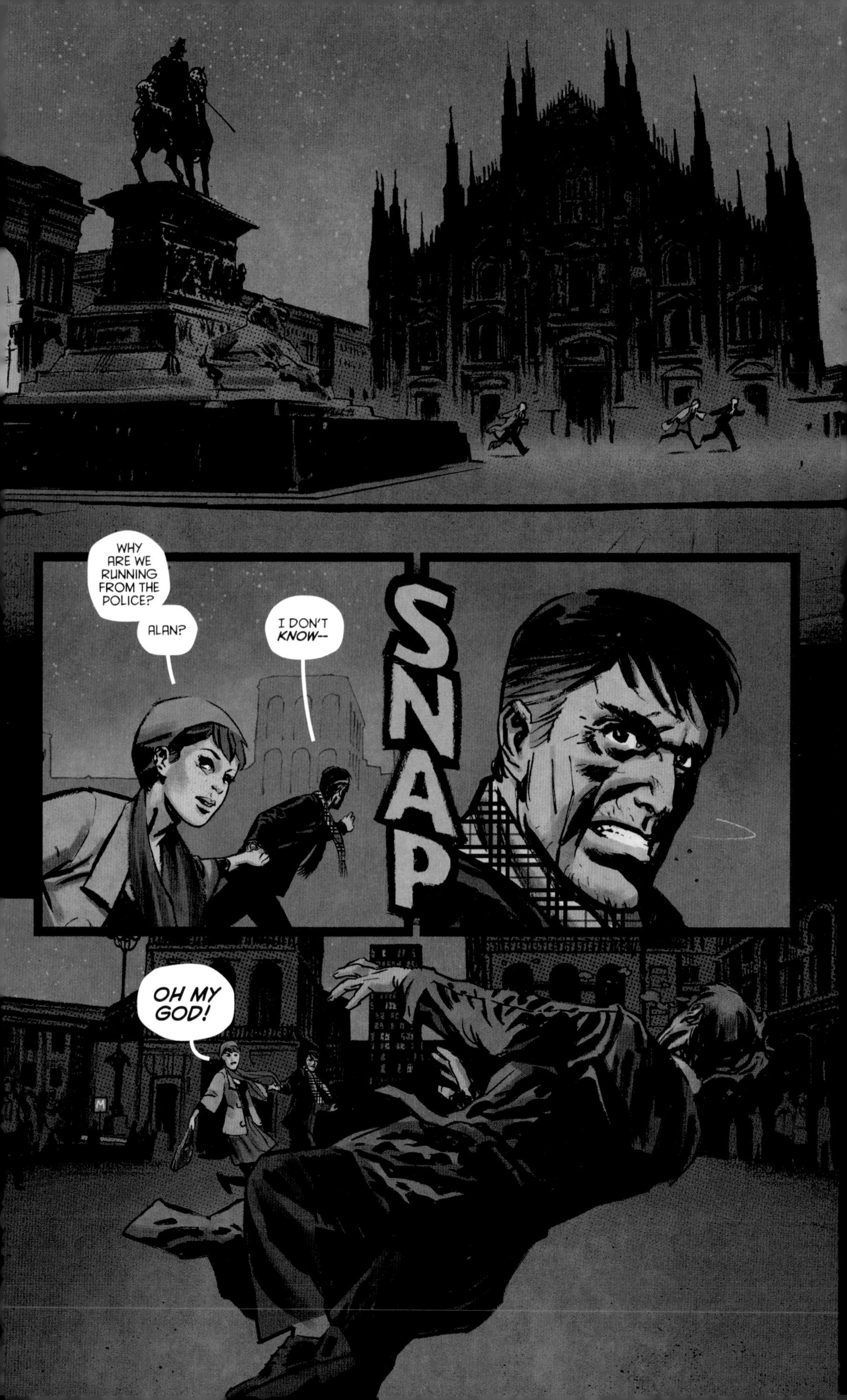

WHY ARE WE RUNNING FROM THE POLICE?
ALAN?
I DON'T KNOW--
SNAP
OH MY GOD!

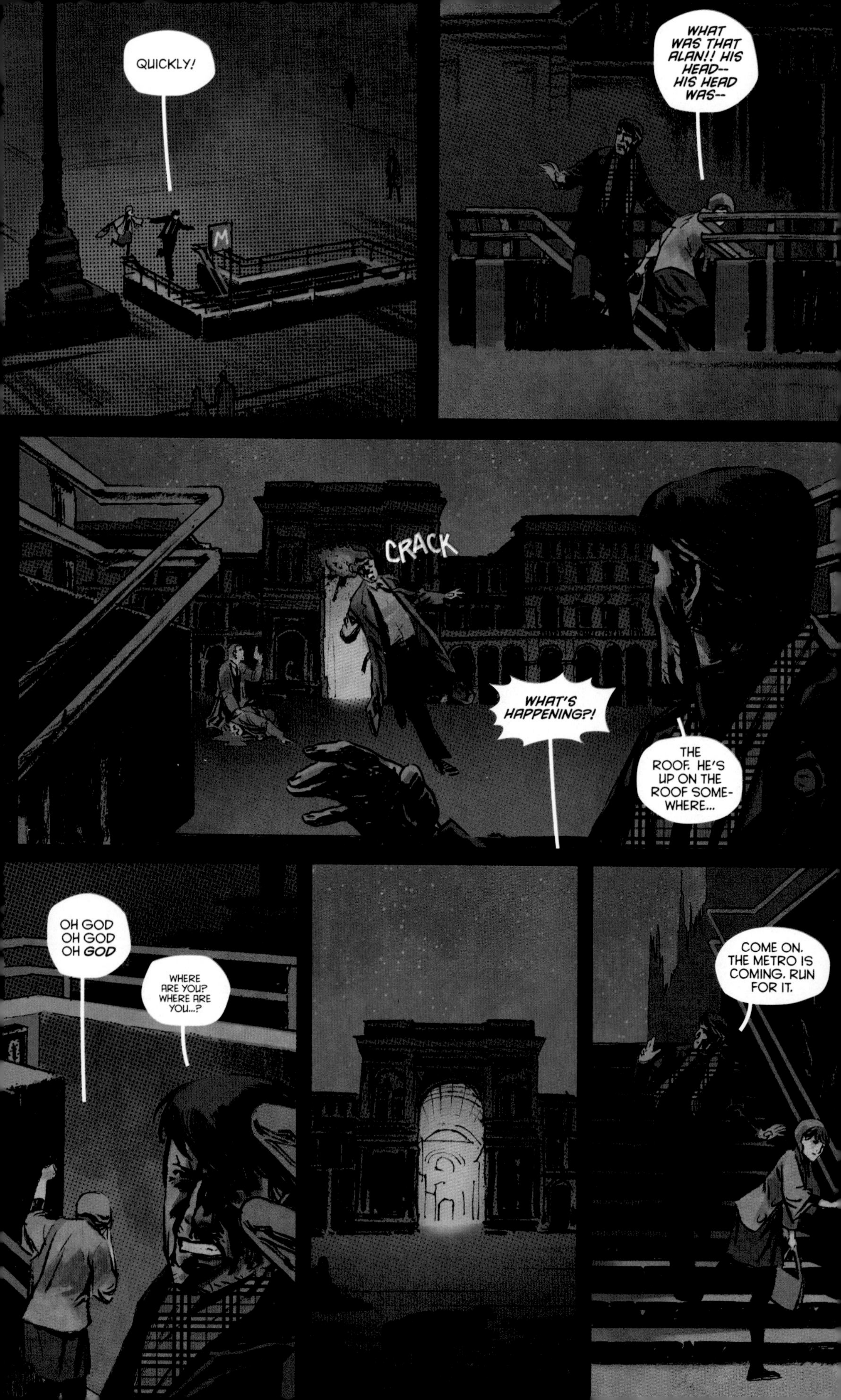
QUICKLY!
WHAT WAS THAT ALAN!! HIS HEAD-- HIS HEAD WAS--
CRACK
WHAT'S HAPPENING?!
THE ROOF. HE'S UP ON THE ROOF SOME-WHERE...
OH GOD OH GOD OH *GOD*
WHERE ARE YOU? WHERE ARE YOU...?
COME ON. THE METRO IS COMING. RUN FOR IT.

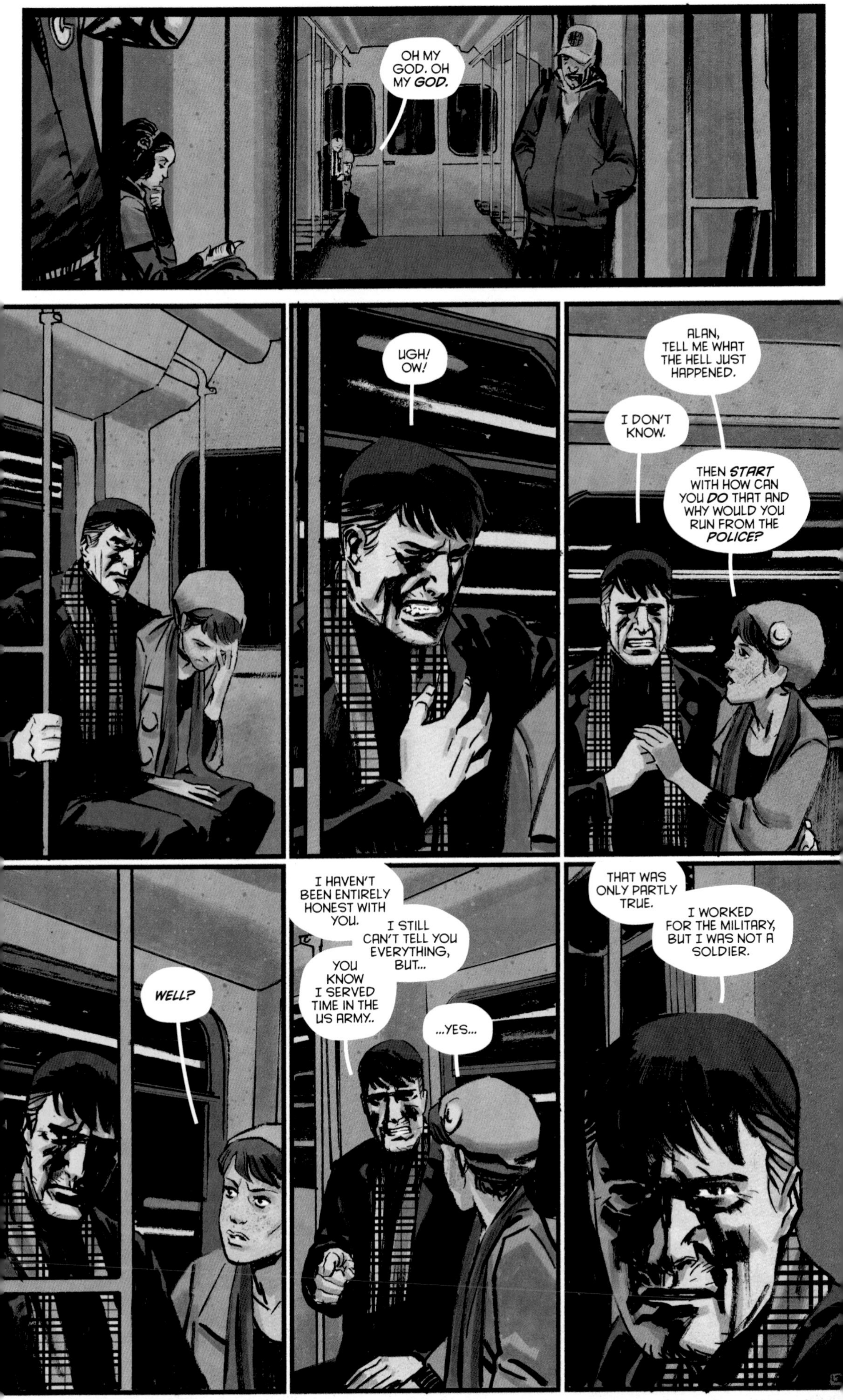
OH MY GOD. OH MY GOD.
UGH! OW!
ALAN, TELL ME WHAT THE HELL JUST HAPPENED.
I DON'T KNOW.
THEN START WITH HOW CAN YOU DO THAT AND WHY WOULD YOU RUN FROM THE POLICE?
WELL?
I HAVEN'T BEEN ENTIRELY HONEST WITH YOU.
I STILL CAN'T TELL YOU EVERYTHING, BUT...
YOU KNOW I SERVED TIME IN THE US ARMY..
...YES...
THAT WAS ONLY PARTLY TRUE.
I WORKED FOR THE MILITARY, BUT I WAS NOT A SOLDIER.

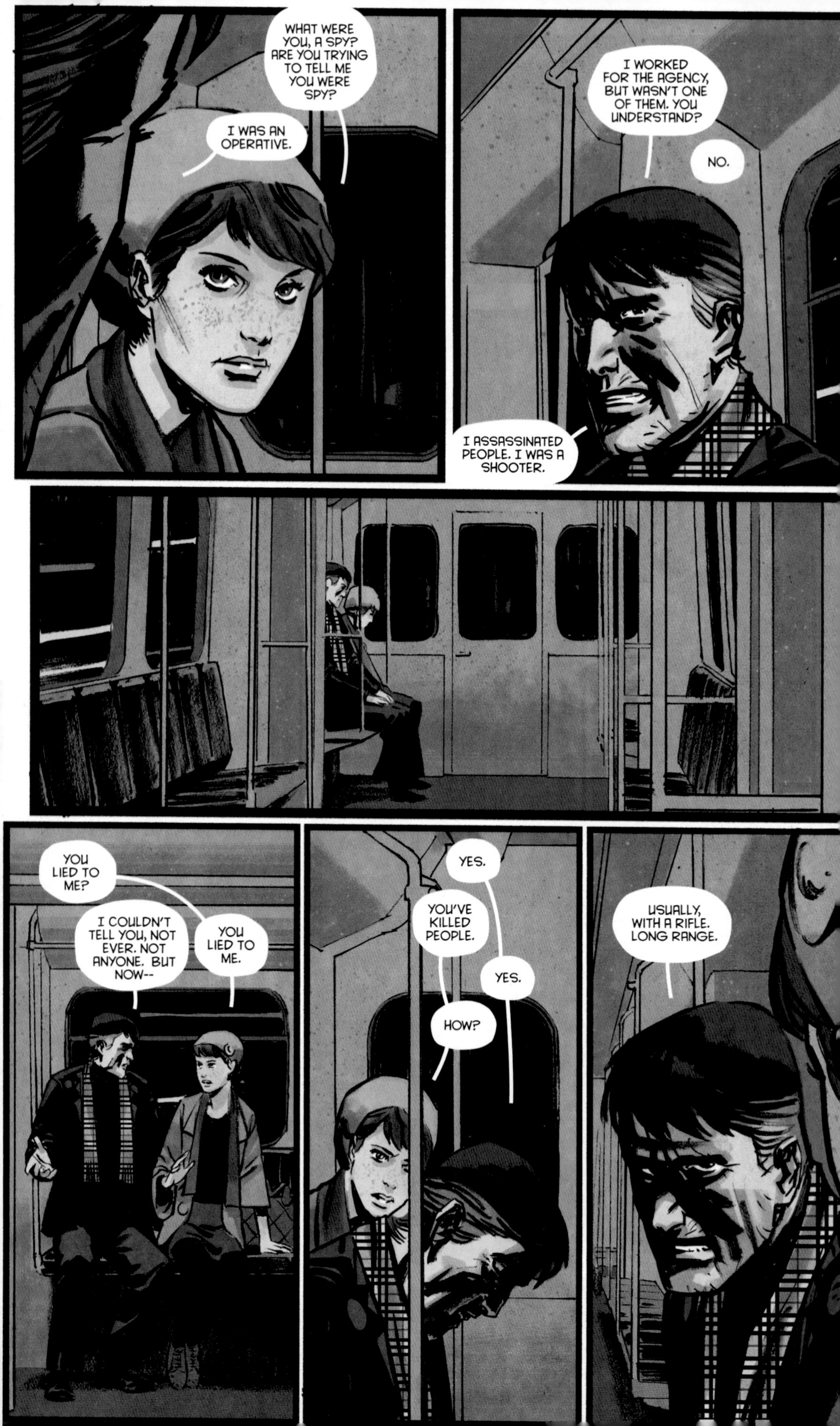

WHAT WERE YOU, A SPY? ARE YOU TRYING TO TELL ME YOU WERE SPY?
I WAS AN OPERATIVE.
I WORKED FOR THE AGENCY, BUT WASN'T ONE OF THEM. YOU UNDERSTAND?
NO.
I ASSASSINATED PEOPLE. I WAS A SHOOTER.
YOU LIED TO ME?
I COULDN'T TELL YOU, NOT EVER. NOT ANYONE. BUT NOW--
YOU LIED TO ME.
YES.
YOU'VE KILLED PEOPLE.
YES.
HOW?
USUALLY, WITH A RIFLE. LONG RANGE.

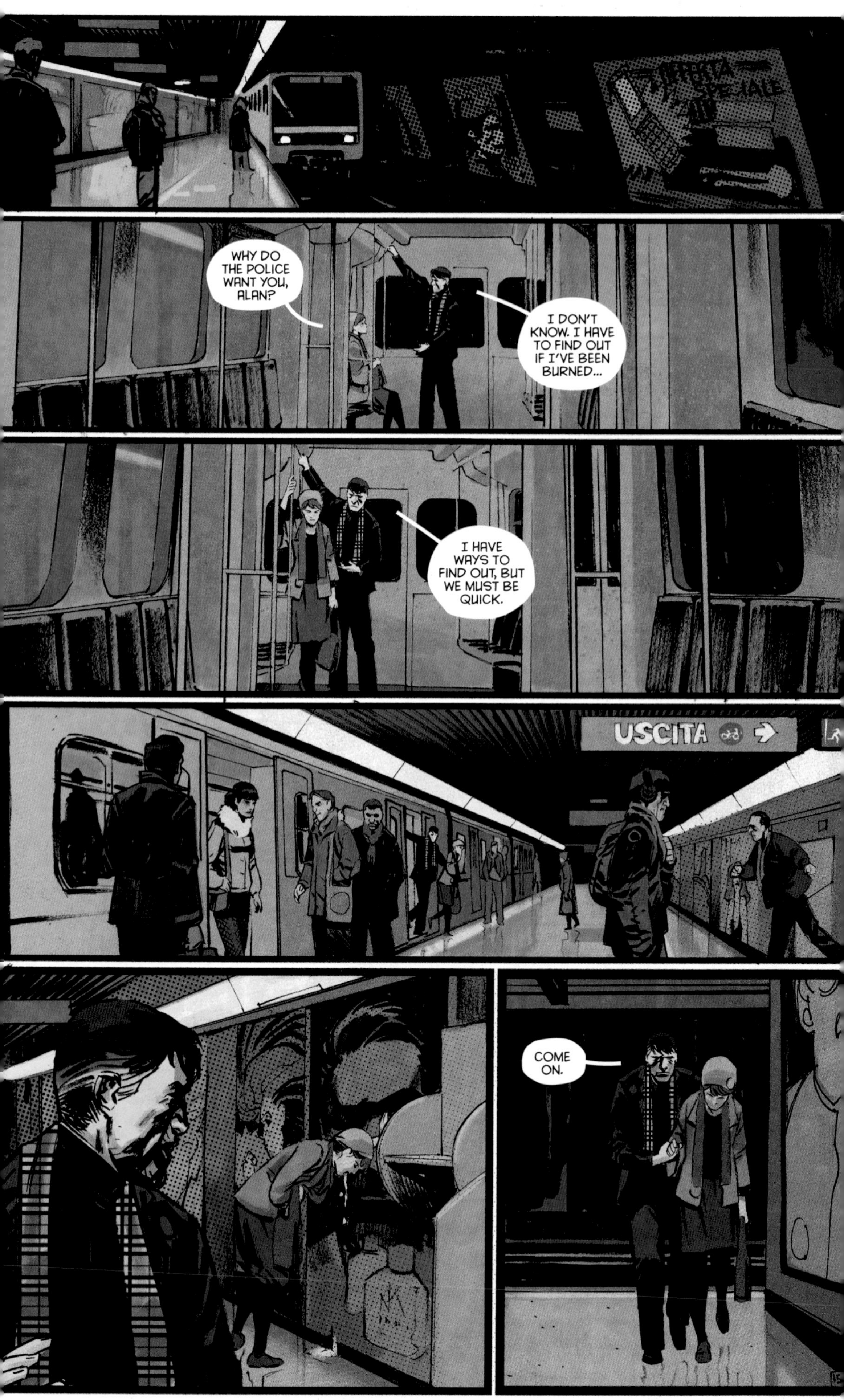

WHY DO THE POLICE WANT YOU, ALAN?
I DON'T KNOW. I HAVE TO FIND OUT IF I'VE BEEN BURNED...
I HAVE WAYS TO FIND OUT, BUT WE MUST BE QUICK.
USCITA
COME ON.

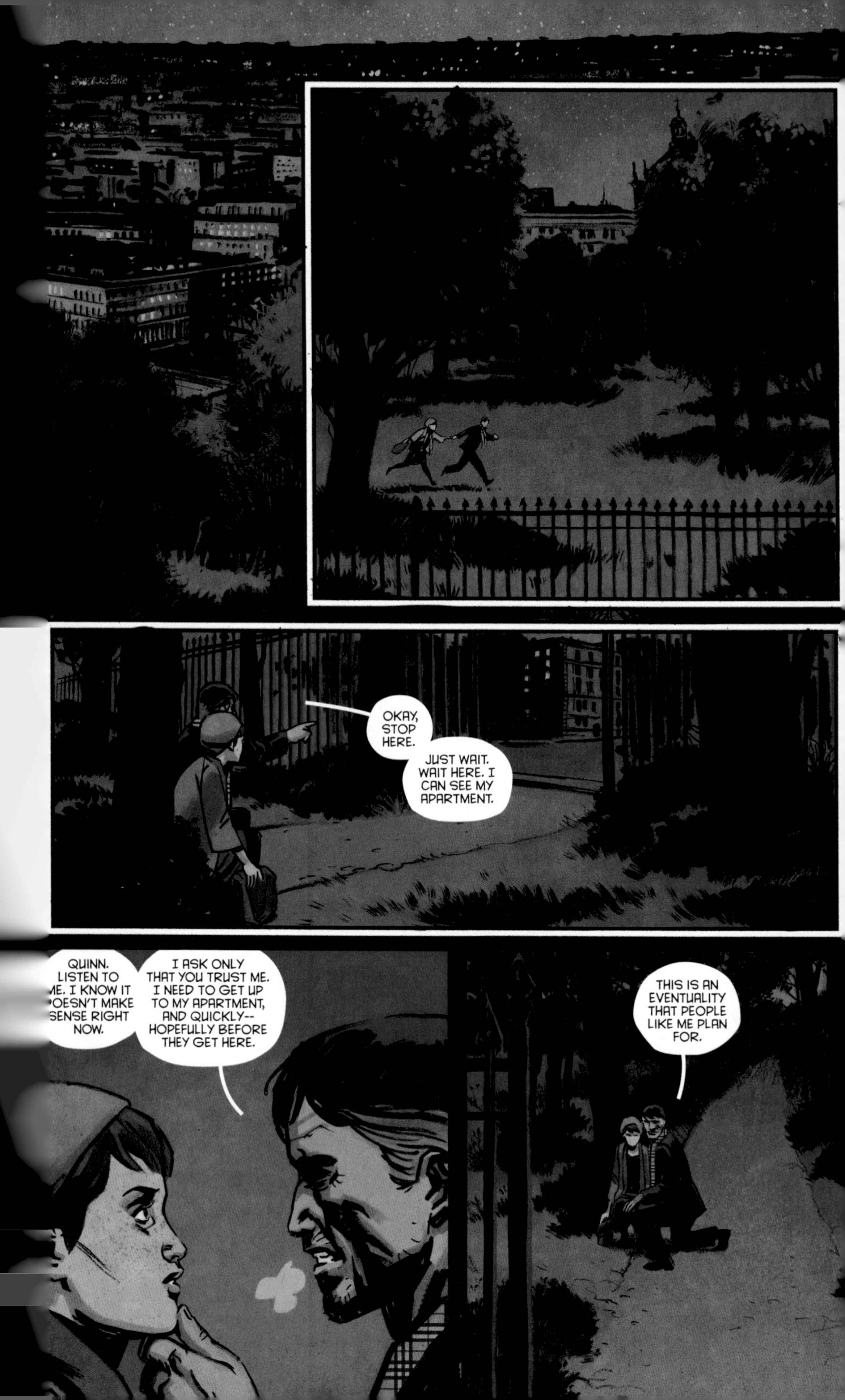
OKAY, STOP HERE.
JUST WAIT. WAIT HERE. I CAN SEE MY APARTMENT.
QUINN. LISTEN TO ME. I KNOW IT DOESN'T MAKE SENSE RIGHT NOW.
I ASK ONLY THAT YOU TRUST ME. I NEED TO GET UP TO MY APARTMENT, AND QUICKLY-- HOPEFULLY BEFORE THEY GET HERE.
THIS IS AN EVENTUALITY THAT PEOPLE LIKE ME PLAN FOR.

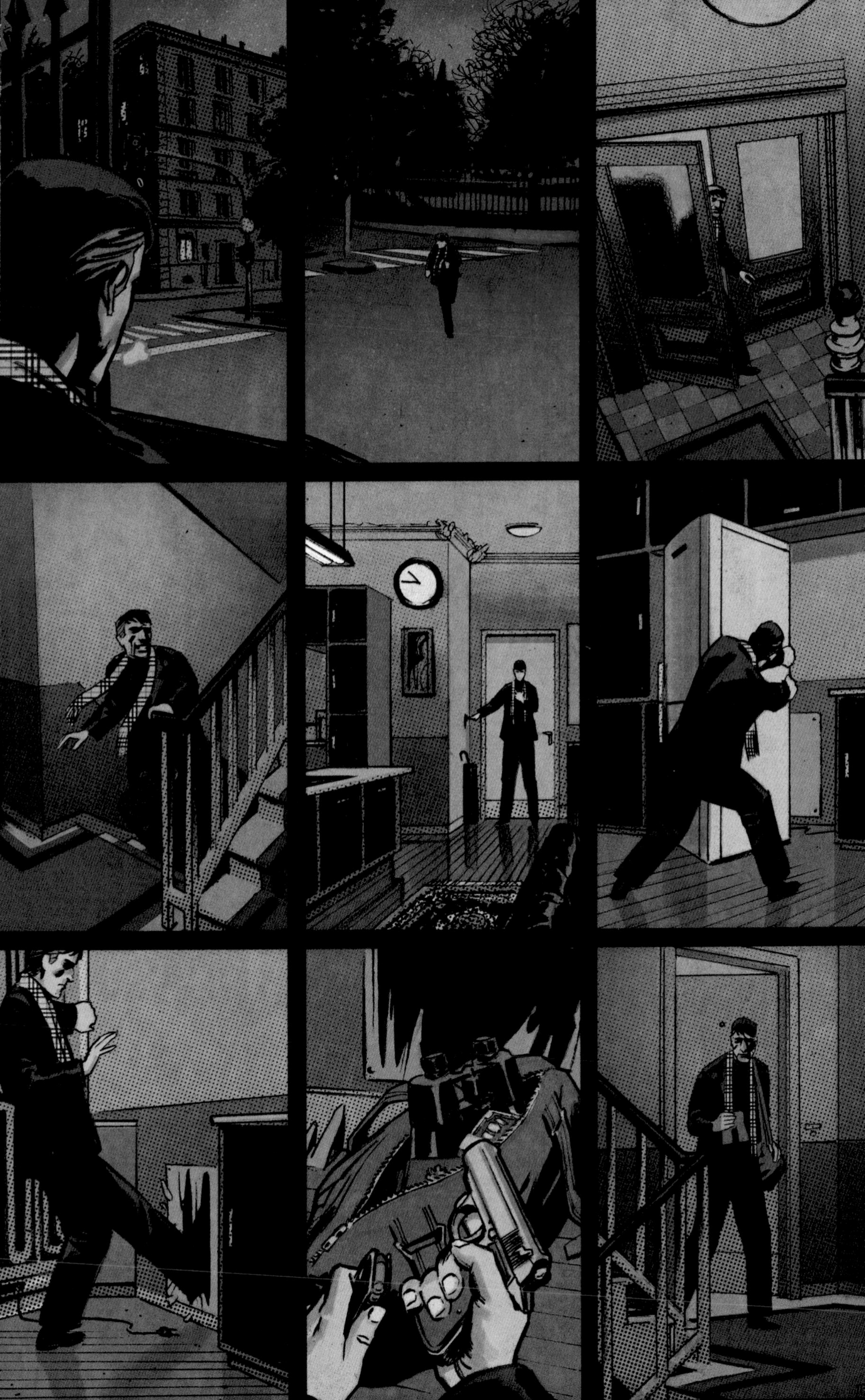

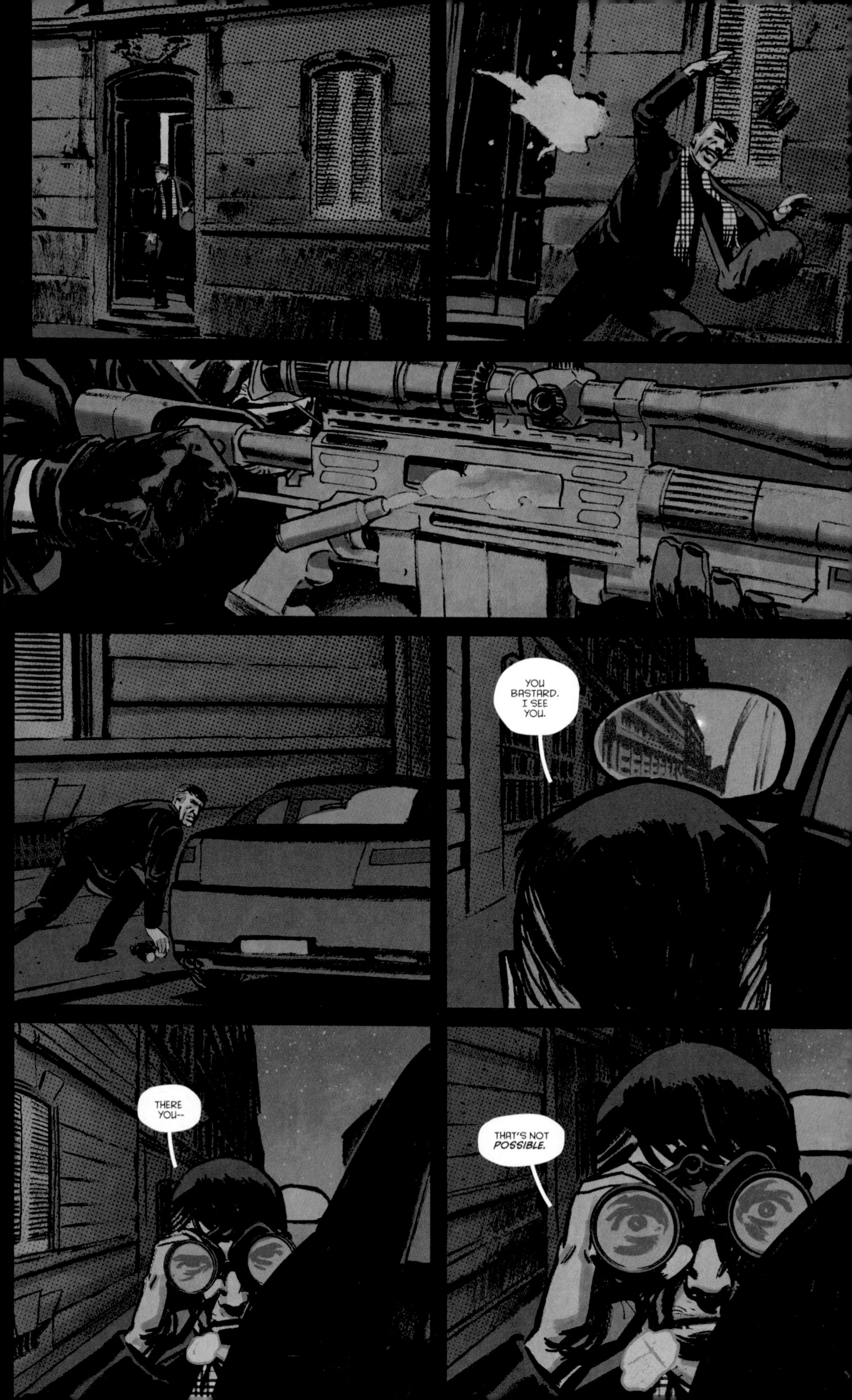
YOU BASTARD. I SEE YOU.
THERE YOU--
THAT'S NOT *POSSIBLE.*

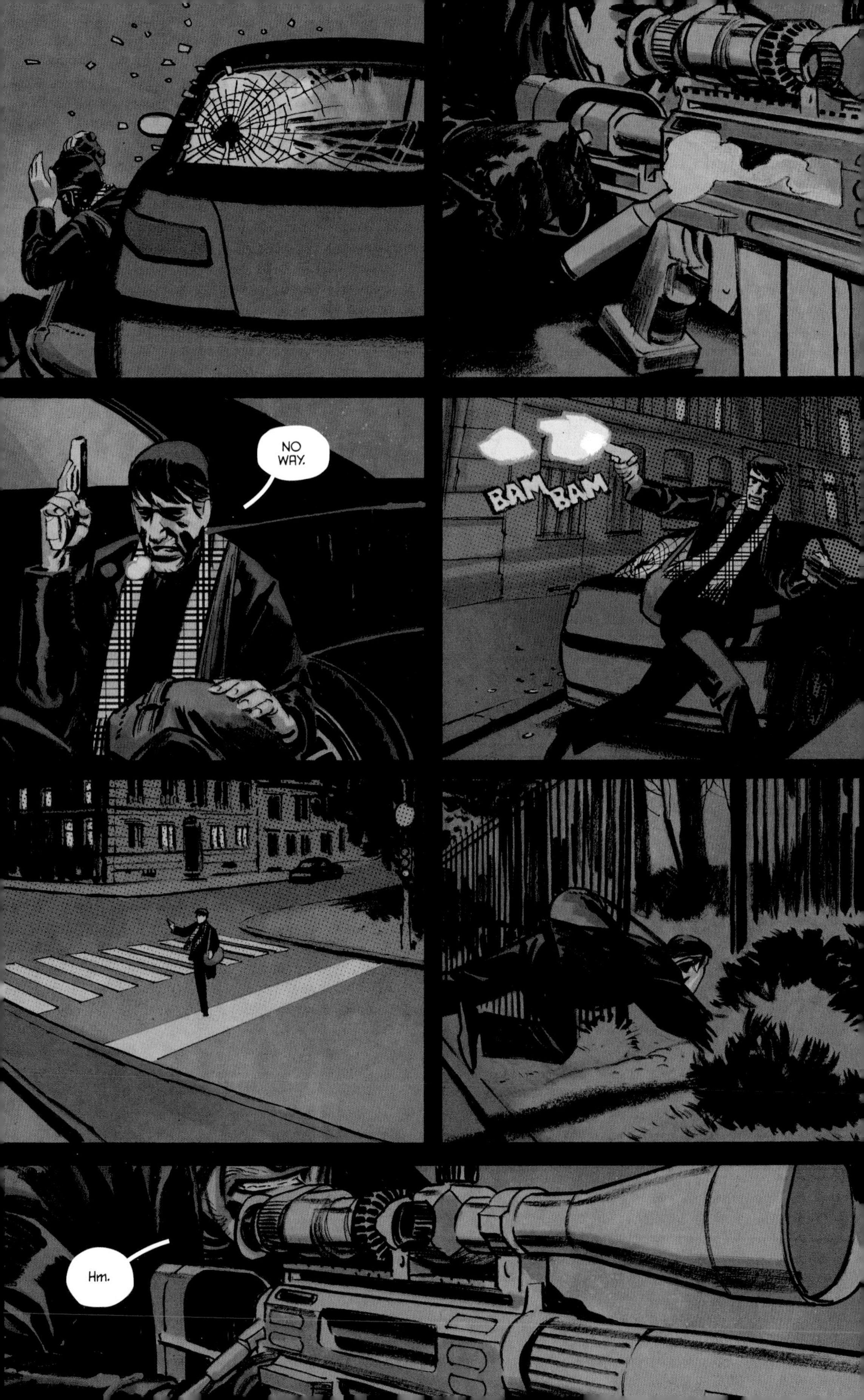
NO WAY.
BAM BAM
Hm.

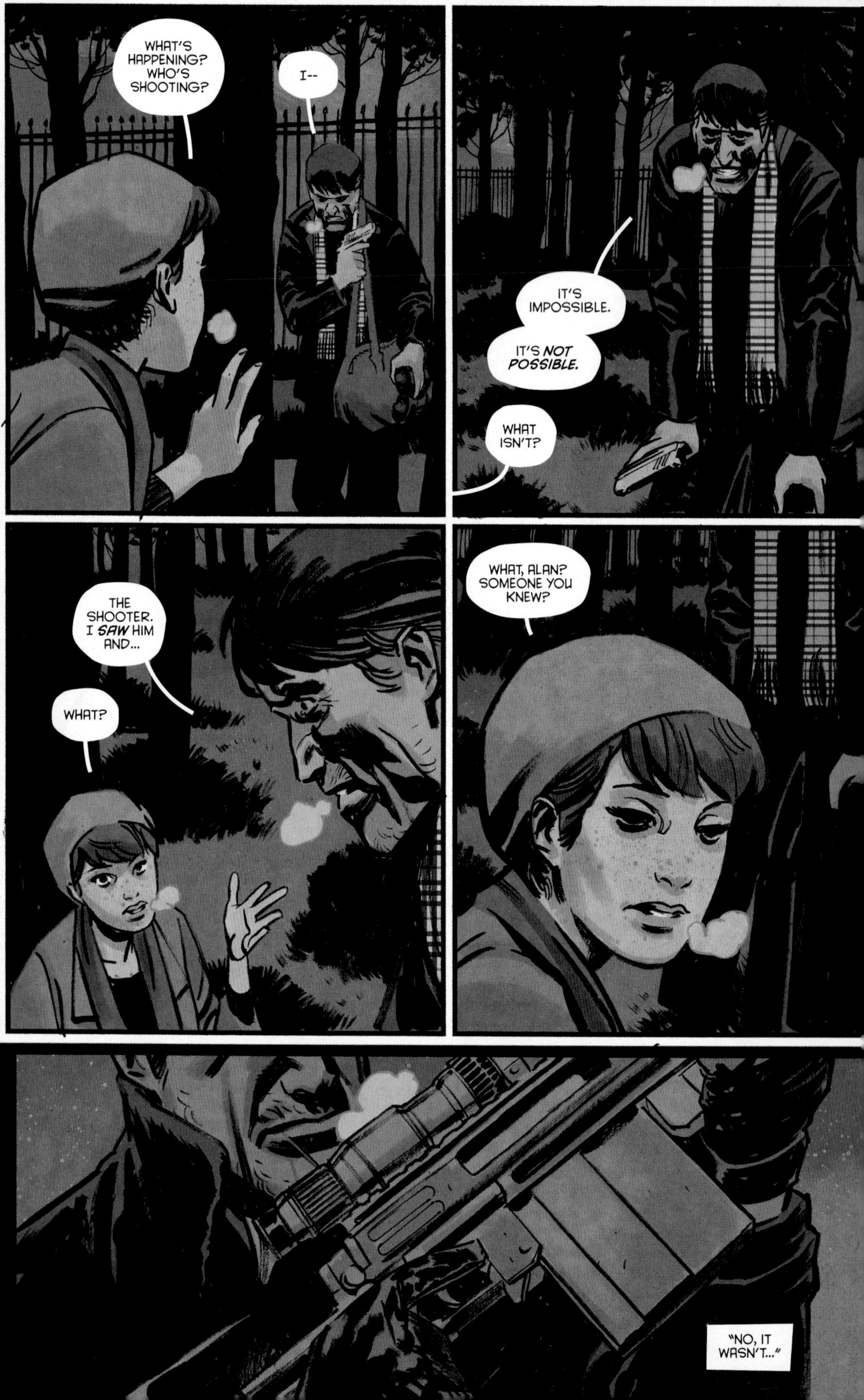
WHAT'S HAPPENING? WHO'S SHOOTING?
I--
IT'S IMPOSSIBLE.
IT'S *NOT POSSIBLE.*
WHAT ISN'T?
THE SHOOTER. I *SAW* HIM AND...
WHAT?
WHAT, ALAN? SOMEONE YOU KNEW?
"NO, IT WASN'T..."

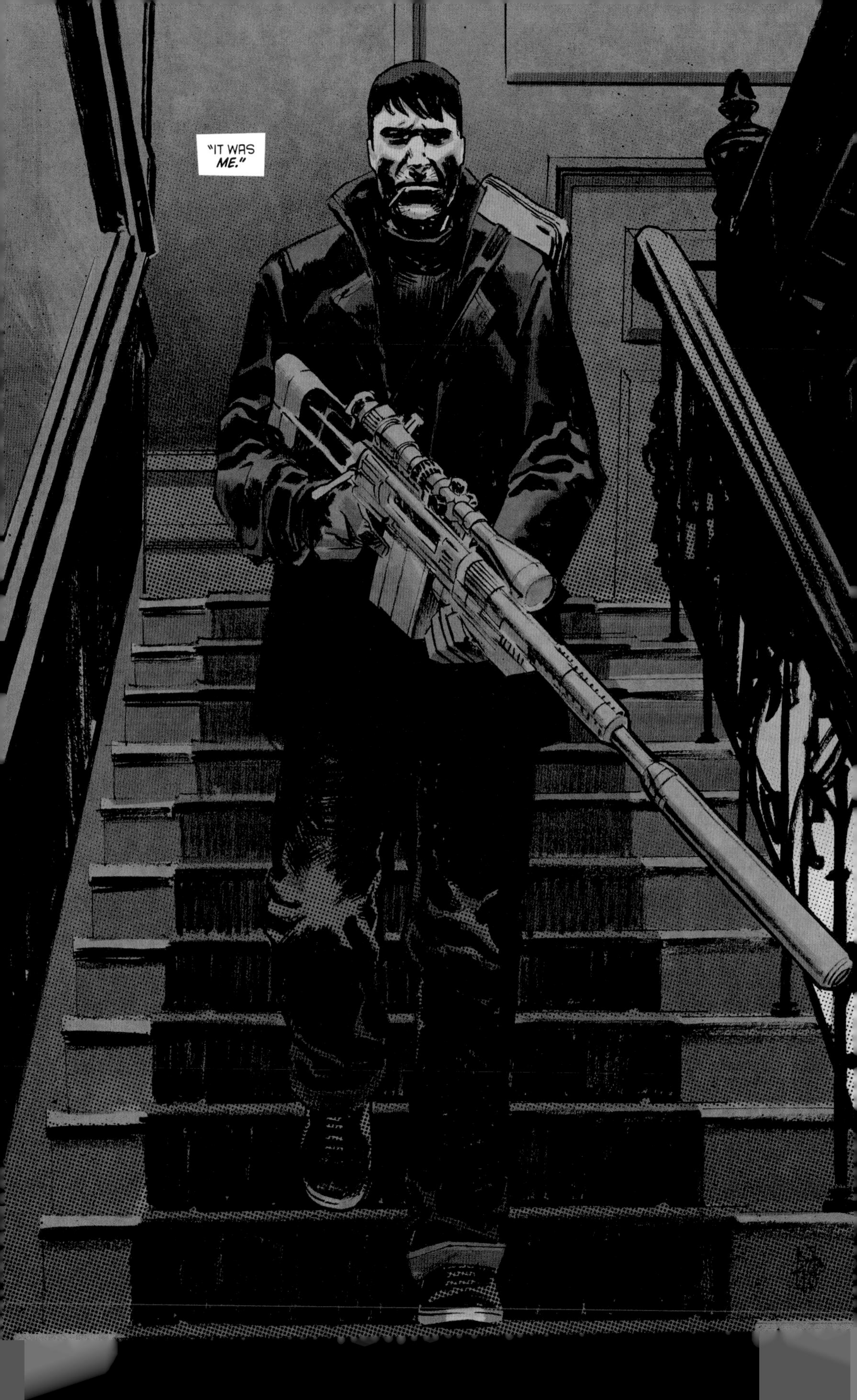
"IT WAS ME."

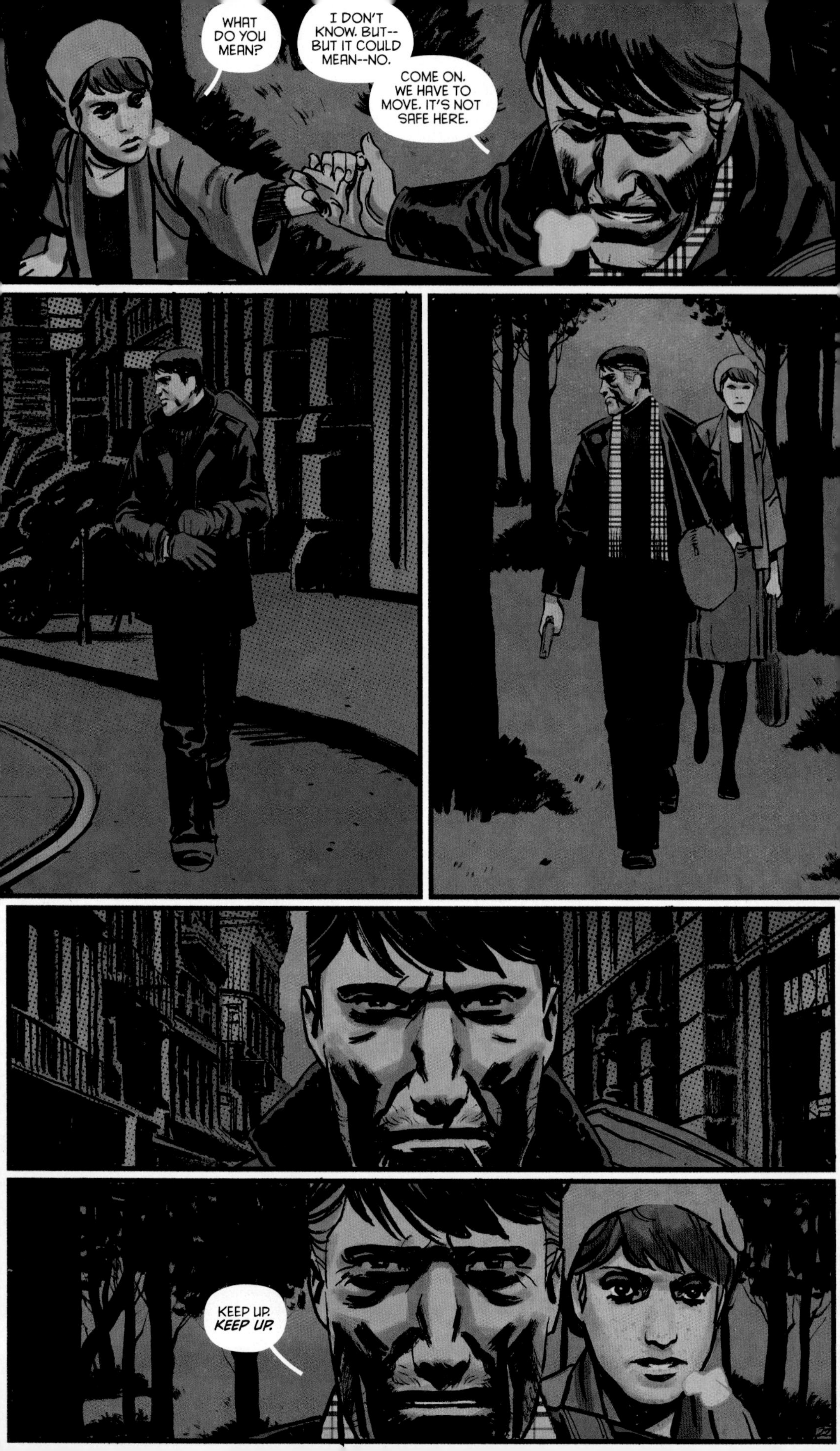
WHAT DO YOU MEAN?
I DON'T KNOW. BUT--BUT IT COULD MEAN--NO.
COME ON. WE HAVE TO MOVE. IT'S NOT SAFE HERE.
KEEP UP.
KEEP UP.

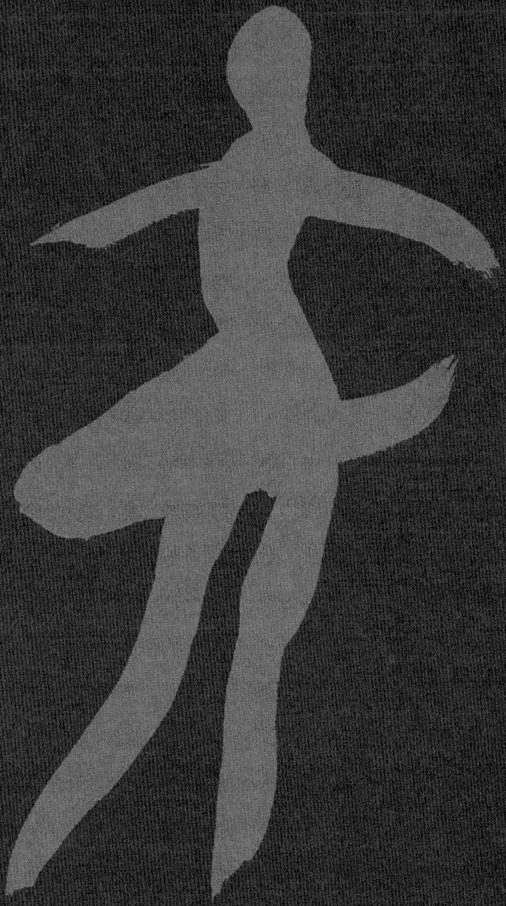

BALANCÉ

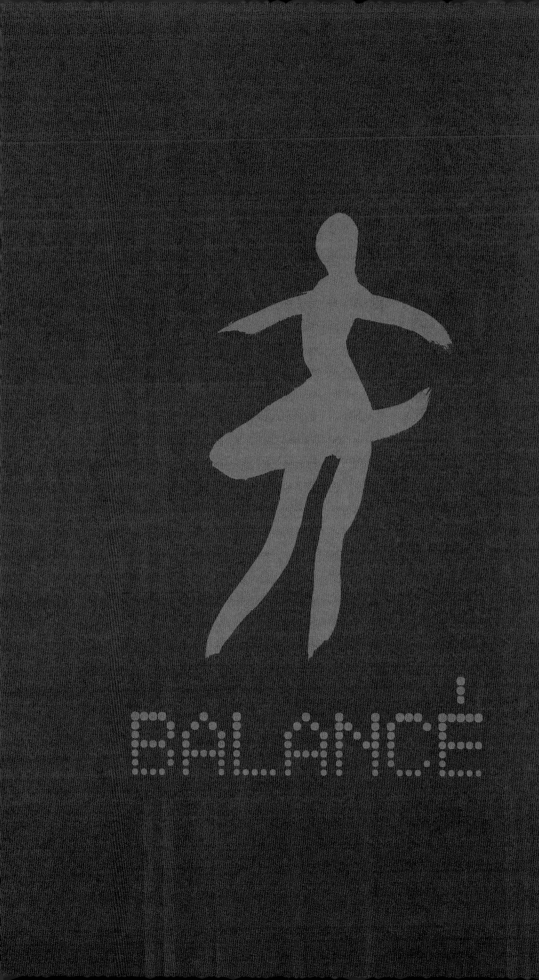

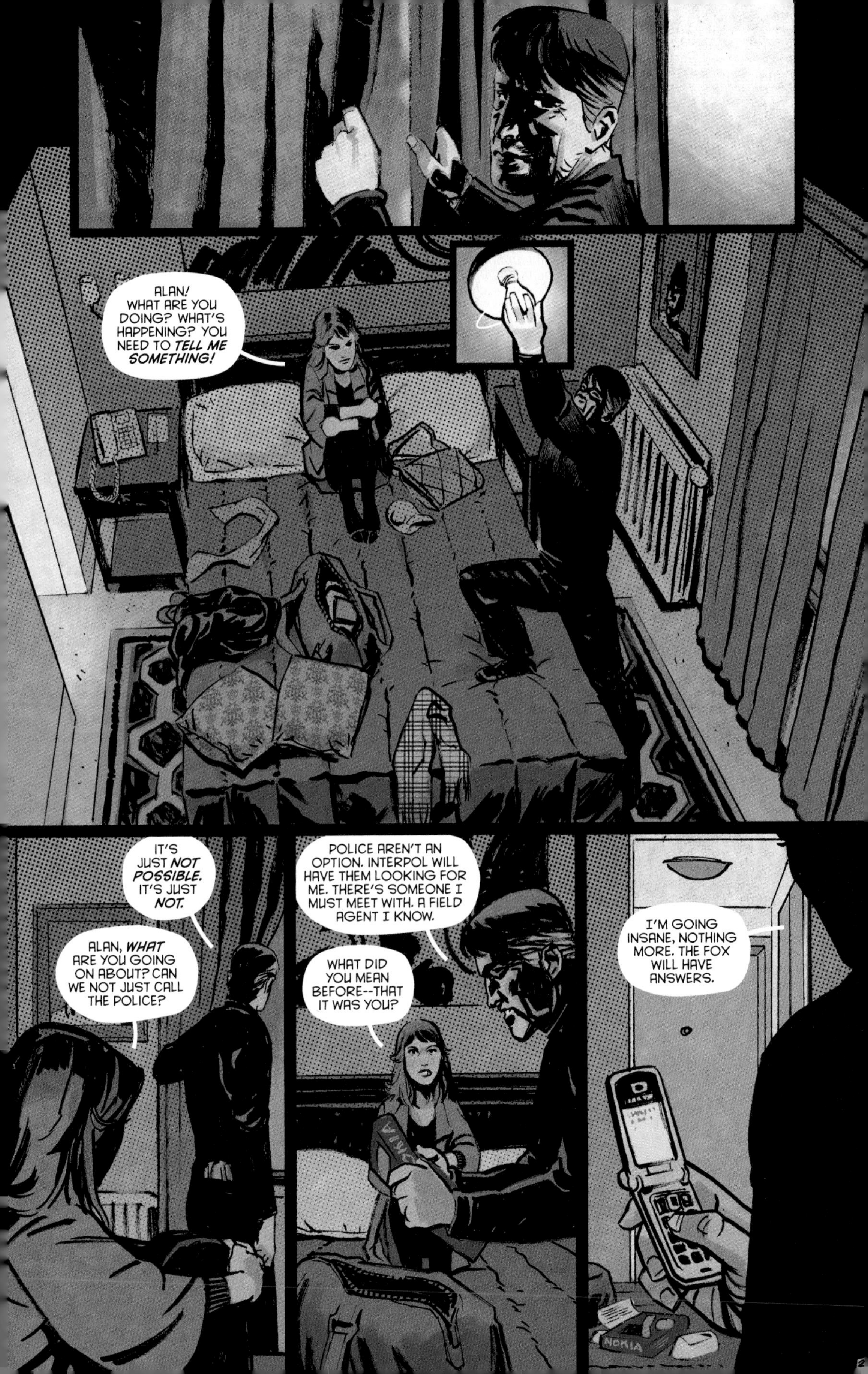
ALAN! WHAT ARE YOU DOING? WHAT'S HAPPENING? YOU NEED TO TELL ME SOMETHING!
IT'S JUST NOT POSSIBLE. IT'S JUST NOT.
ALAN, WHAT ARE YOU GOING ON ABOUT? CAN WE NOT JUST CALL THE POLICE?
POLICE AREN'T AN OPTION. INTERPOL WILL HAVE THEM LOOKING FOR ME. THERE'S SOMEONE I MUST MEET WITH. A FIELD AGENT I KNOW.
WHAT DID YOU MEAN BEFORE--THAT IT WAS YOU?
I'M GOING INSANE, NOTHING MORE. THE FOX WILL HAVE ANSWERS.
NOKIA

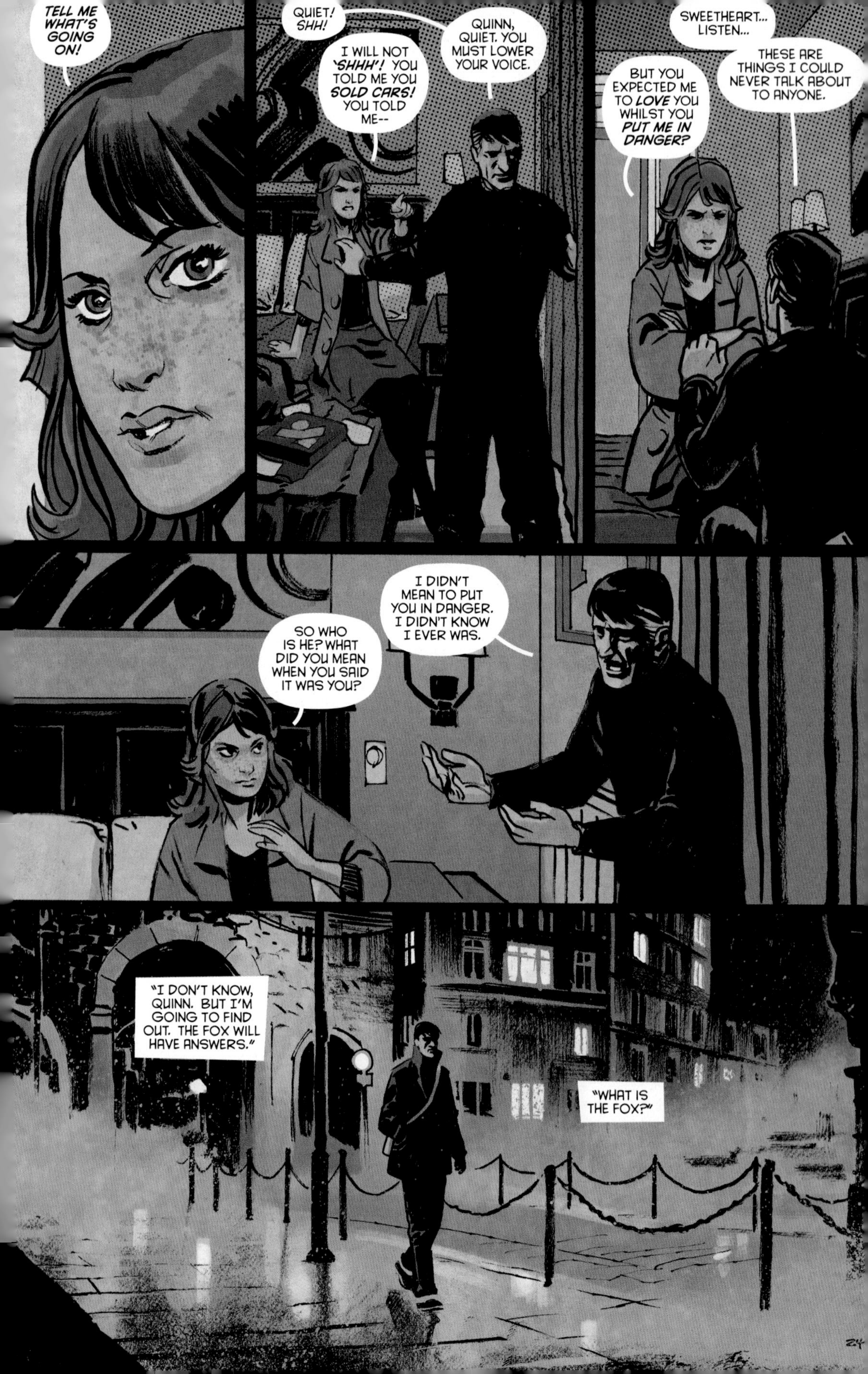

TELL ME WHAT'S GOING ON!
QUIET! SHH!
I WILL NOT *'SHHH'!* YOU TOLD ME YOU *SOLD CARS!* YOU TOLD ME--
QUINN, QUIET. YOU MUST LOWER YOUR VOICE.
SWEETHEART... LISTEN...
BUT YOU EXPECTED ME TO *LOVE* YOU WHILST YOU *PUT ME IN DANGER?*
THESE ARE THINGS I COULD NEVER TALK ABOUT TO ANYONE.
SO WHO IS HE? WHAT DID YOU MEAN WHEN YOU SAID IT WAS YOU?
I DIDN'T MEAN TO PUT YOU IN DANGER. I DIDN'T KNOW I EVER WAS.
"I DON'T KNOW, QUINN. BUT I'M GOING TO FIND OUT. THE FOX WILL HAVE ANSWERS."
"WHAT IS THE FOX?"
24

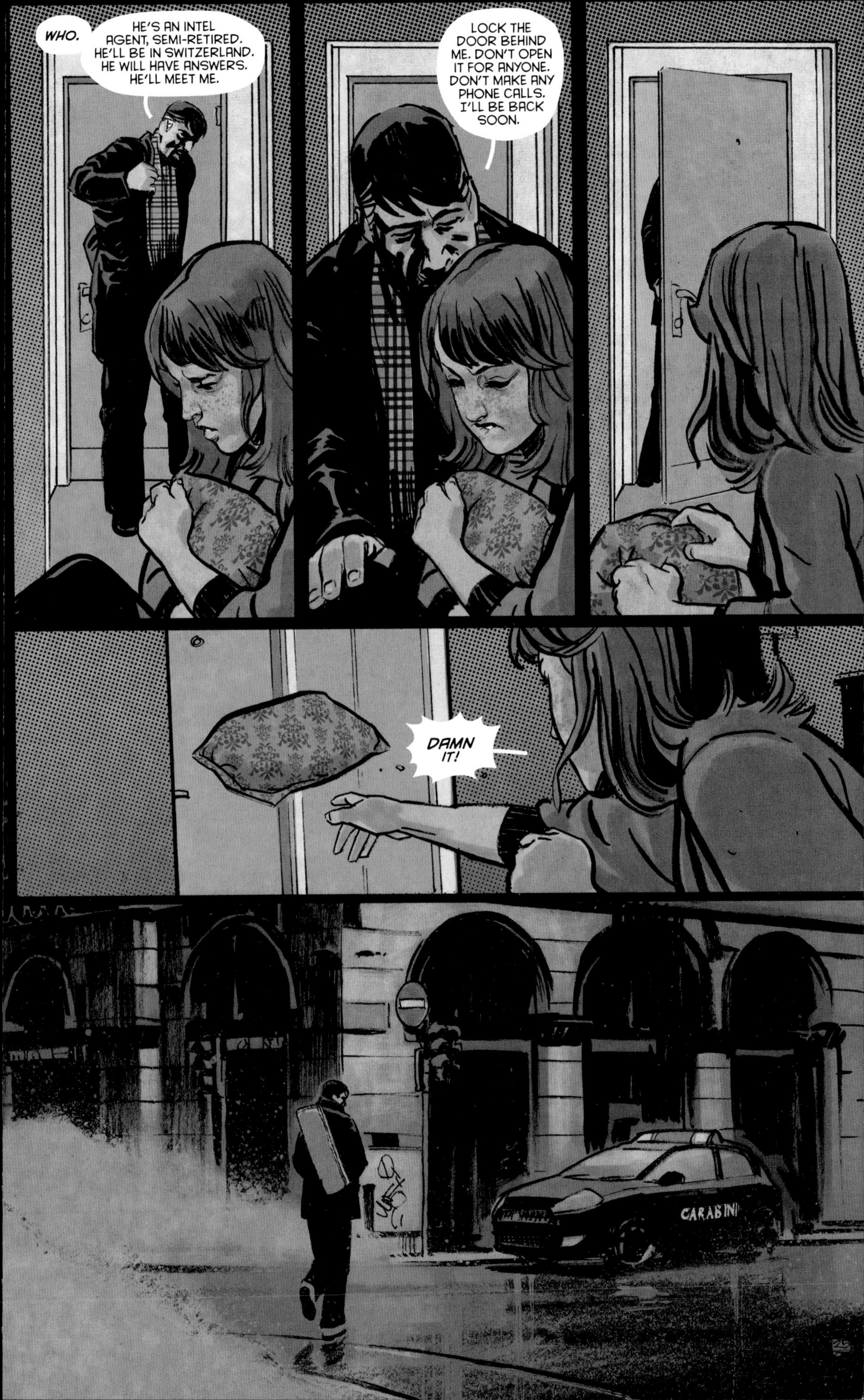
WHO.
HE'S AN INTEL AGENT, SEMI-RETIRED. HE'LL BE IN SWITZERLAND. HE WILL HAVE ANSWERS. HE'LL MEET ME.
LOCK THE DOOR BEHIND ME. DON'T OPEN IT FOR ANYONE. DON'T MAKE ANY PHONE CALLS. I'LL BE BACK SOON.
DAMN IT!
CARABINI

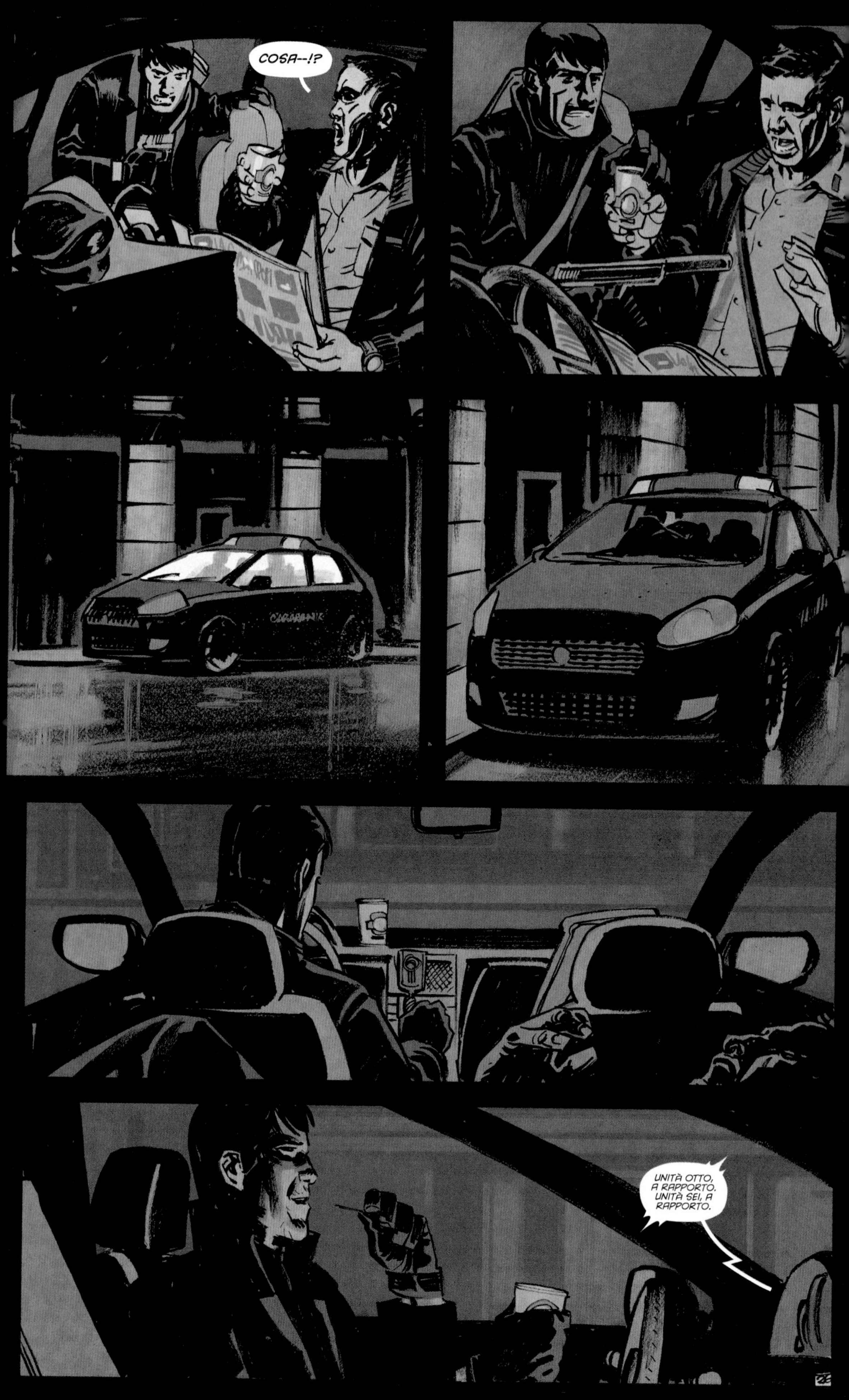
COSA--!?
UNITÀ OTTO, A RAPPORTO. UNITÀ SEI, A RAPPORTO.

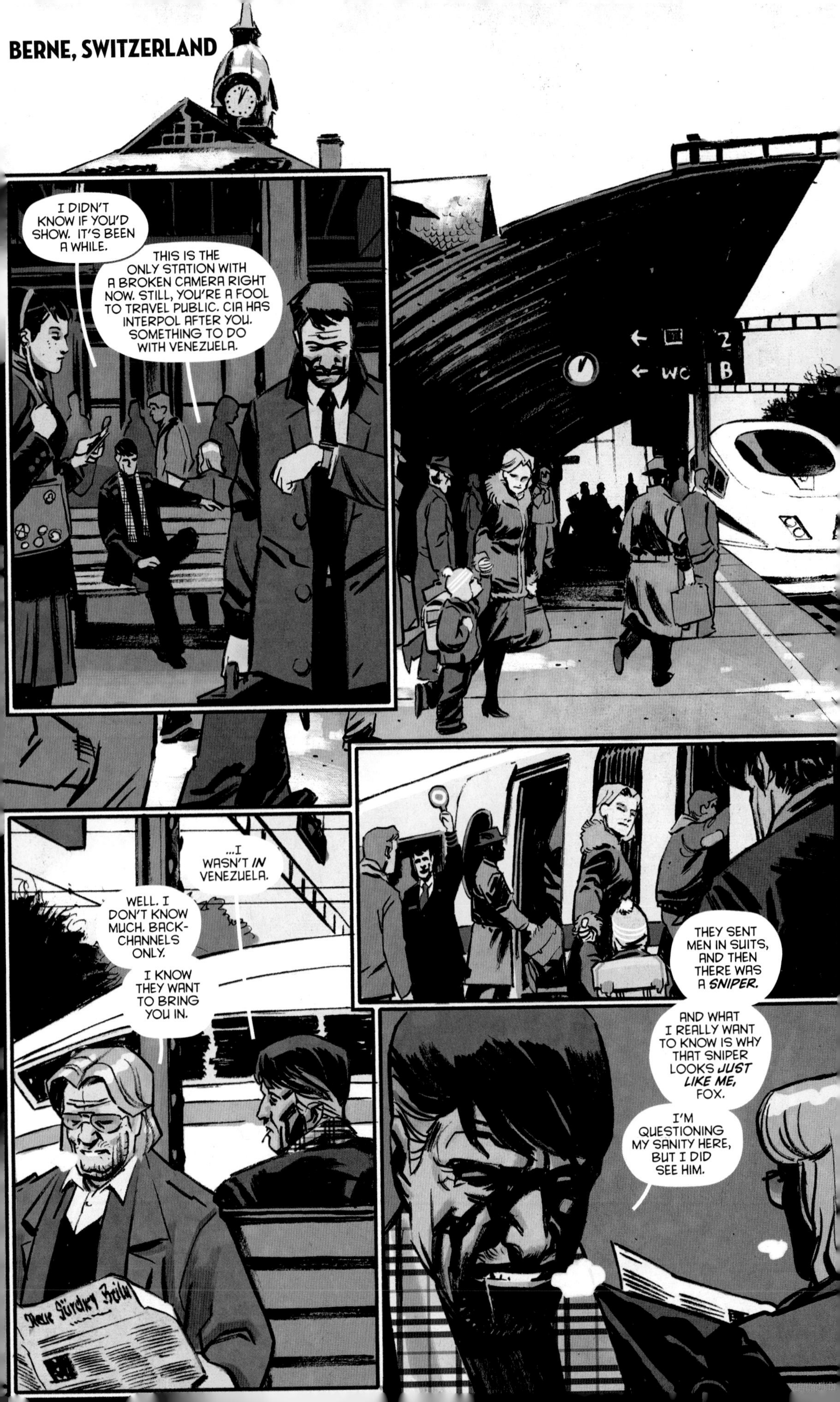

BERNE, SWITZERLAND
I DIDN'T KNOW IF YOU'D SHOW. IT'S BEEN A WHILE.
THIS IS THE ONLY STATION WITH A BROKEN CAMERA RIGHT NOW. STILL, YOU'RE A FOOL TO TRAVEL PUBLIC. CIA HAS INTERPOL AFTER YOU. SOMETHING TO DO WITH VENEZUELA.
WC
B
2
...I WASN'T *IN* VENEZUELA.
WELL. I DON'T KNOW MUCH. BACK-CHANNELS ONLY.
I KNOW THEY WANT TO BRING YOU IN.
THEY SENT MEN IN SUITS, AND THEN THERE WAS A ***SNIPER.***
AND WHAT I REALLY WANT TO KNOW IS WHY THAT SNIPER LOOKS ***JUST LIKE ME,*** FOX.
I'M QUESTIONING MY SANITY HERE, BUT I DID SEE HIM.

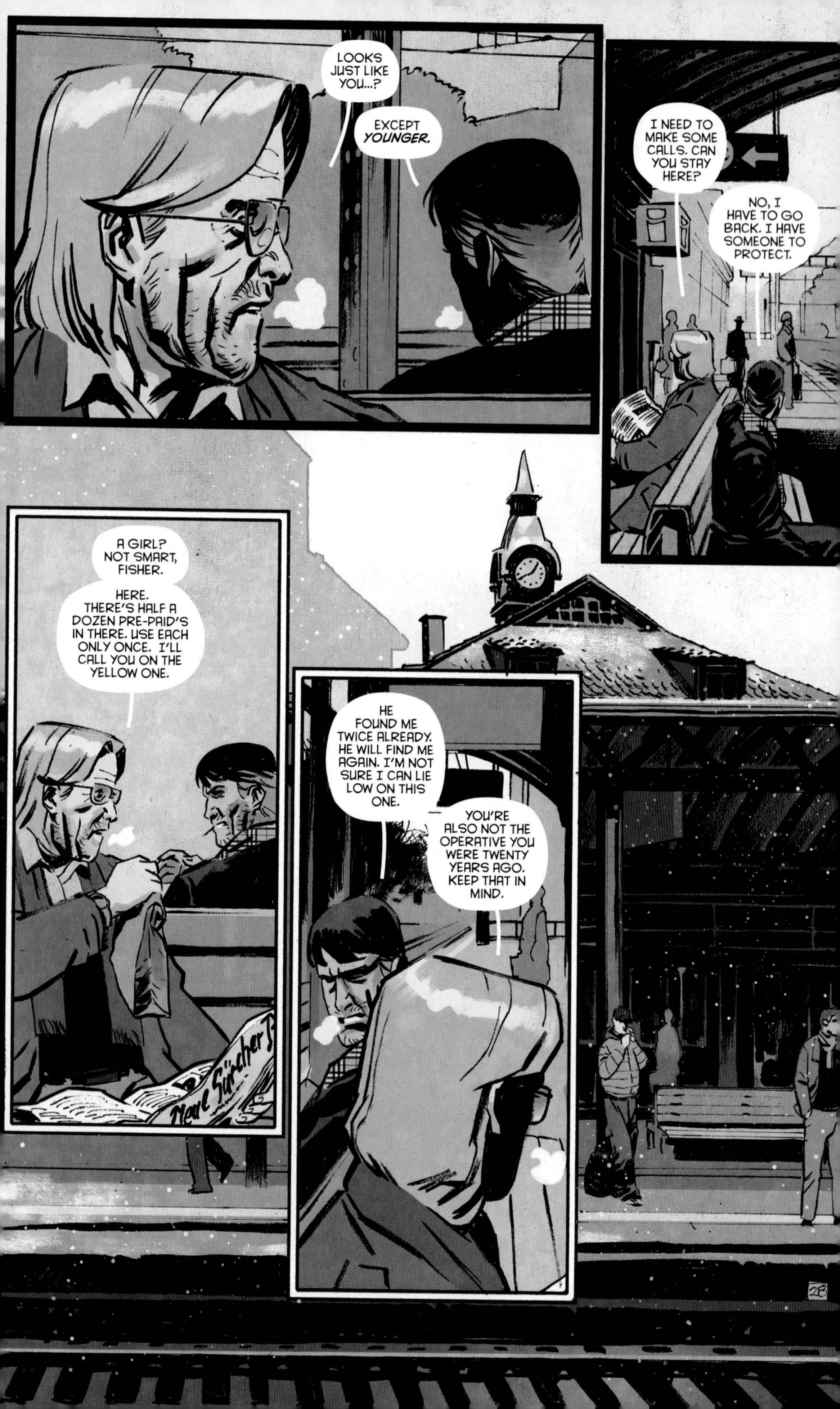

LOOKS JUST LIKE YOU...?
EXCEPT *YOUNGER.*
I NEED TO MAKE SOME CALLS. CAN YOU STAY HERE?
NO, I HAVE TO GO BACK. I HAVE SOMEONE TO PROTECT.
A GIRL? NOT SMART, FISHER.
HERE. THERE'S HALF A DOZEN PRE-PAID'S IN THERE. USE EACH ONLY ONCE. I'LL CALL YOU ON THE YELLOW ONE.
Neue Zürcher
HE FOUND ME TWICE ALREADY. HE WILL FIND ME AGAIN. I'M NOT SURE I CAN LIE LOW ON THIS ONE.
YOU'RE ALSO NOT THE OPERATIVE YOU WERE TWENTY YEARS AGO. KEEP THAT IN MIND.

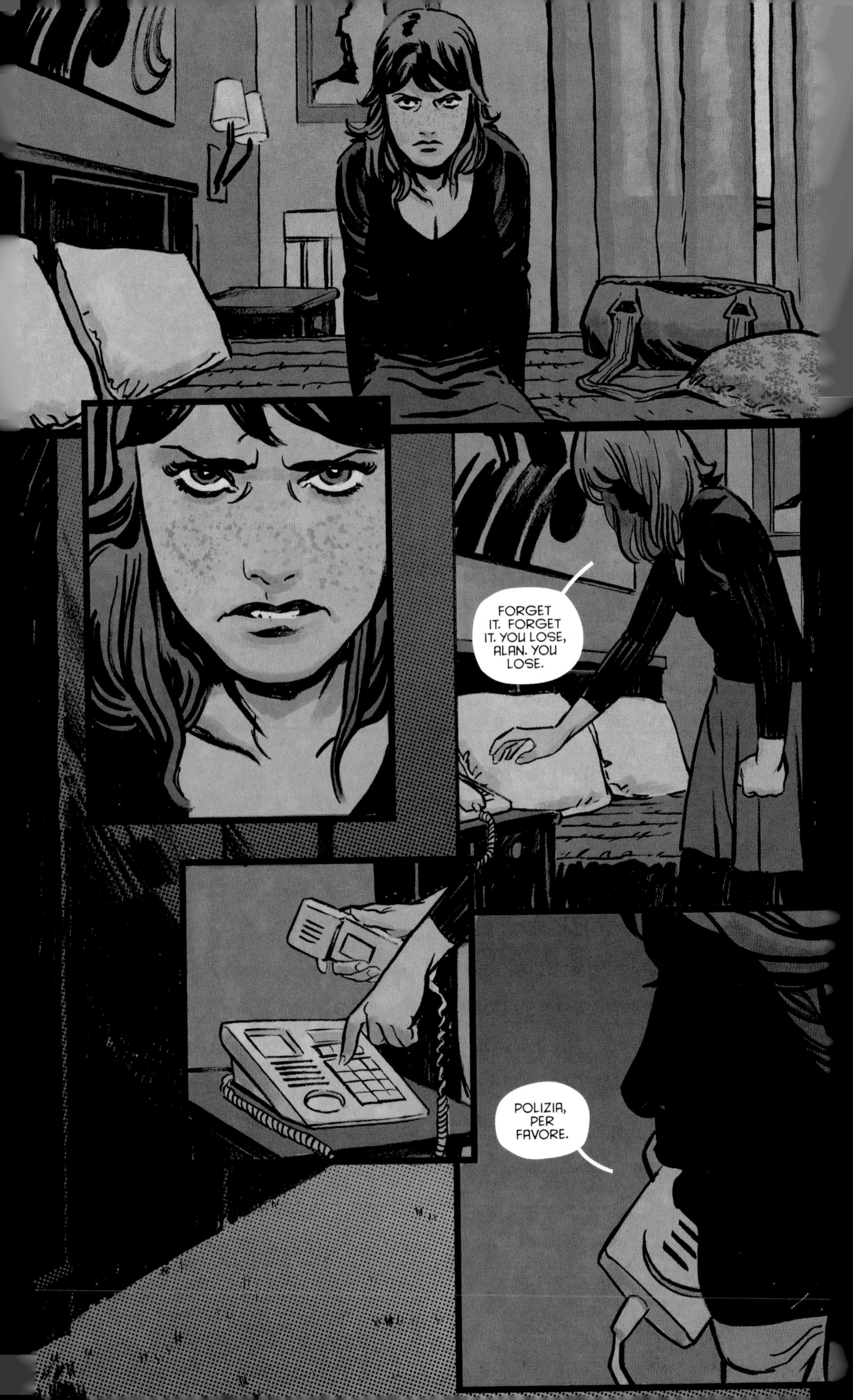
FORGET IT. FORGET IT. YOU LOSE, ALAN. YOU LOSE.
POLIZIA, PER FAVORE.

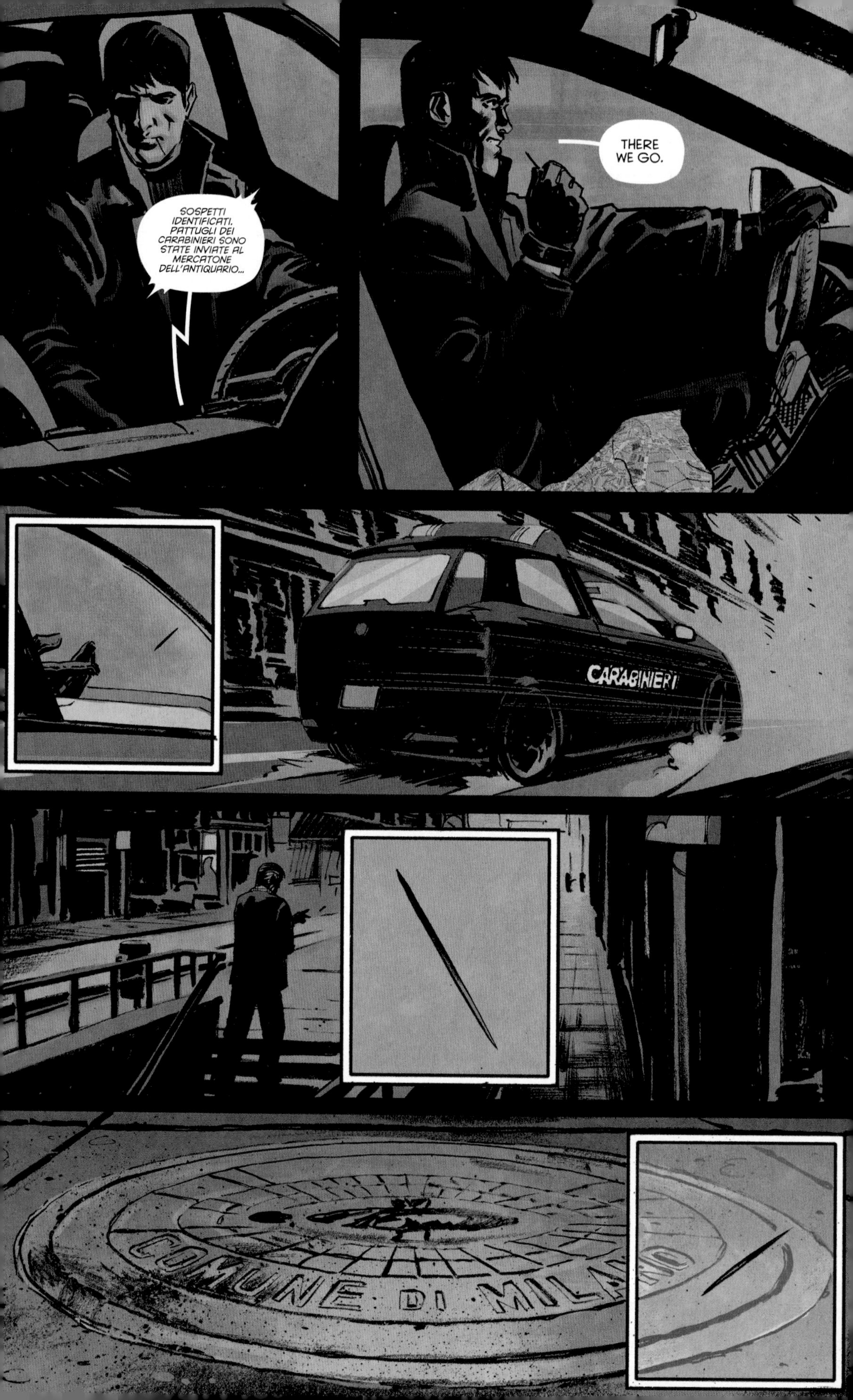
SOSPETTI IDENTIFICATI. PATTUGLI DEI CARABINIERI SONO STATE INVIATE AL MERCATONE DELL'ANTIQUARIO...
THERE WE GO.
CARABINIERI
COMUNE DI MILANO

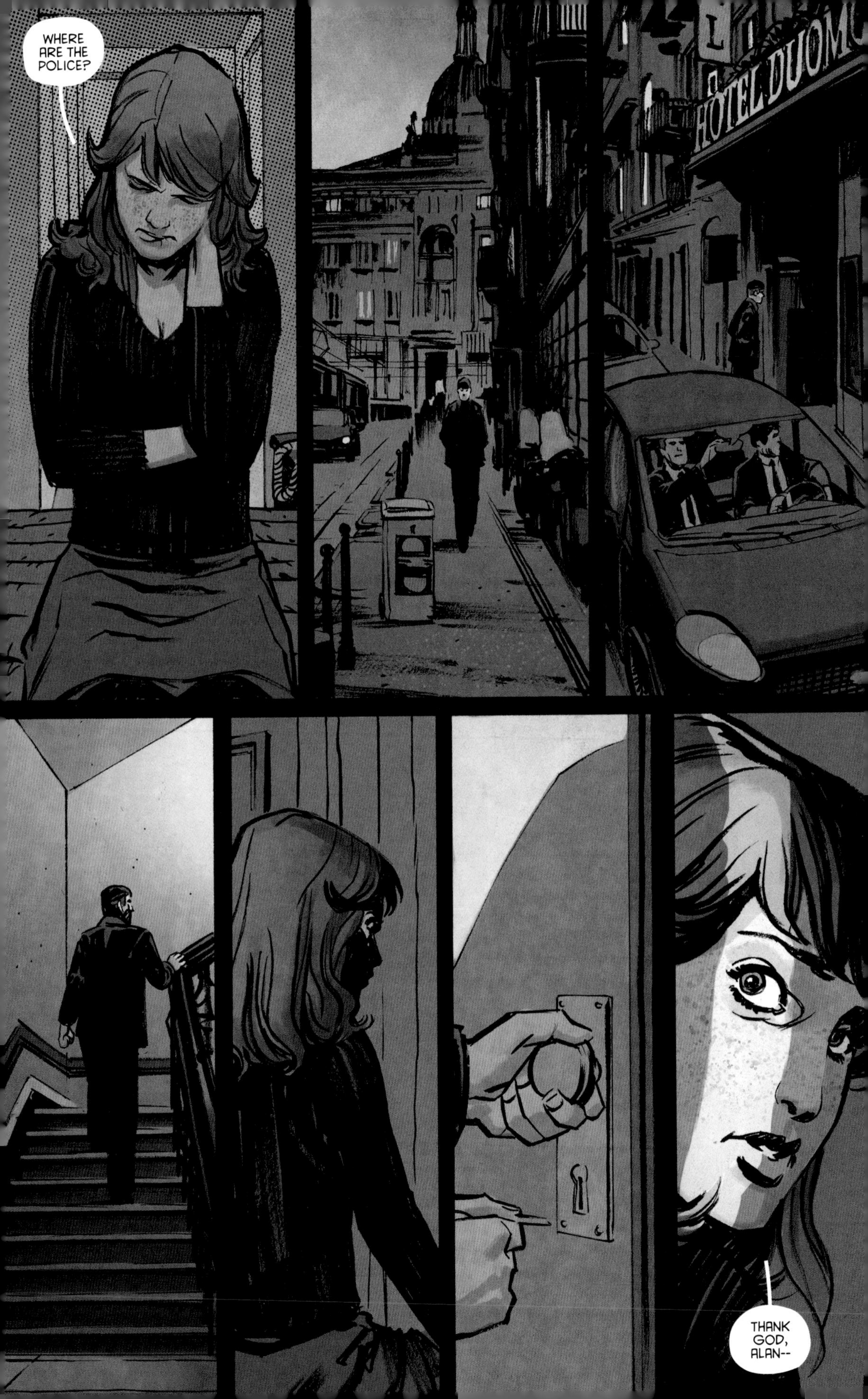
WHERE ARE THE POLICE?
HOTEL DUOMO
THANK GOD, ALAN--

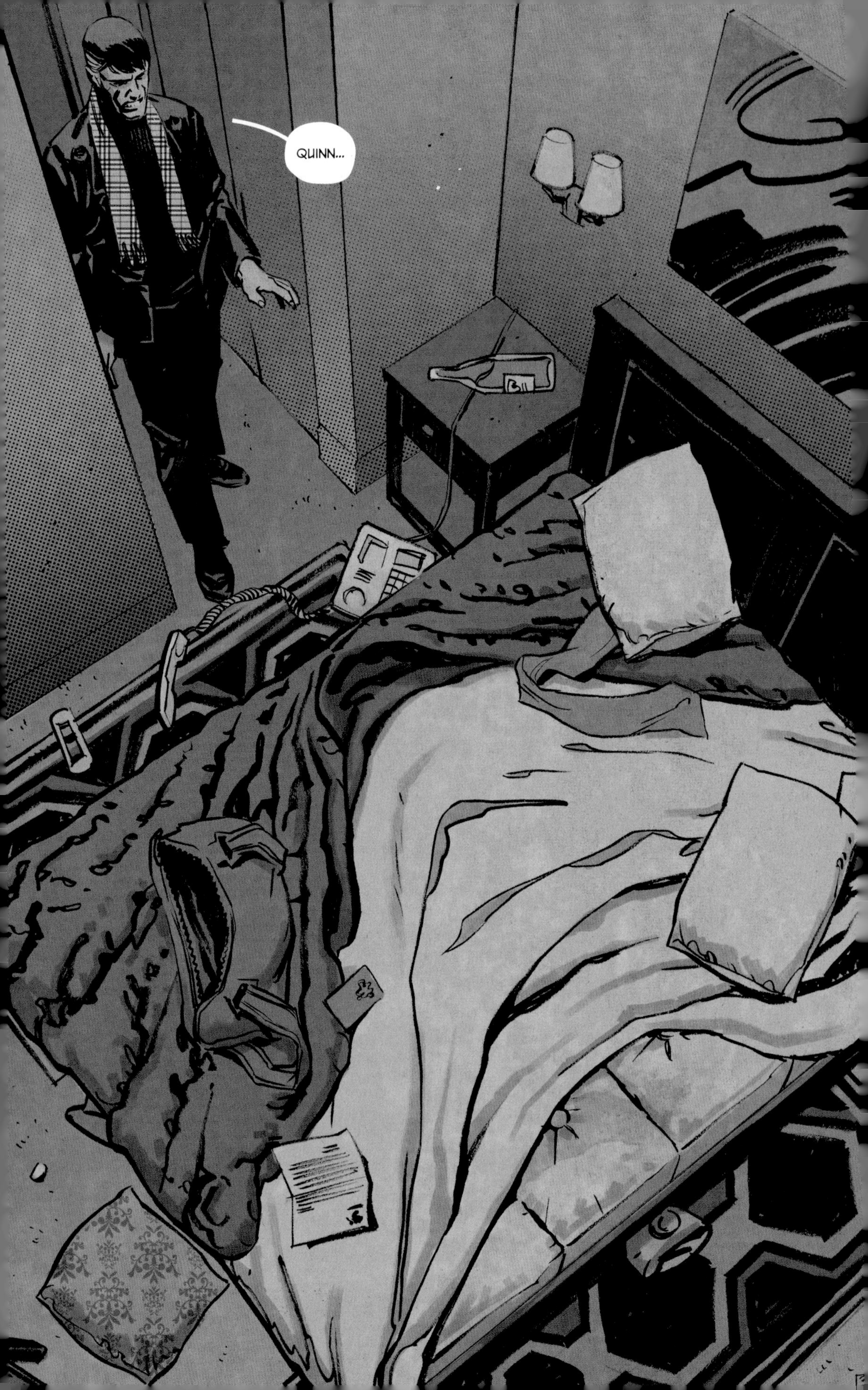
QUINN...

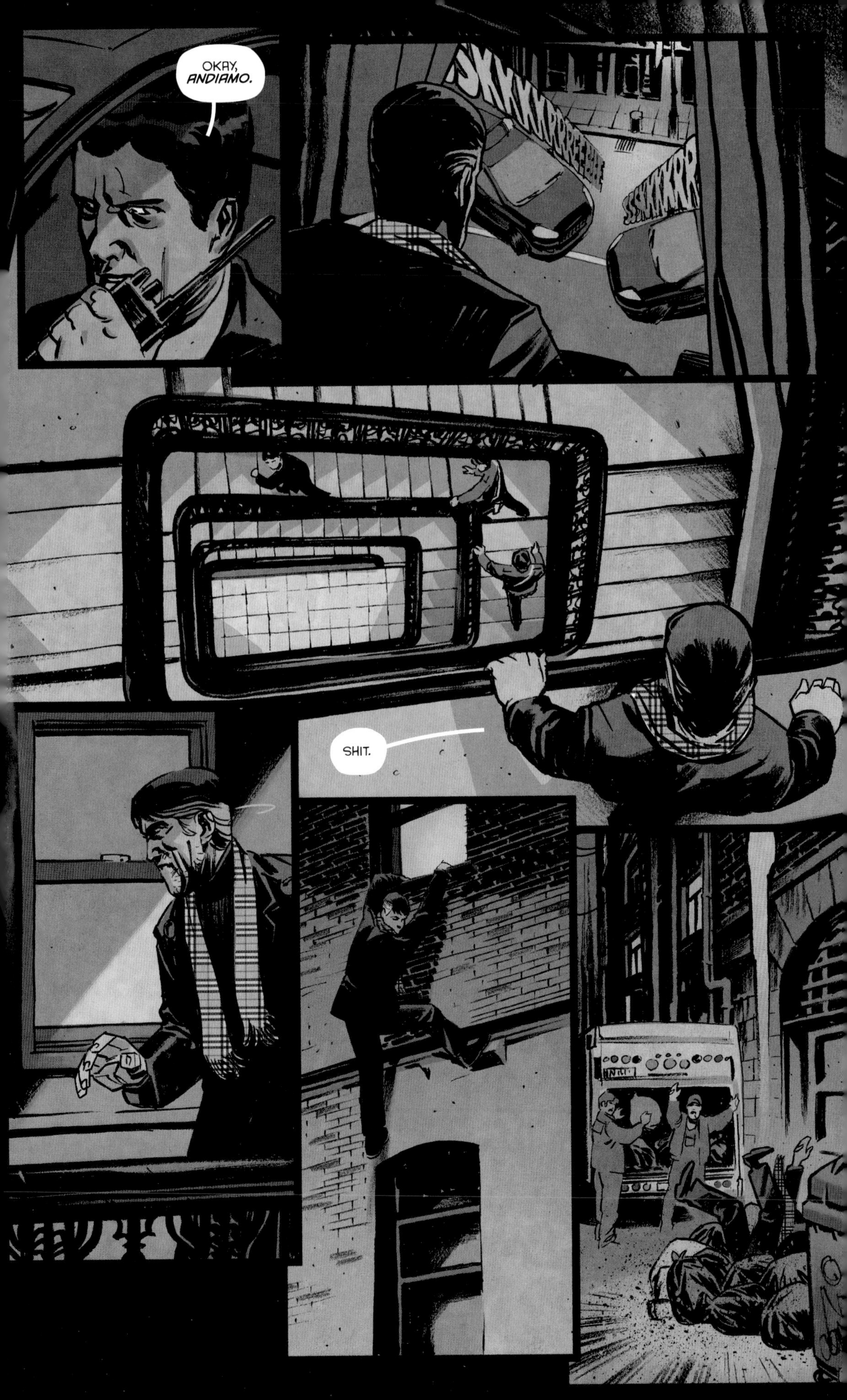
OKAY, *ANDIAMO.*
SKKKKRREEEEE
SSKKKKRR
SHIT.

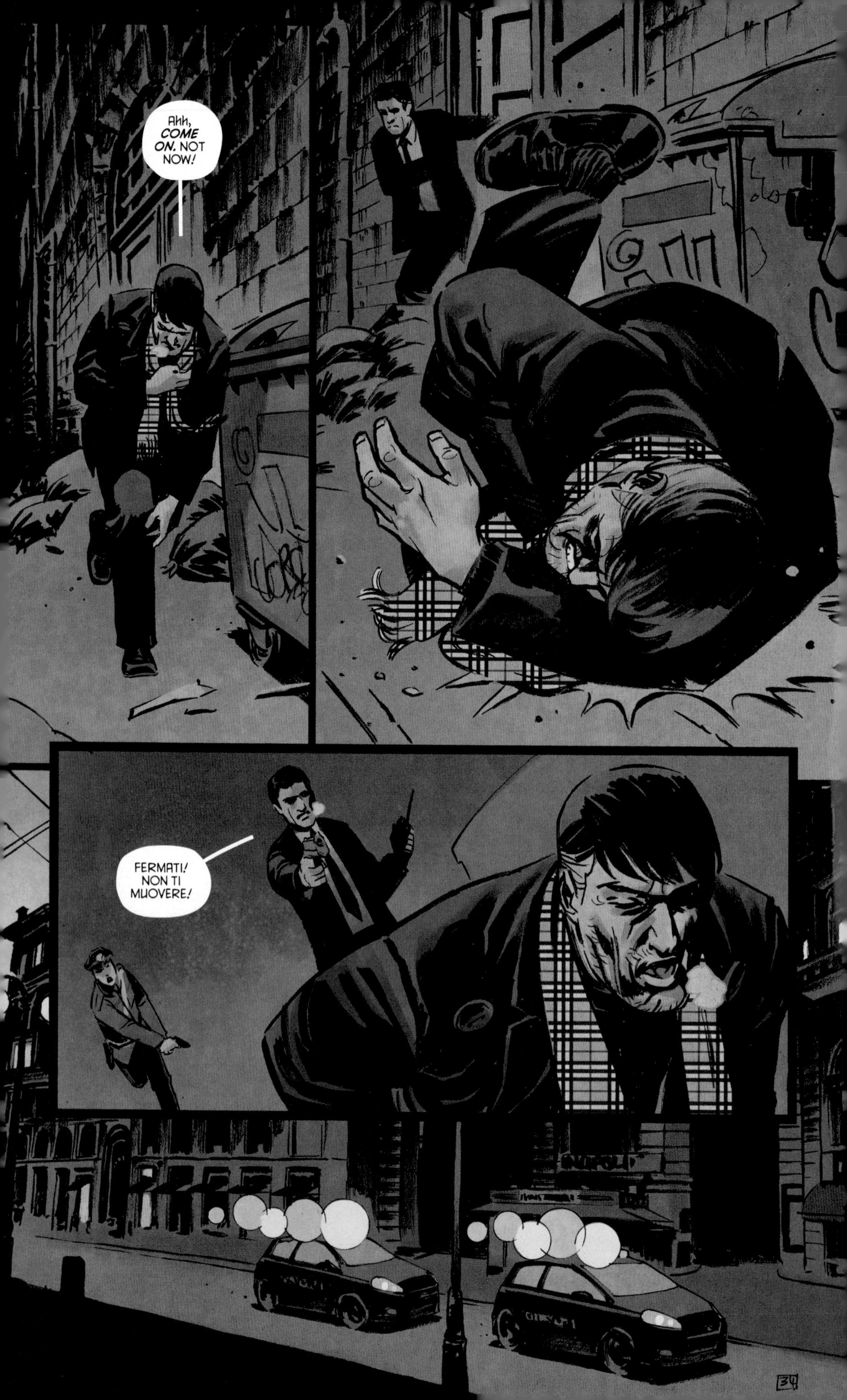
Ahh, COME ON. NOT NOW!
FERMATI! NON TI MUOVERE!

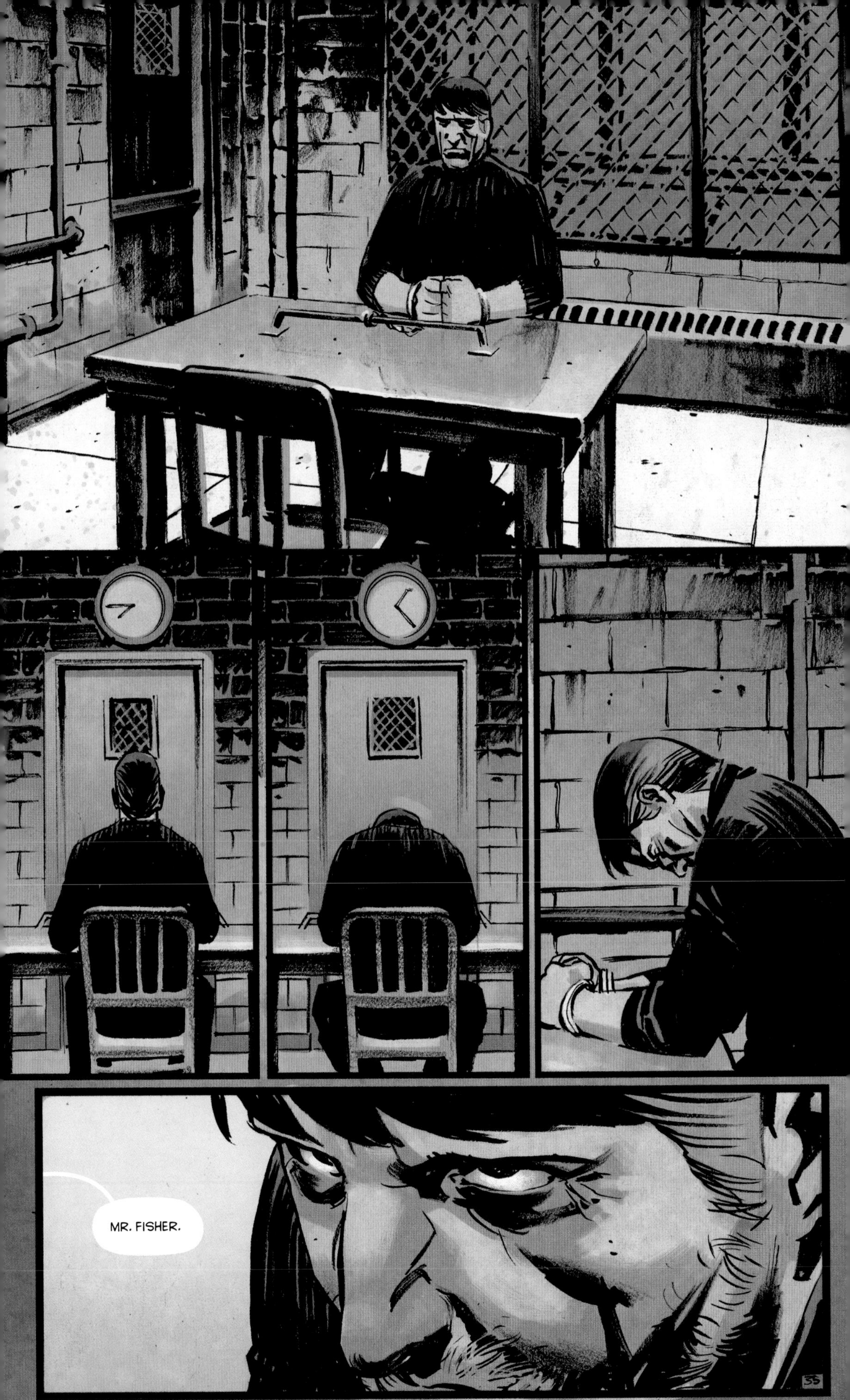
MR. FISHER.

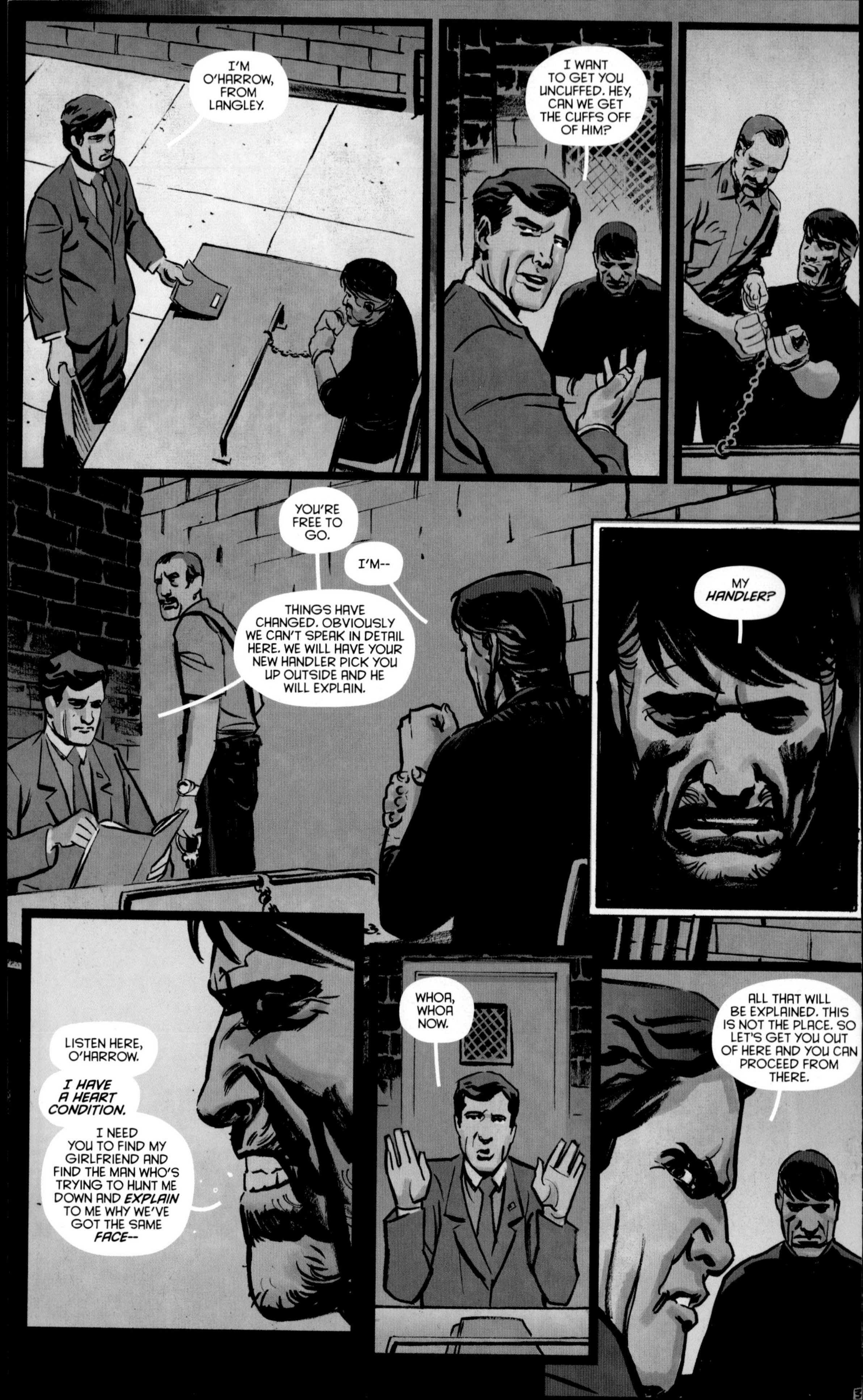
I'M O'HARROW, FROM LANGLEY.
I WANT TO GET YOU UNCUFFED. HEY, CAN WE GET THE CUFFS OFF OF HIM?
YOU'RE FREE TO GO.
I'M--
THINGS HAVE CHANGED. OBVIOUSLY WE CAN'T SPEAK IN DETAIL HERE. WE WILL HAVE YOUR NEW HANDLER PICK YOU UP OUTSIDE AND HE WILL EXPLAIN.
MY HANDLER?
LISTEN HERE, O'HARROW.
I HAVE A HEART CONDITION.
I NEED YOU TO FIND MY GIRLFRIEND AND FIND THE MAN WHO'S TRYING TO HUNT ME DOWN AND EXPLAIN TO ME WHY WE'VE GOT THE SAME FACE--
WHOA, WHOA NOW.
ALL THAT WILL BE EXPLAINED. THIS IS NOT THE PLACE. SO LET'S GET YOU OUT OF HERE AND YOU CAN PROCEED FROM THERE.

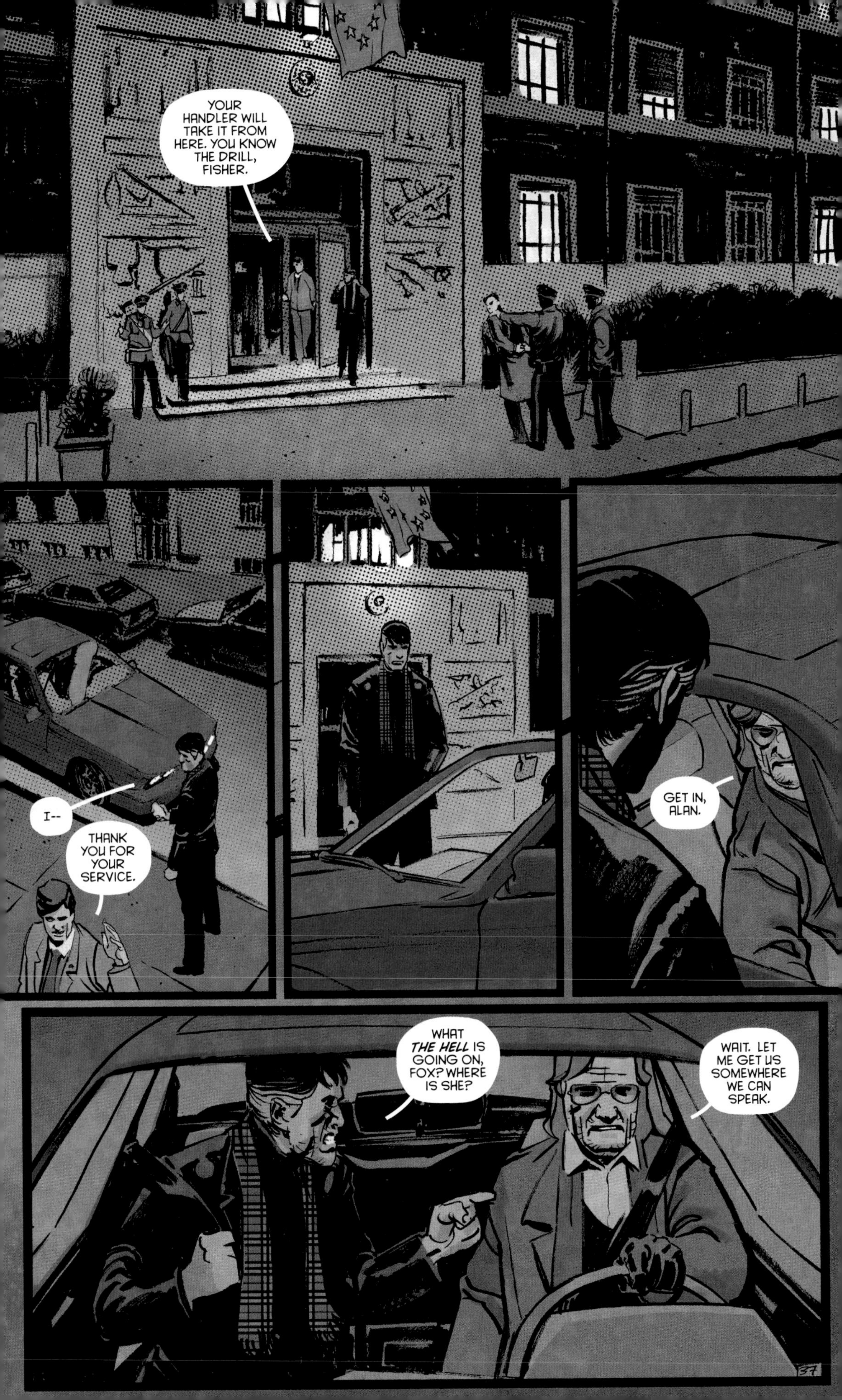
YOUR HANDLER WILL TAKE IT FROM HERE. YOU KNOW THE DRILL, FISHER.
I--
THANK YOU FOR YOUR SERVICE.
GET IN, ALAN.
WHAT *THE HELL* IS GOING ON, FOX? WHERE IS SHE?
WAIT. LET ME GET US SOMEWHERE WE CAN SPEAK.
37

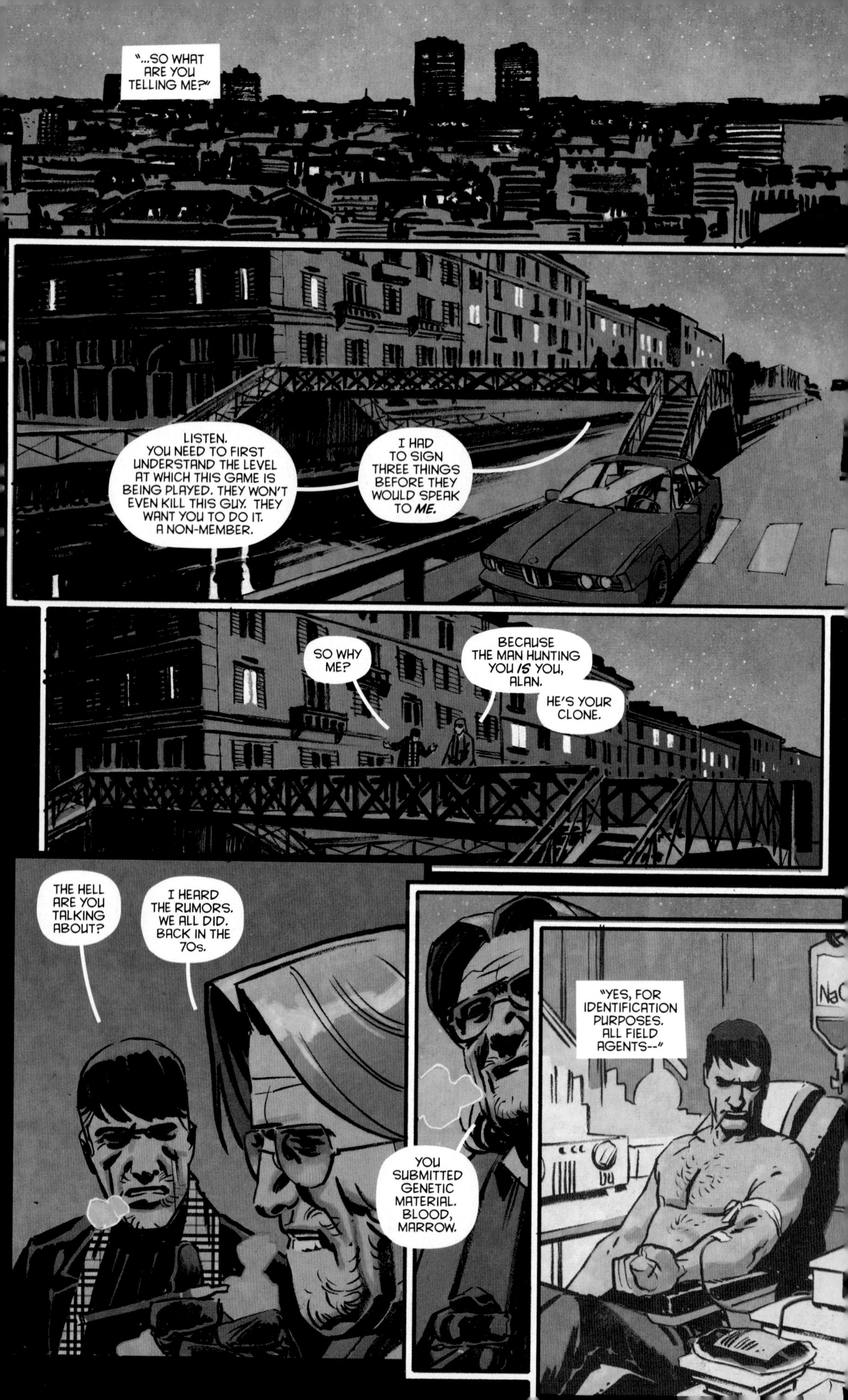
"...SO WHAT ARE YOU TELLING ME?"
LISTEN. YOU NEED TO FIRST UNDERSTAND THE LEVEL AT WHICH THIS GAME IS BEING PLAYED. THEY WON'T EVEN KILL THIS GUY. THEY WANT YOU TO DO IT. A NON-MEMBER.
I HAD TO SIGN THREE THINGS BEFORE THEY WOULD SPEAK TO *ME.*
SO WHY ME?
BECAUSE THE MAN HUNTING YOU *IS* YOU, ALAN.
HE'S YOUR CLONE.
THE HELL ARE YOU TALKING ABOUT?
I HEARD THE RUMORS. WE ALL DID. BACK IN THE 70s.
YOU SUBMITTED GENETIC MATERIAL. BLOOD, MARROW.
"YES, FOR IDENTIFICATION PURPOSES. ALL FIELD AGENTS--"
NaC

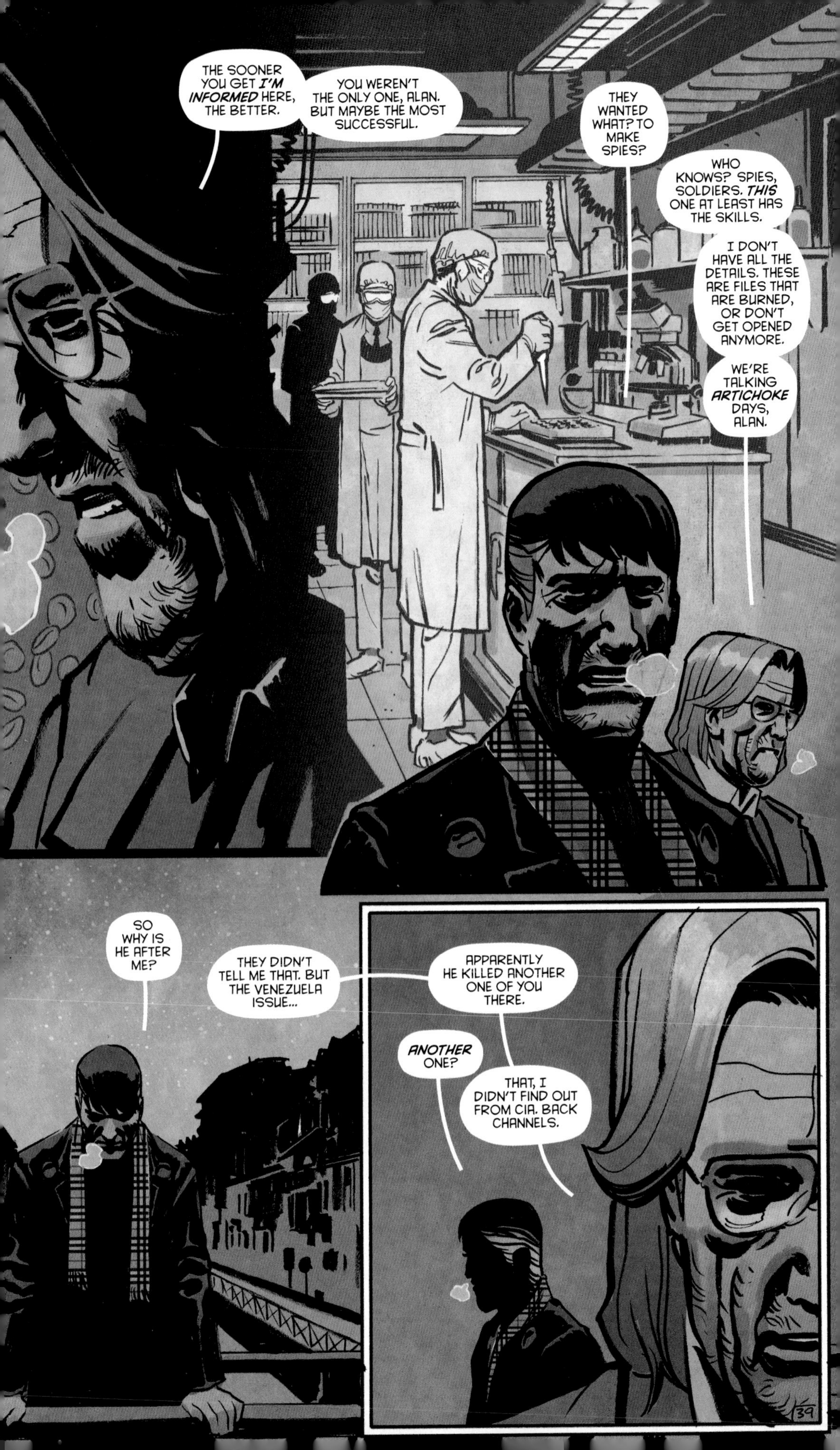
THE SOONER YOU GET I'M INFORMED HERE, THE BETTER.
YOU WEREN'T THE ONLY ONE, ALAN. BUT MAYBE THE MOST SUCCESSFUL.
THEY WANTED WHAT? TO MAKE SPIES?
WHO KNOWS? SPIES, SOLDIERS. THIS ONE AT LEAST HAS THE SKILLS.
I DON'T HAVE ALL THE DETAILS. THESE ARE FILES THAT ARE BURNED, OR DON'T GET OPENED ANYMORE.
WE'RE TALKING ARTICHOKE DAYS, ALAN.
SO WHY IS HE AFTER ME?
THEY DIDN'T TELL ME THAT. BUT THE VENEZUELA ISSUE...
APPARENTLY HE KILLED ANOTHER ONE OF YOU THERE.
ANOTHER ONE?
THAT, I DIDN'T FIND OUT FROM CIA. BACK CHANNELS.

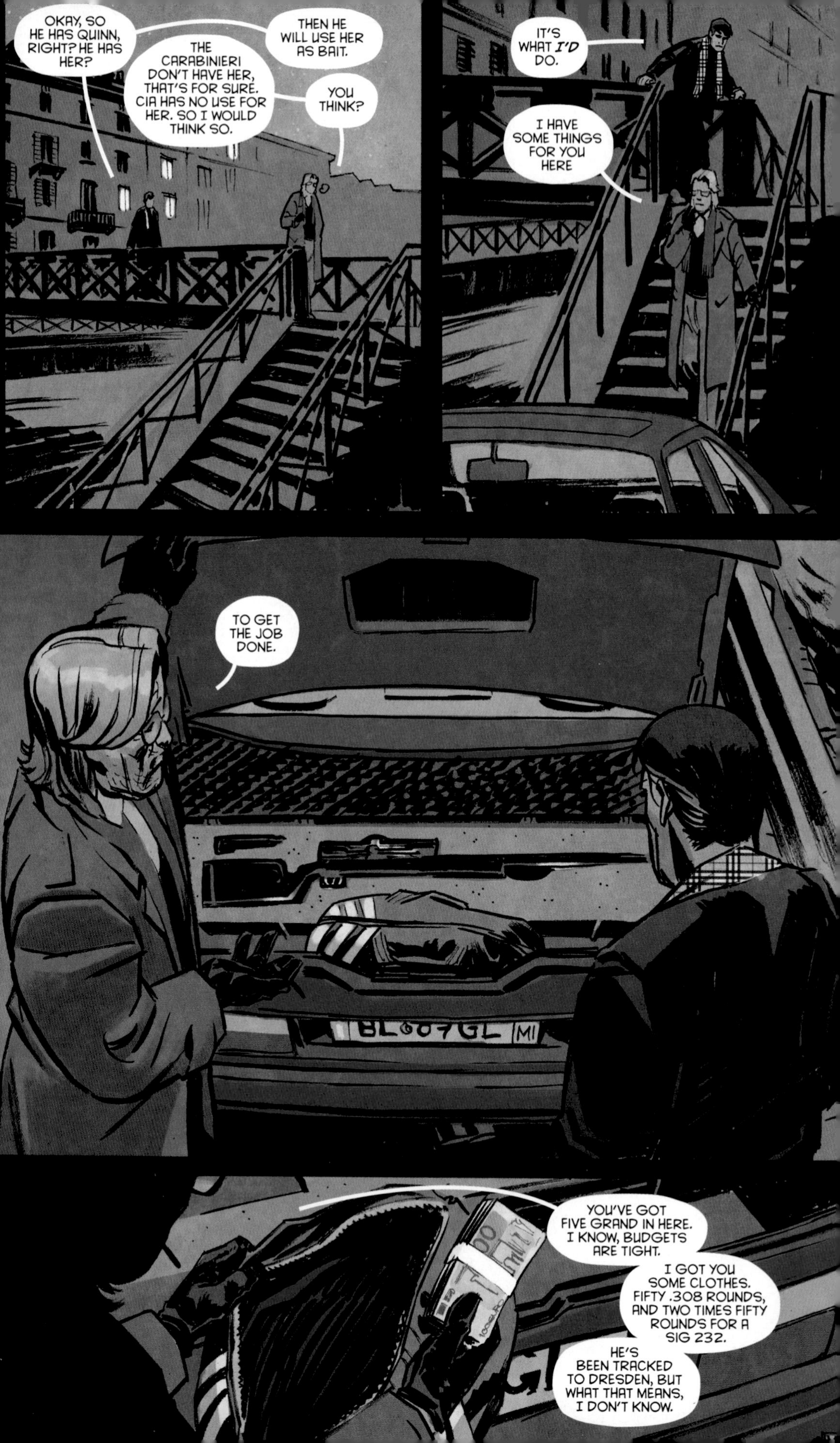
OKAY, SO HE HAS QUINN, RIGHT? HE HAS HER?
THEN HE WILL USE HER AS BAIT.
THE CARABINIERI DON'T HAVE HER, THAT'S FOR SURE. CIA HAS NO USE FOR HER. SO I WOULD THINK SO.
YOU THINK?
IT'S WHAT *I'D* DO.
I HAVE SOME THINGS FOR YOU HERE
TO GET THE JOB DONE.
BL 607GL MI
YOU'VE GOT FIVE GRAND IN HERE. I KNOW, BUDGETS ARE TIGHT.
I GOT YOU SOME CLOTHES. FIFTY .308 ROUNDS, AND TWO TIMES FIFTY ROUNDS FOR A SIG 232.
HE'S BEEN TRACKED TO DRESDEN, BUT WHAT THAT MEANS, I DON'T KNOW.

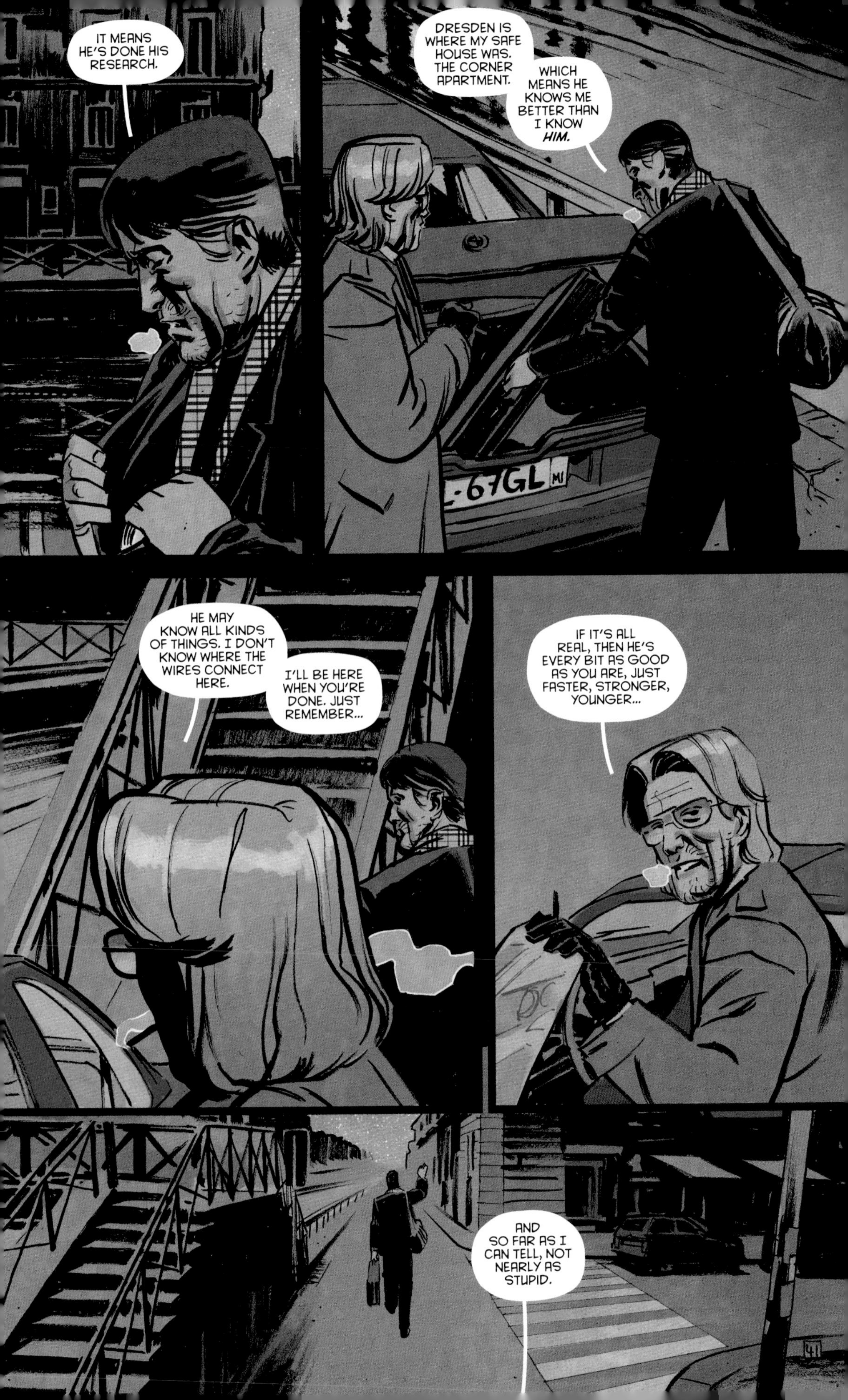
IT MEANS HE'S DONE HIS RESEARCH.
DRESDEN IS WHERE MY SAFE HOUSE WAS. THE CORNER APARTMENT.
WHICH MEANS HE KNOWS ME BETTER THAN I KNOW *HIM.*
L-67GL MI
HE MAY KNOW ALL KINDS OF THINGS. I DON'T KNOW WHERE THE WIRES CONNECT HERE.
I'LL BE HERE WHEN YOU'RE DONE. JUST REMEMBER...
IF IT'S ALL REAL, THEN HE'S EVERY BIT AS GOOD AS YOU ARE, JUST FASTER, STRONGER, YOUNGER...
AND SO FAR AS I CAN TELL, NOT NEARLY AS STUPID.

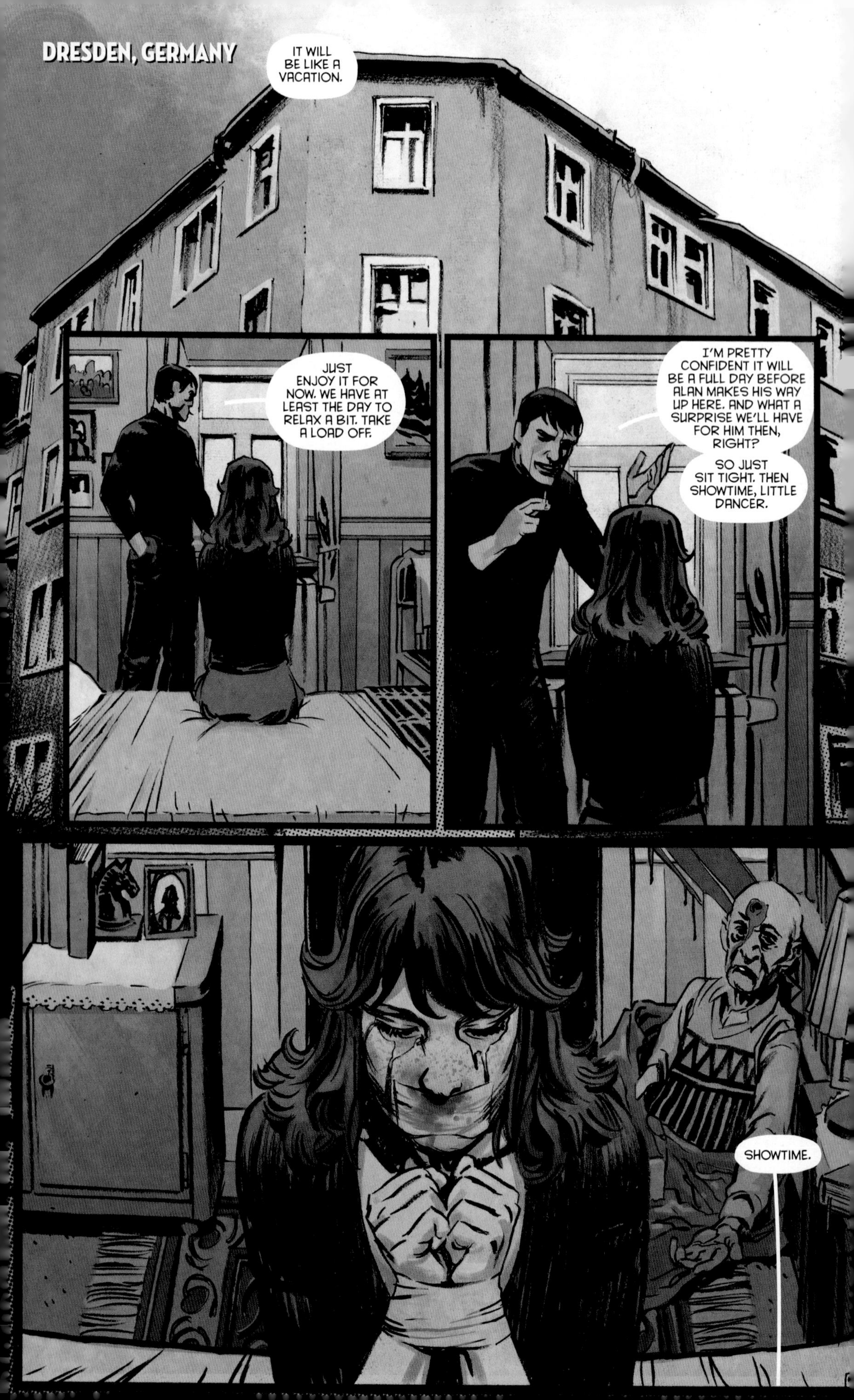
DRESDEN, GERMANY
IT WILL BE LIKE A VACATION.
JUST ENJOY IT FOR NOW. WE HAVE AT LEAST THE DAY TO RELAX A BIT. TAKE A LOAD OFF.
I'M PRETTY CONFIDENT IT WILL BE A FULL DAY BEFORE ALAN MAKES HIS WAY UP HERE. AND WHAT A SURPRISE WE'LL HAVE FOR HIM THEN, RIGHT?
SO JUST SIT TIGHT. THEN SHOWTIME, LITTLE DANCER.
SHOWTIME.

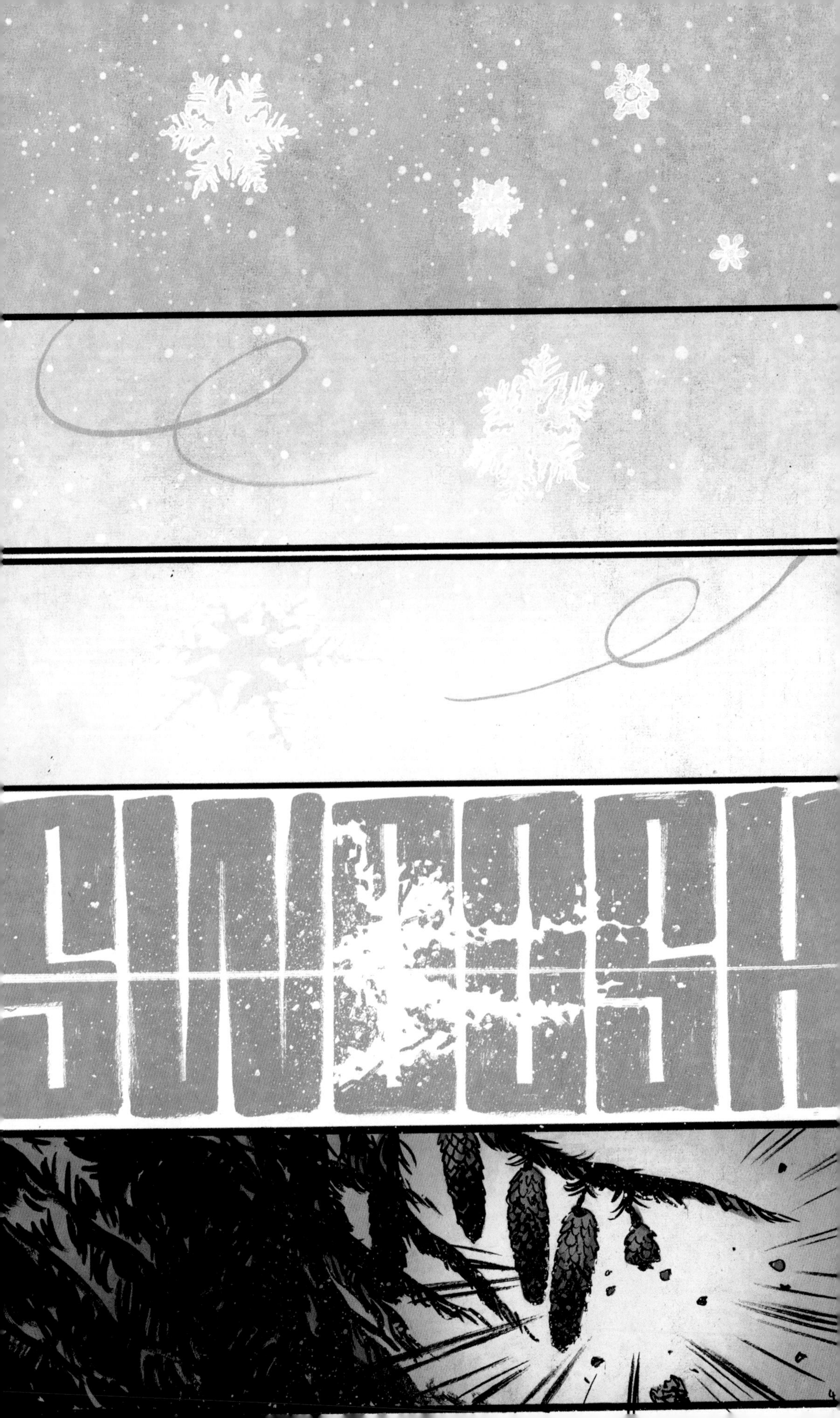
SWOOSH

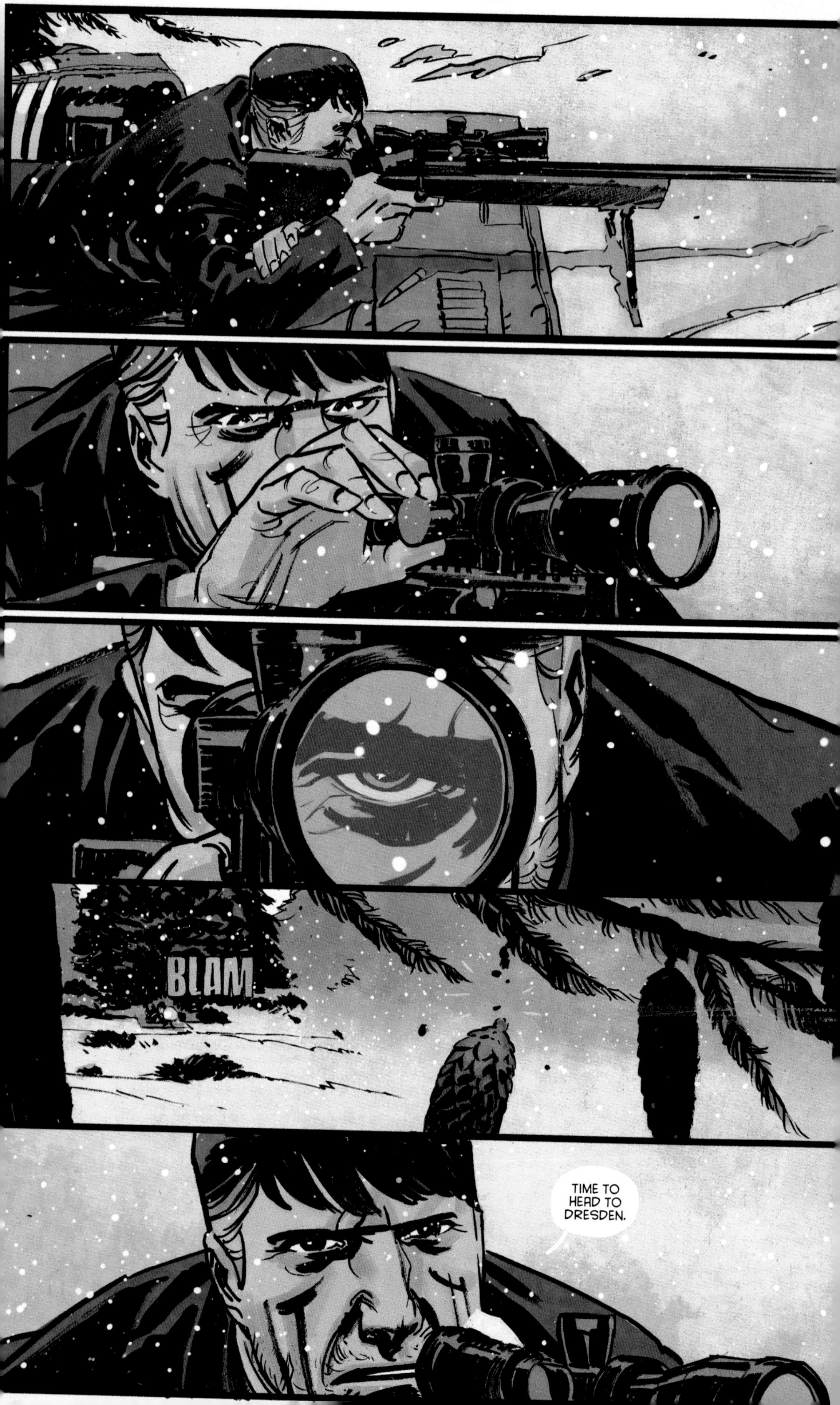
BLAM
TIME TO HEAD TO DRESDEN.

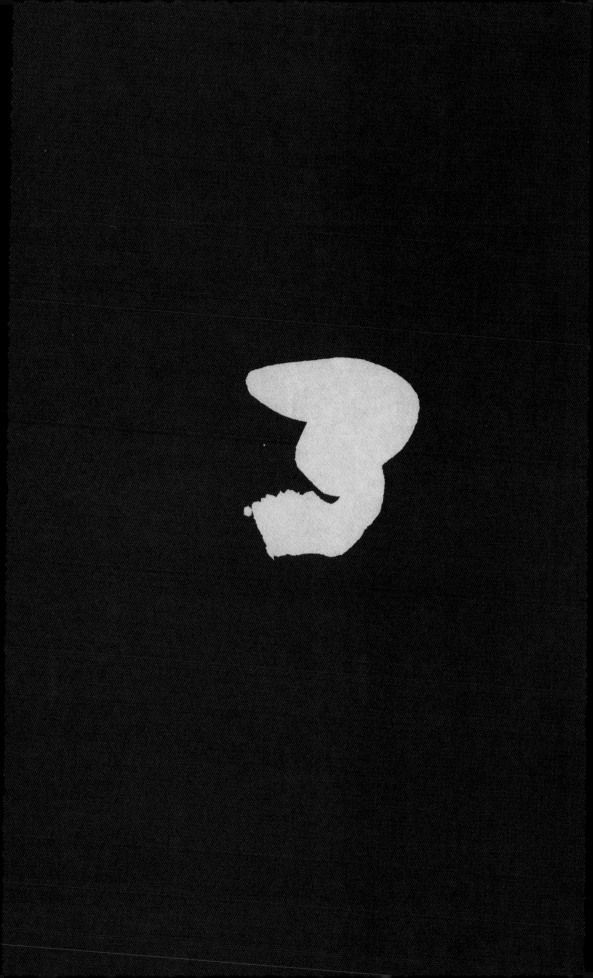

CAVALIER

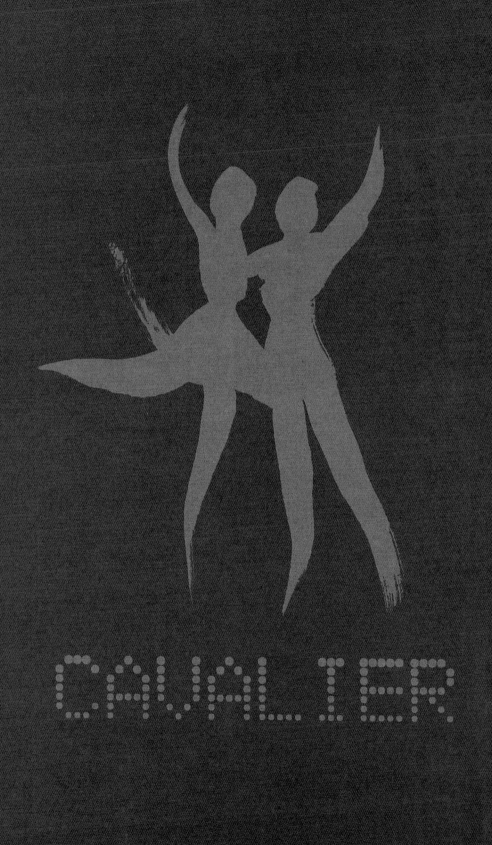

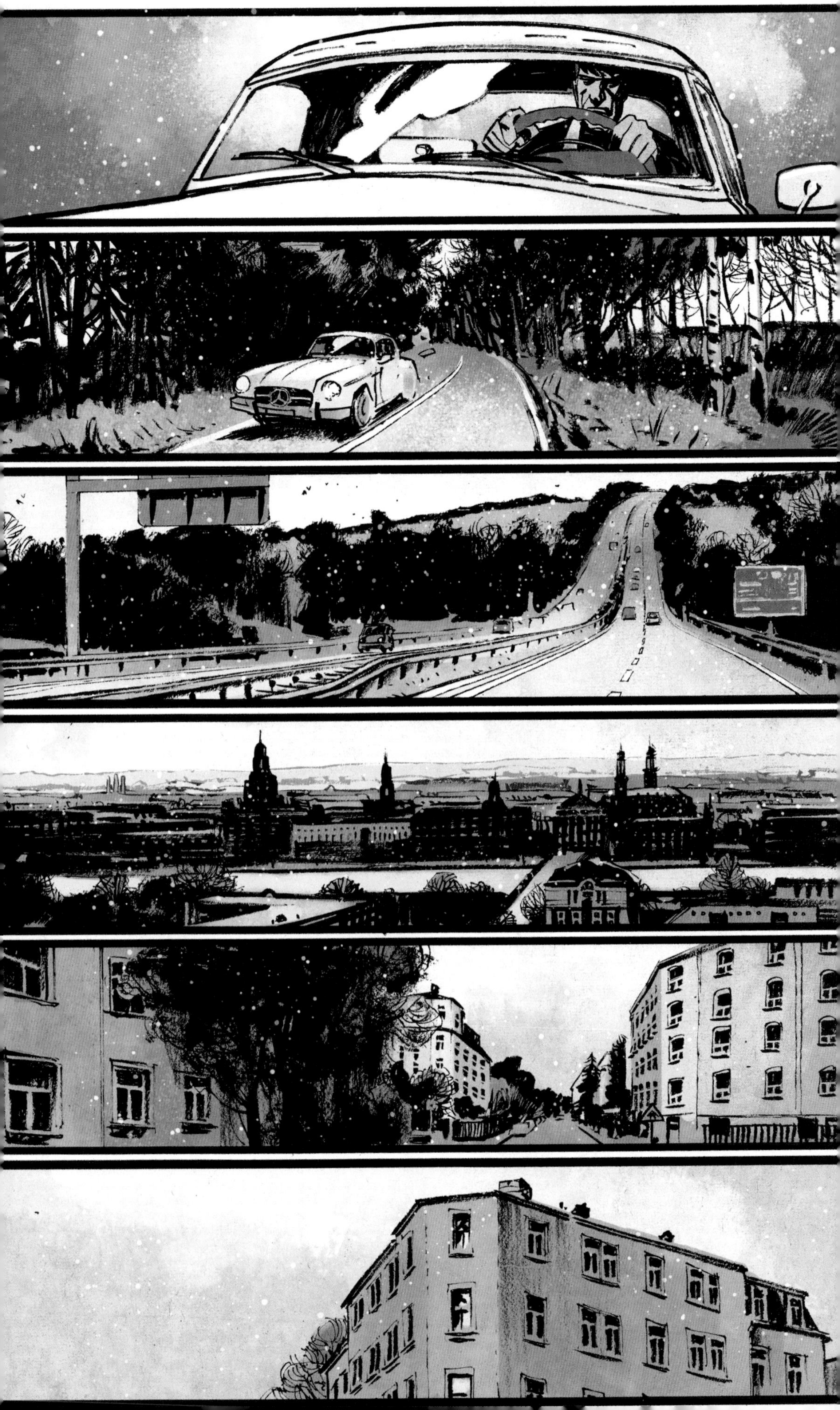

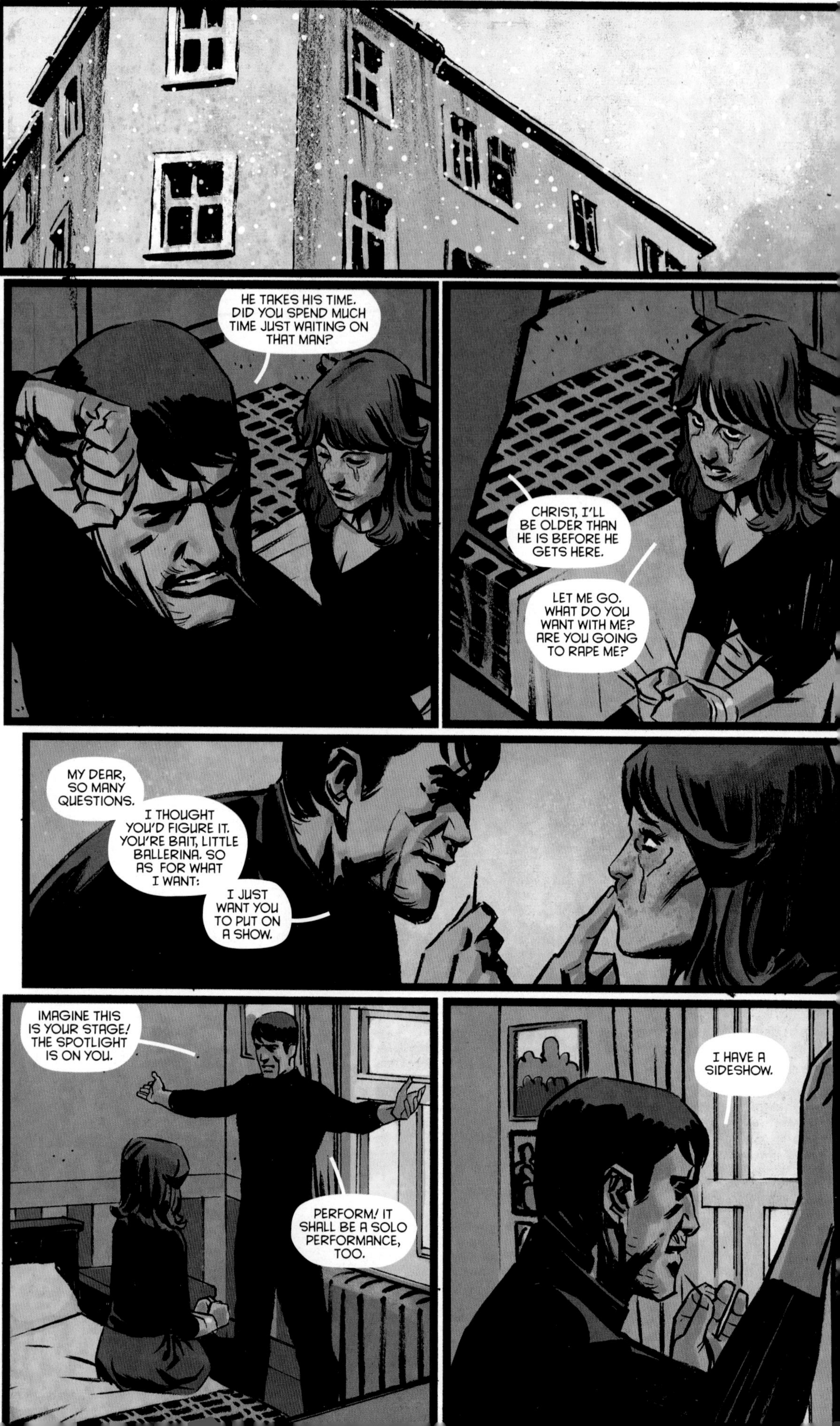
HE TAKES HIS TIME. DID YOU SPEND MUCH TIME JUST WAITING ON THAT MAN?
CHRIST, I'LL BE OLDER THAN HE IS BEFORE HE GETS HERE.
LET ME GO. WHAT DO YOU WANT WITH ME? ARE YOU GOING TO RAPE ME?
MY DEAR, SO MANY QUESTIONS.
I THOUGHT YOU'D FIGURE IT. YOU'RE BAIT, LITTLE BALLERINA. SO AS FOR WHAT I WANT:
I JUST WANT YOU TO PUT ON A SHOW.
IMAGINE THIS IS YOUR STAGE! THE SPOTLIGHT IS ON YOU.
PERFORM! IT SHALL BE A SOLO PERFORMANCE, TOO.
I HAVE A SIDESHOW.

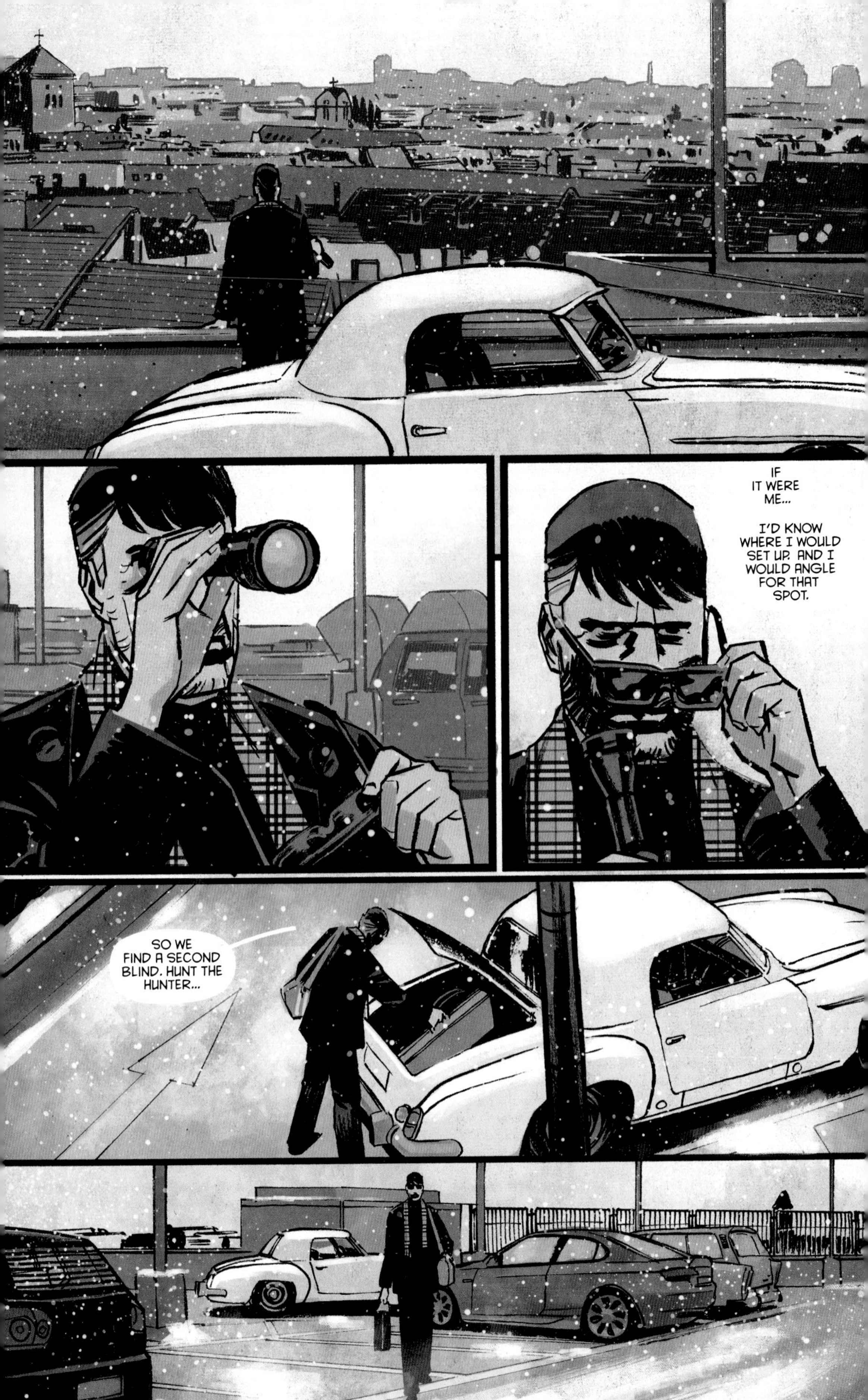
IF IT WERE ME...
I'D KNOW WHERE I WOULD SET UP. AND I WOULD ANGLE FOR THAT SPOT.
SO WE FIND A SECOND BLIND. HUNT THE HUNTER...

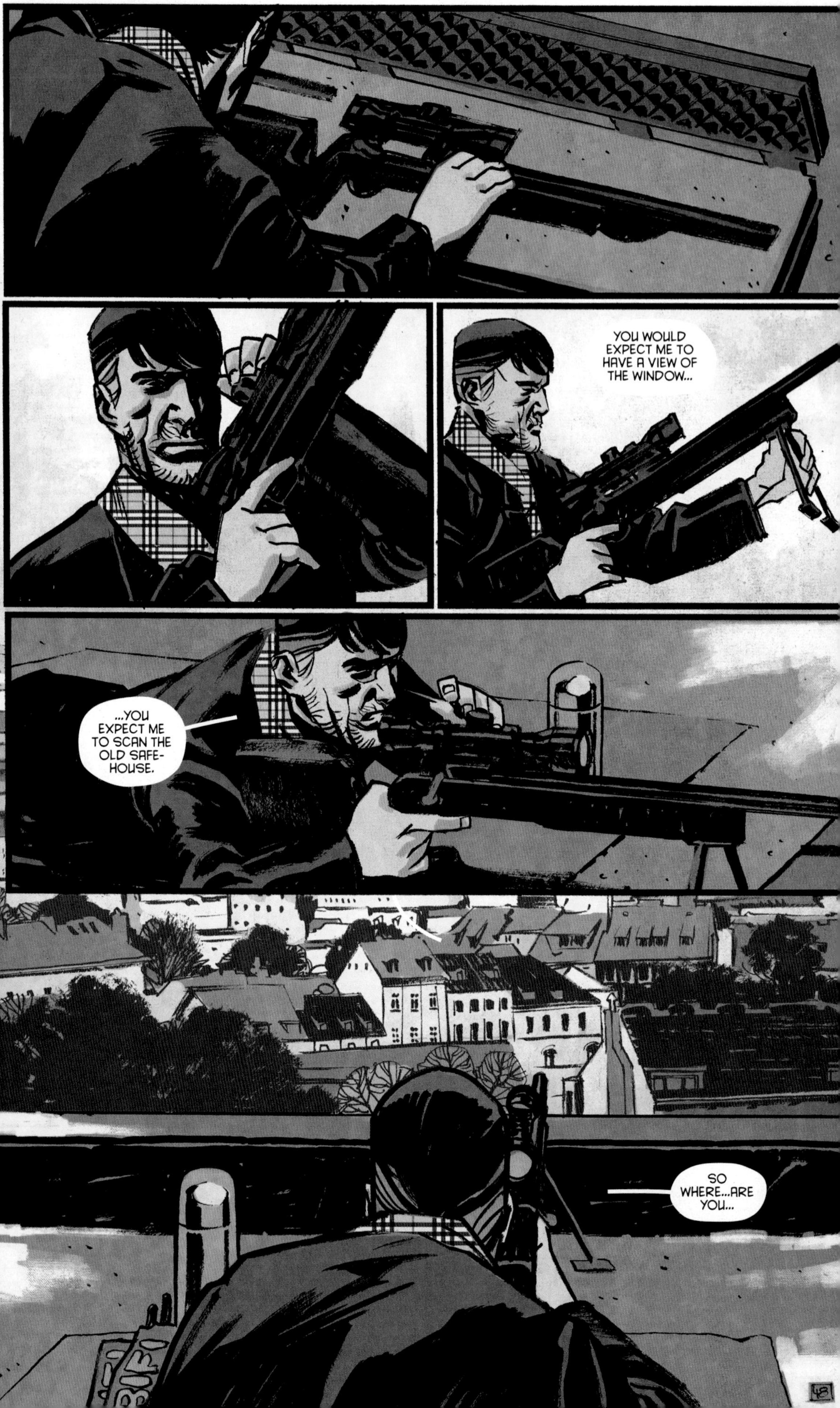
YOU WOULD EXPECT ME TO HAVE A VIEW OF THE WINDOW...
...YOU EXPECT ME TO SCAN THE OLD SAFE-HOUSE.
SO WHERE...ARE YOU...

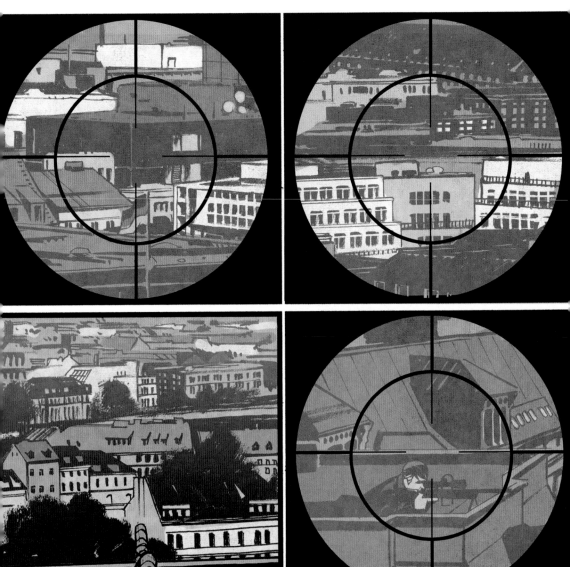

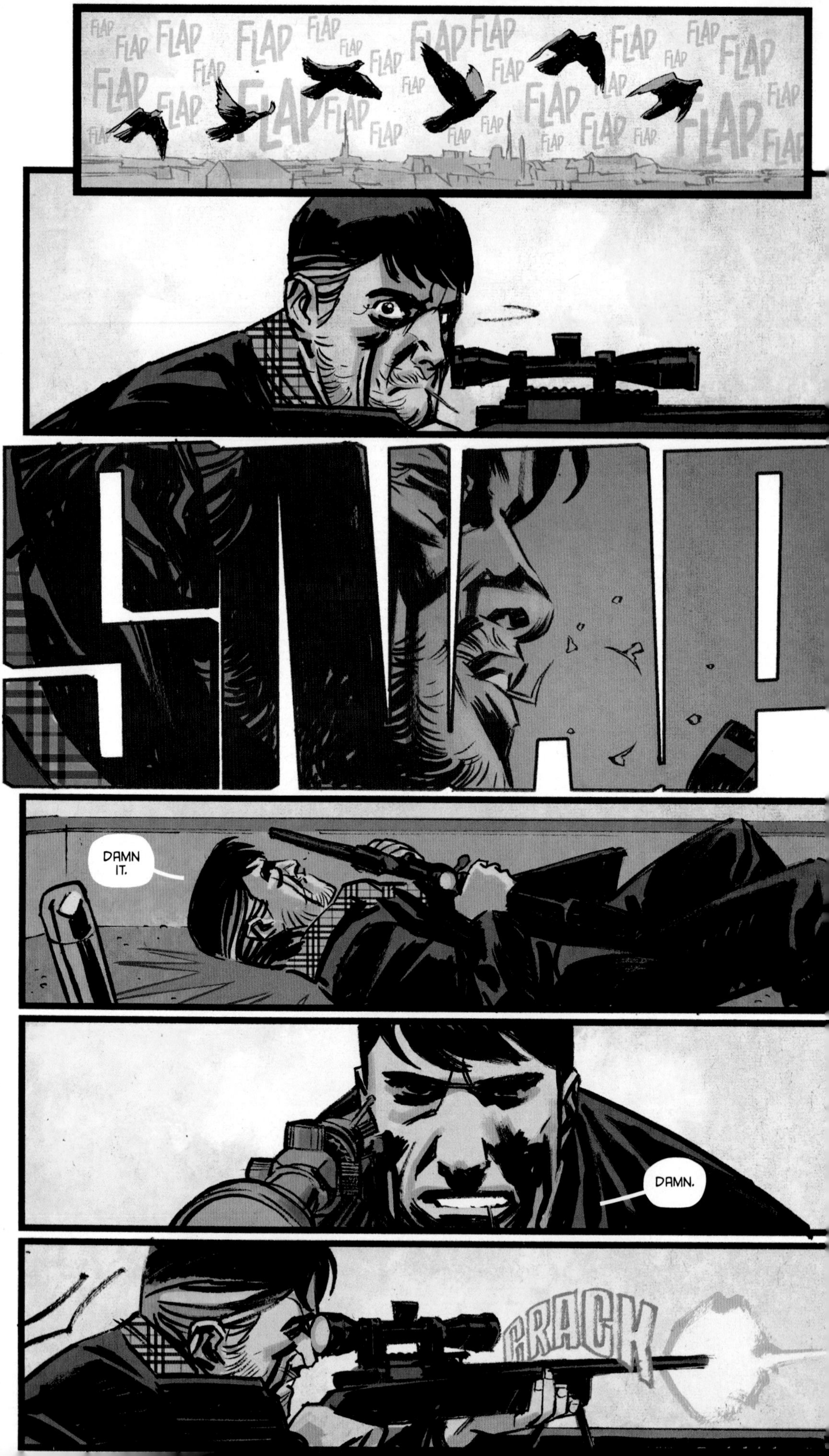
FLAP FLAP FLAP FLAP FLAP FLAP FLAP FLAP
DAMN IT.
DAMN.
CRACK

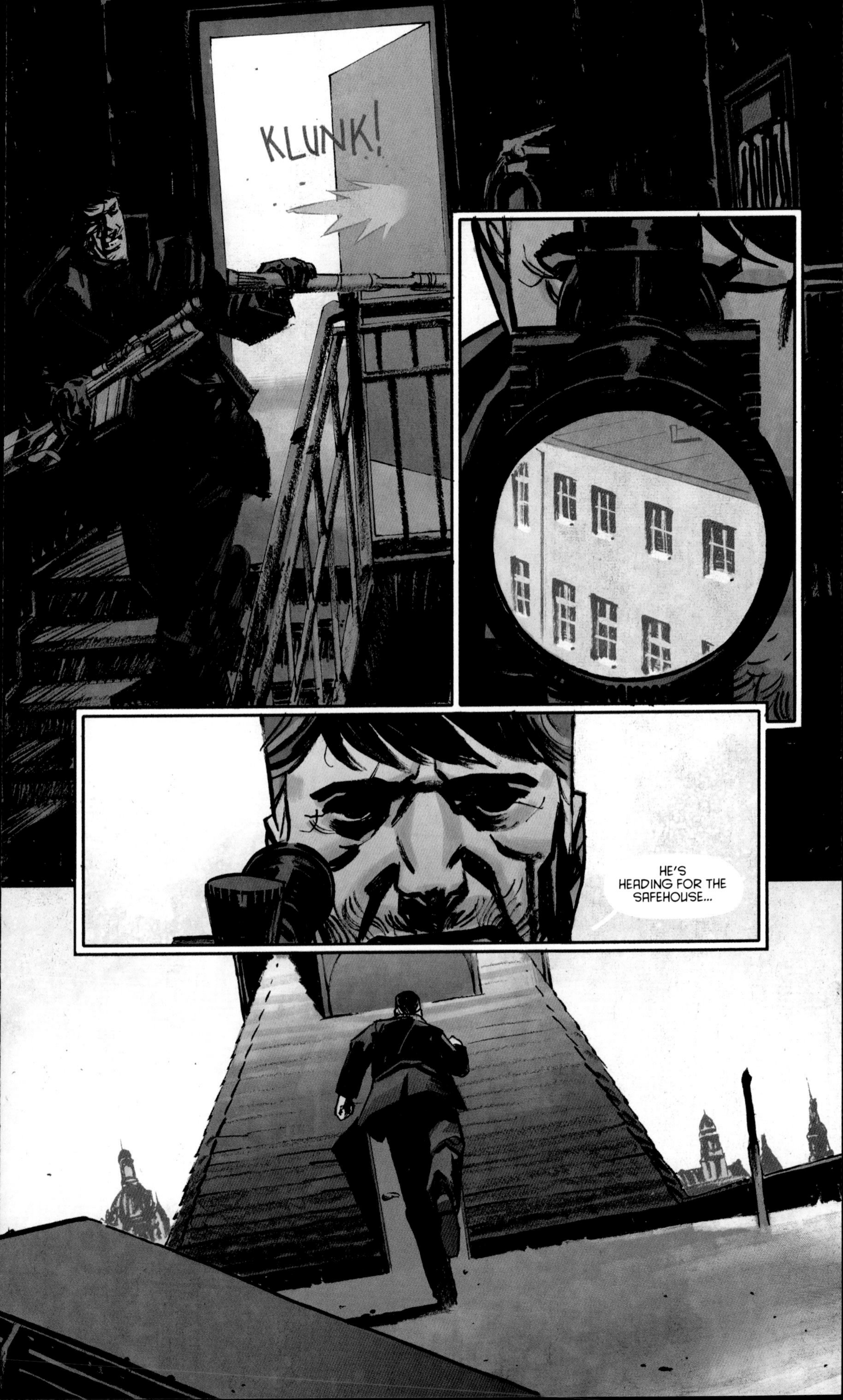
KLUNK!
HE'S HEADING FOR THE SAFEHOUSE...

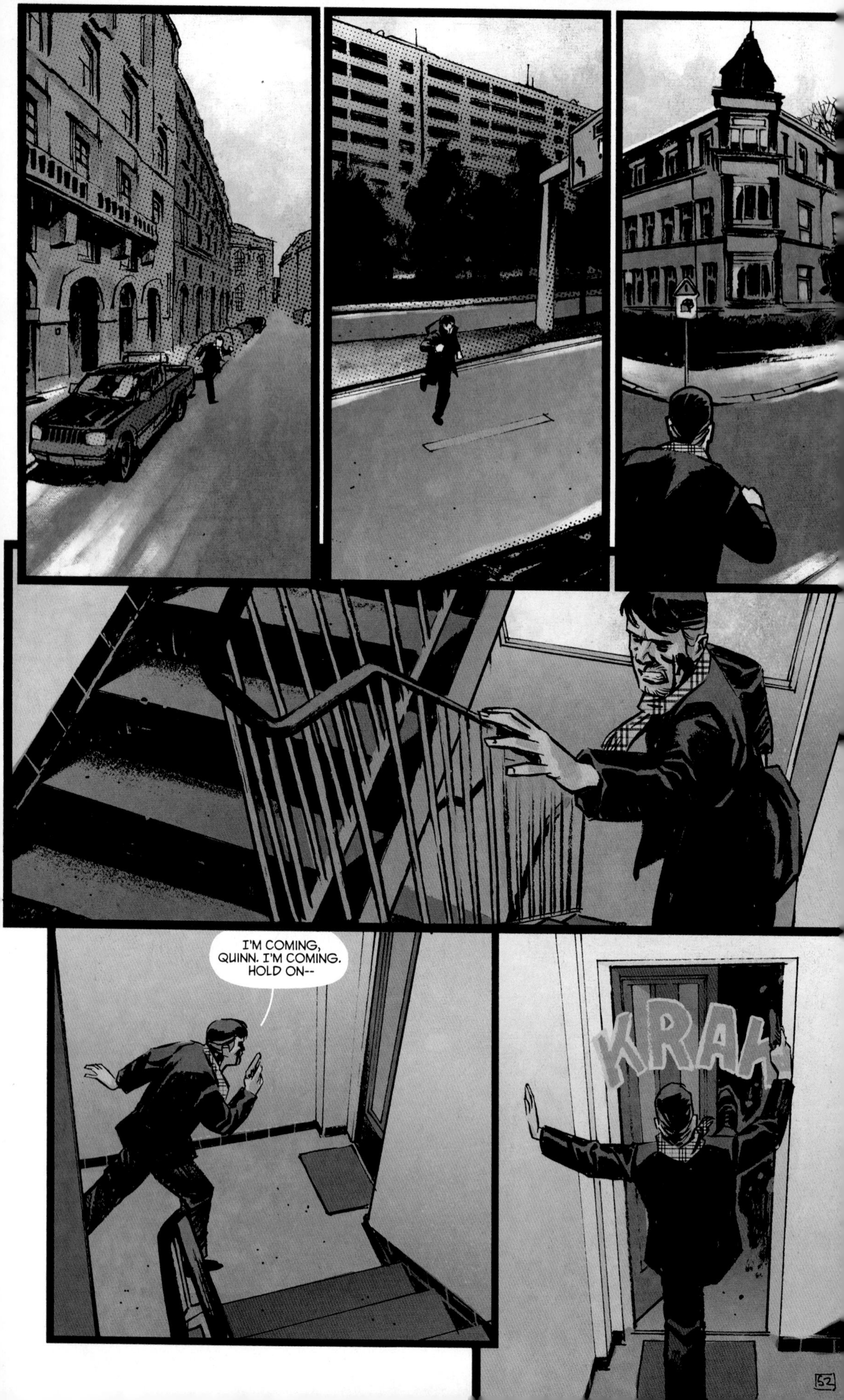
I'M COMING, QUINN. I'M COMING. HOLD ON--
KRAK!

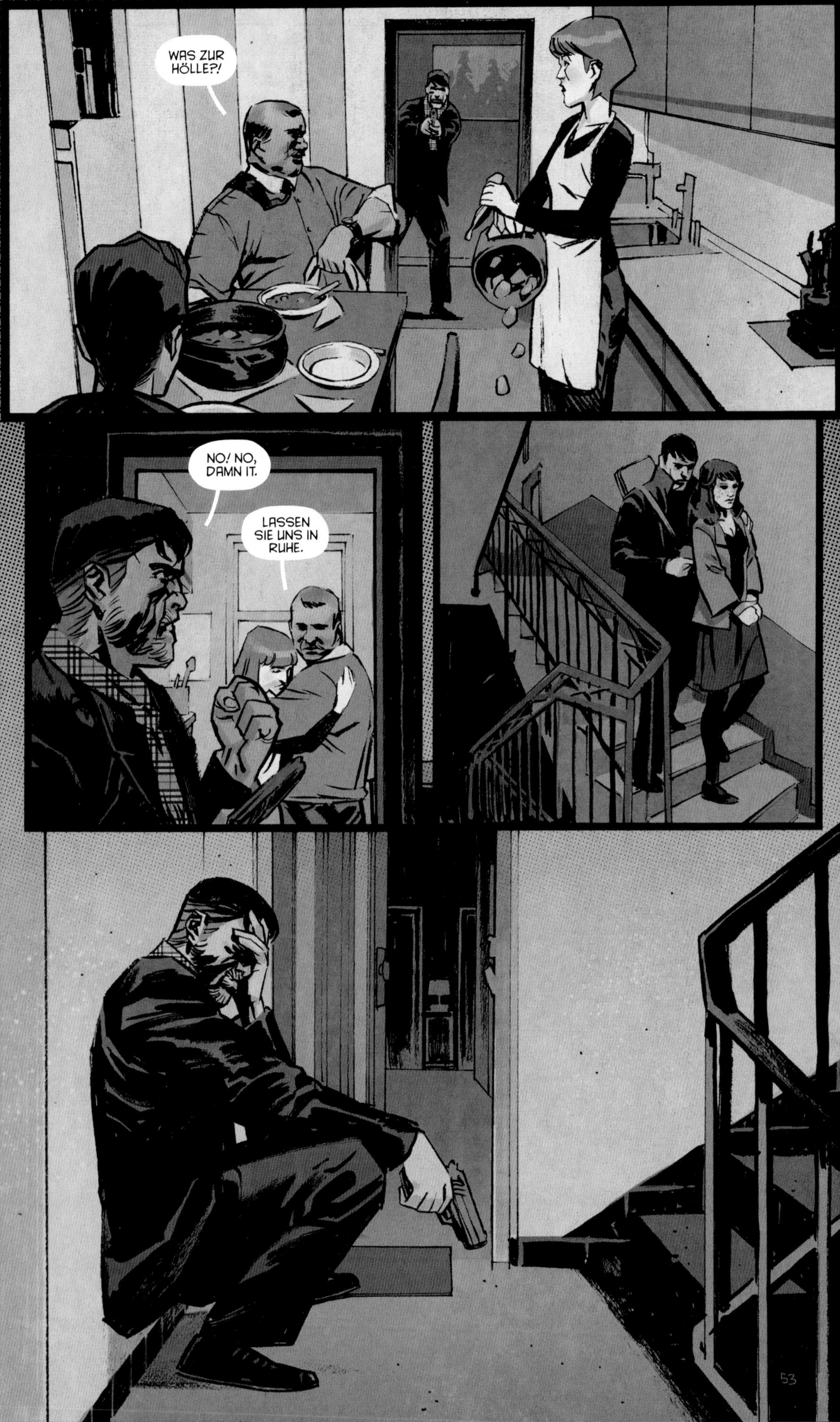
WAS ZUR HÖLLE?!
NO! NO, DAMN IT.
LASSEN SIE UNS IN RUHE.

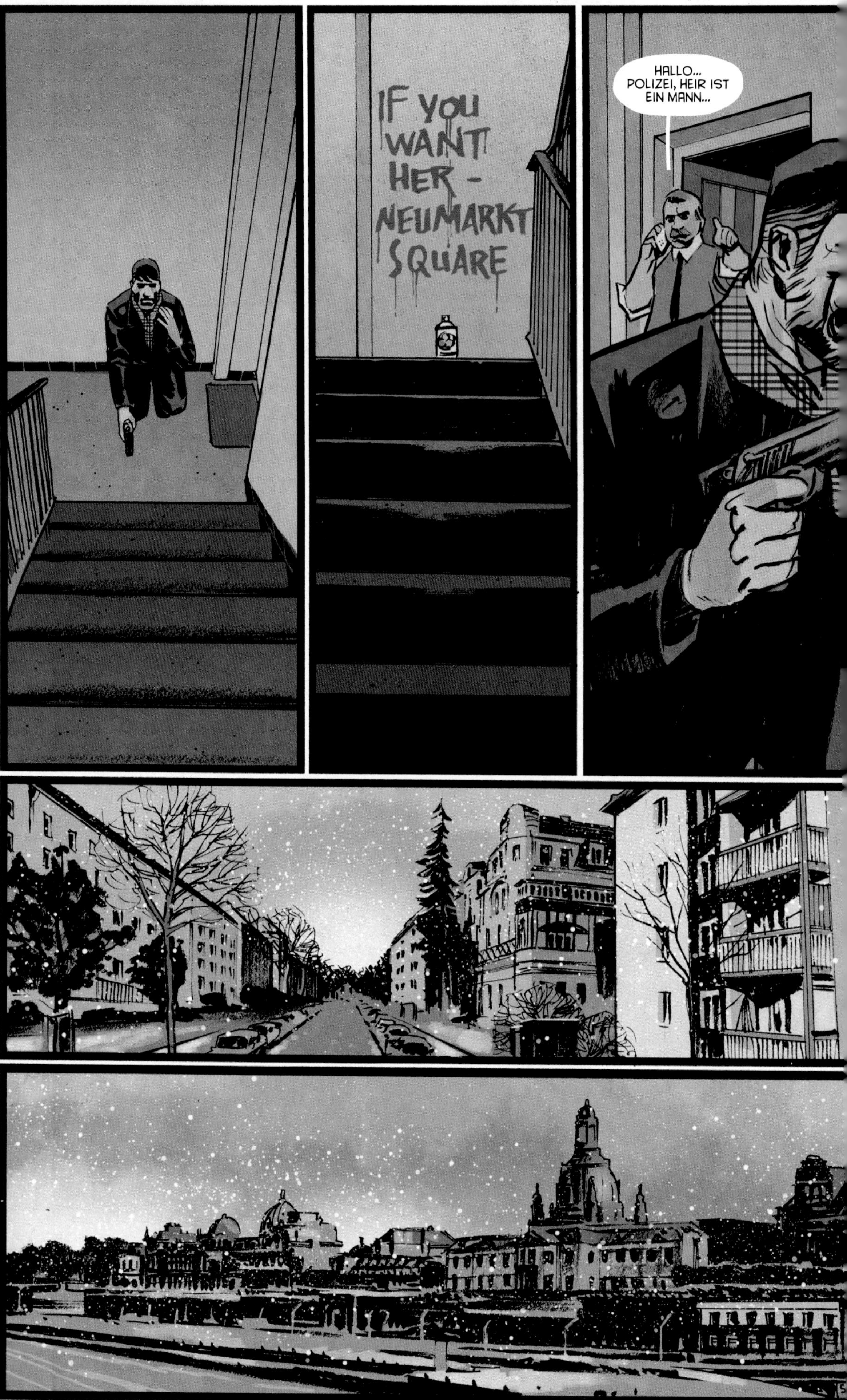
IF you WANT HER - NEUMARKT SQUARE
HALLO... POLIZEI, HEIR IST EIN MANN...

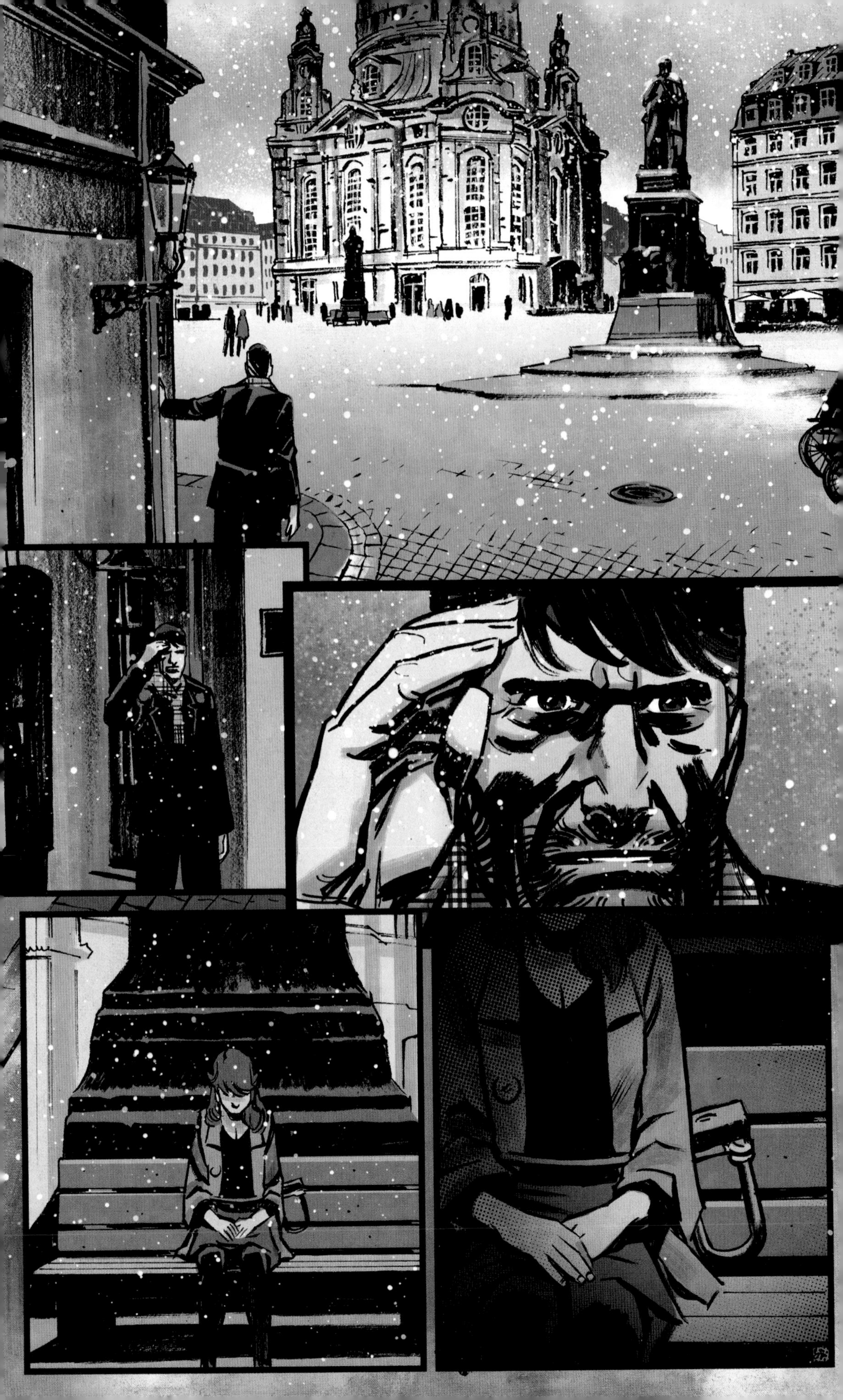

MARTIN LUTHER
56

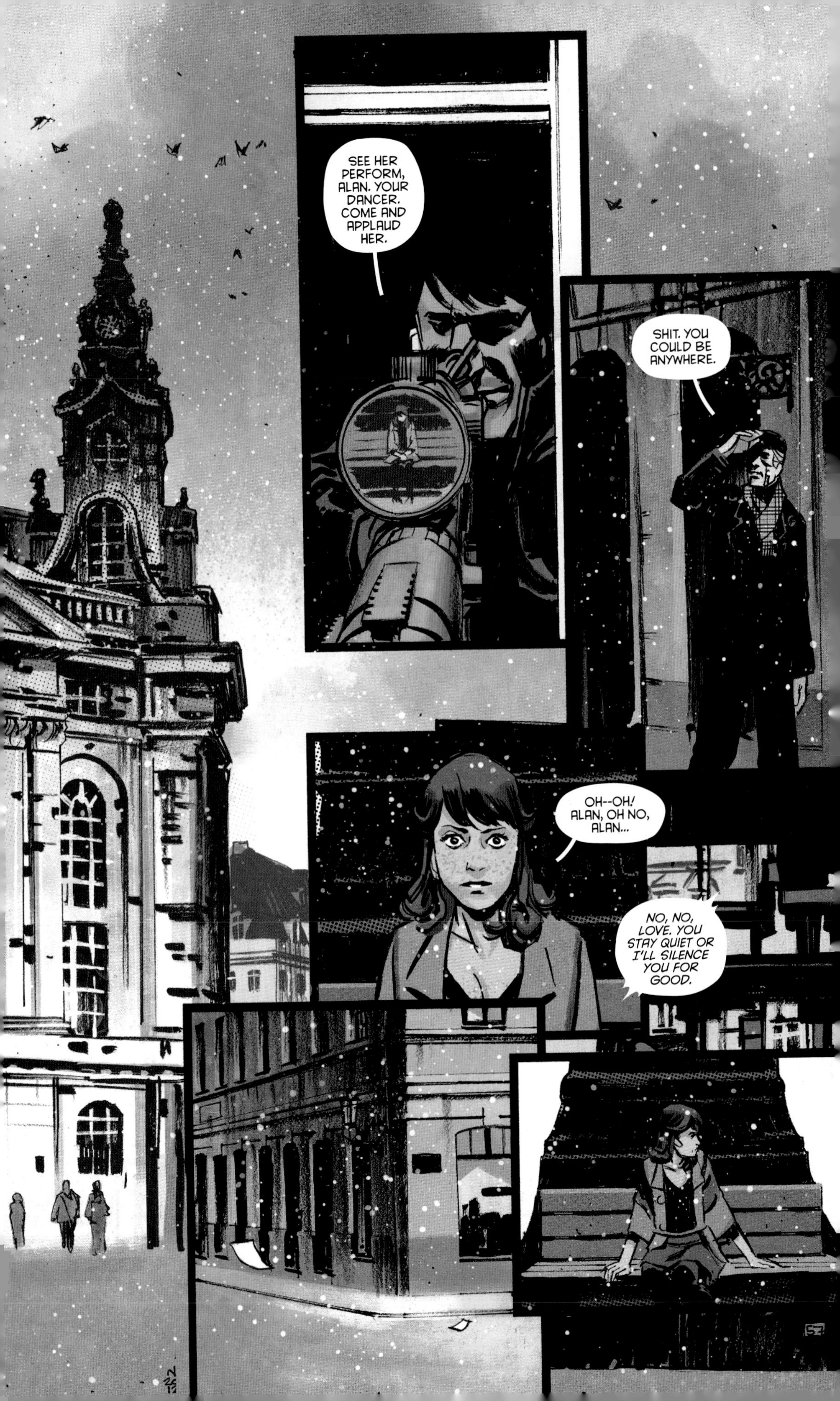
SEE HER PERFORM, ALAN. YOUR DANCER. COME AND APPLAUD HER.
SHIT. YOU COULD BE ANYWHERE.
OH--OH! ALAN, OH NO, ALAN...
NO, NO, LOVE. YOU STAY QUIET OR I'LL SILENCE YOU FOR GOOD.

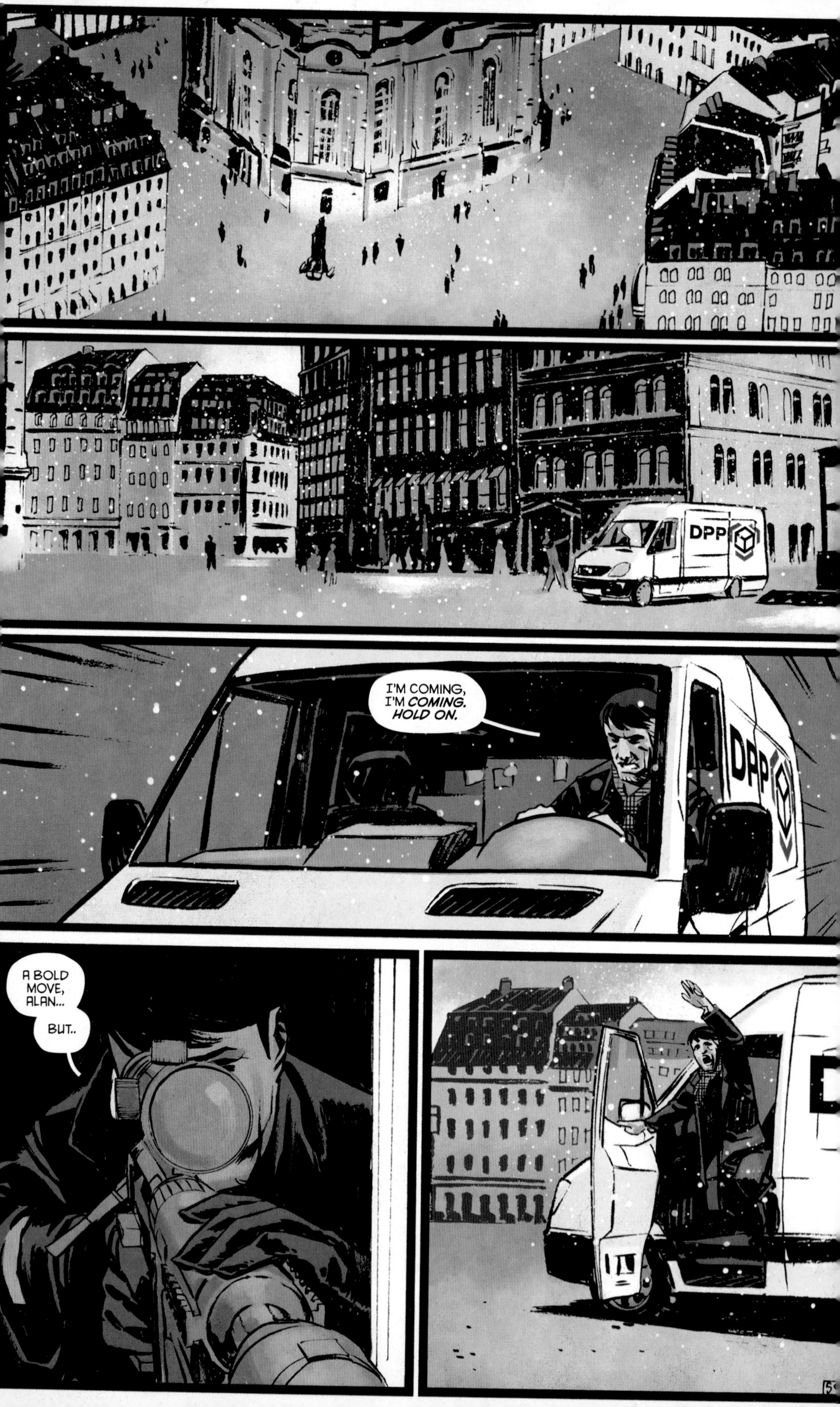
DPP
DPP
I'M COMING, I'M COMING. HOLD ON.
A BOLD MOVE, ALAN...
BUT..

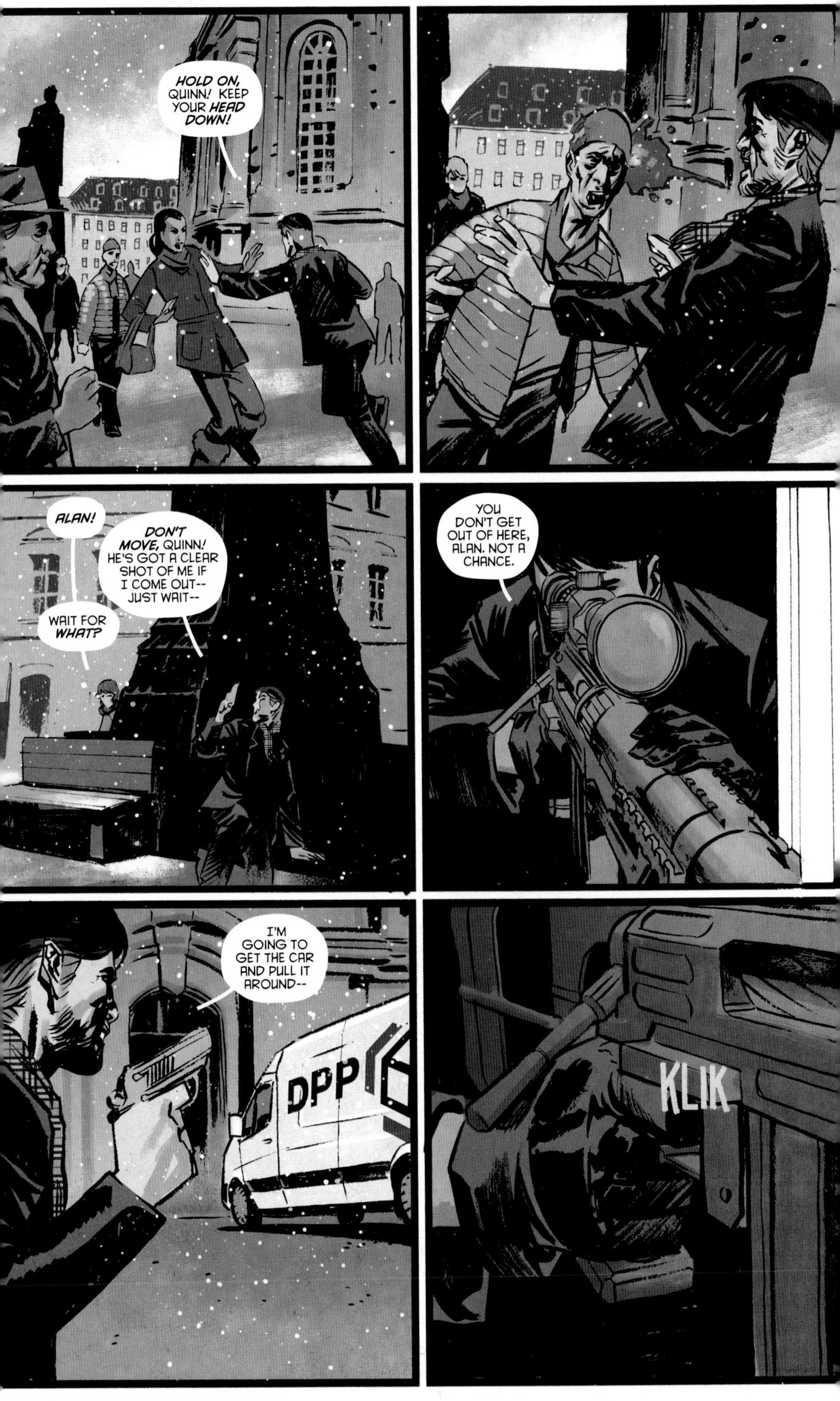
HOLD ON, QUINN! KEEP YOUR HEAD DOWN!
ALAN!
DON'T MOVE, QUINN! HE'S GOT A CLEAR SHOT OF ME IF I COME OUT-- JUST WAIT--
WAIT FOR WHAT?
YOU DON'T GET OUT OF HERE, ALAN. NOT A CHANCE.
I'M GOING TO GET THE CAR AND PULL IT AROUND--
DPP
KLIK

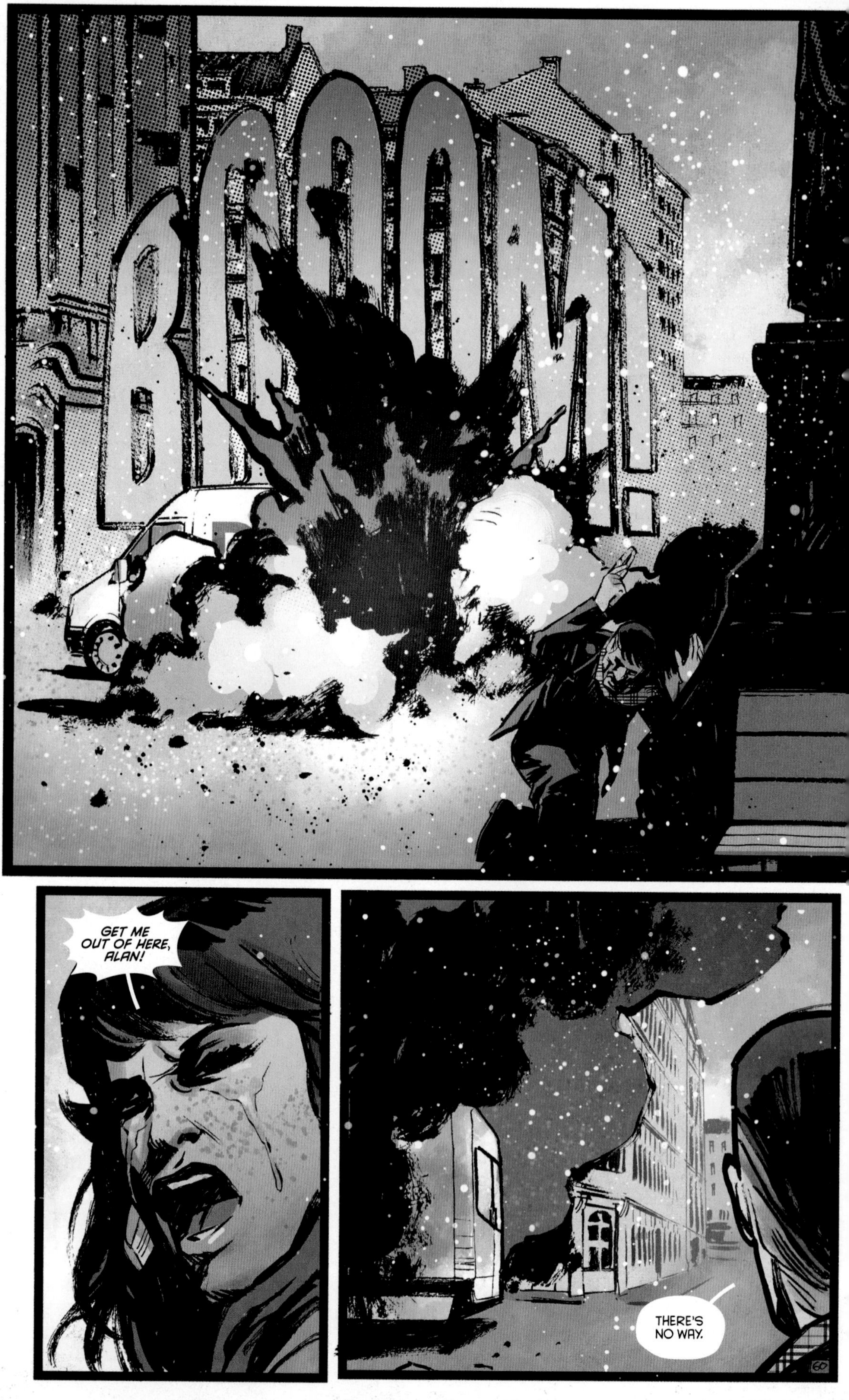
BOOOM!
GET ME OUT OF HERE, ALAN!
THERE'S NO WAY.
60

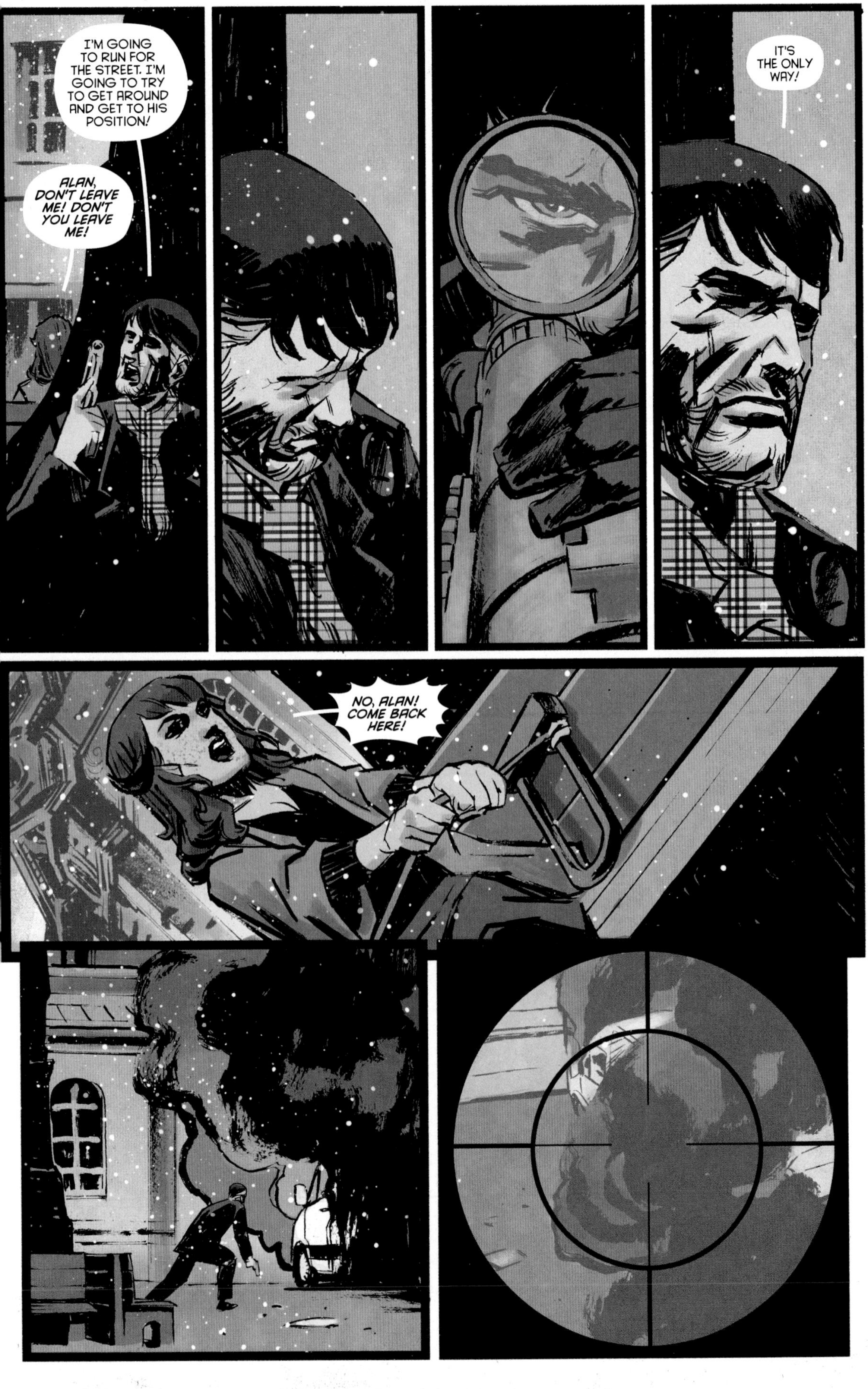
I'M GOING TO RUN FOR THE STREET. I'M GOING TO TRY TO GET AROUND AND GET TO HIS POSITION!
ALAN, DON'T LEAVE ME! DON'T YOU LEAVE ME!
IT'S THE ONLY WAY!
NO, ALAN! COME BACK HERE!

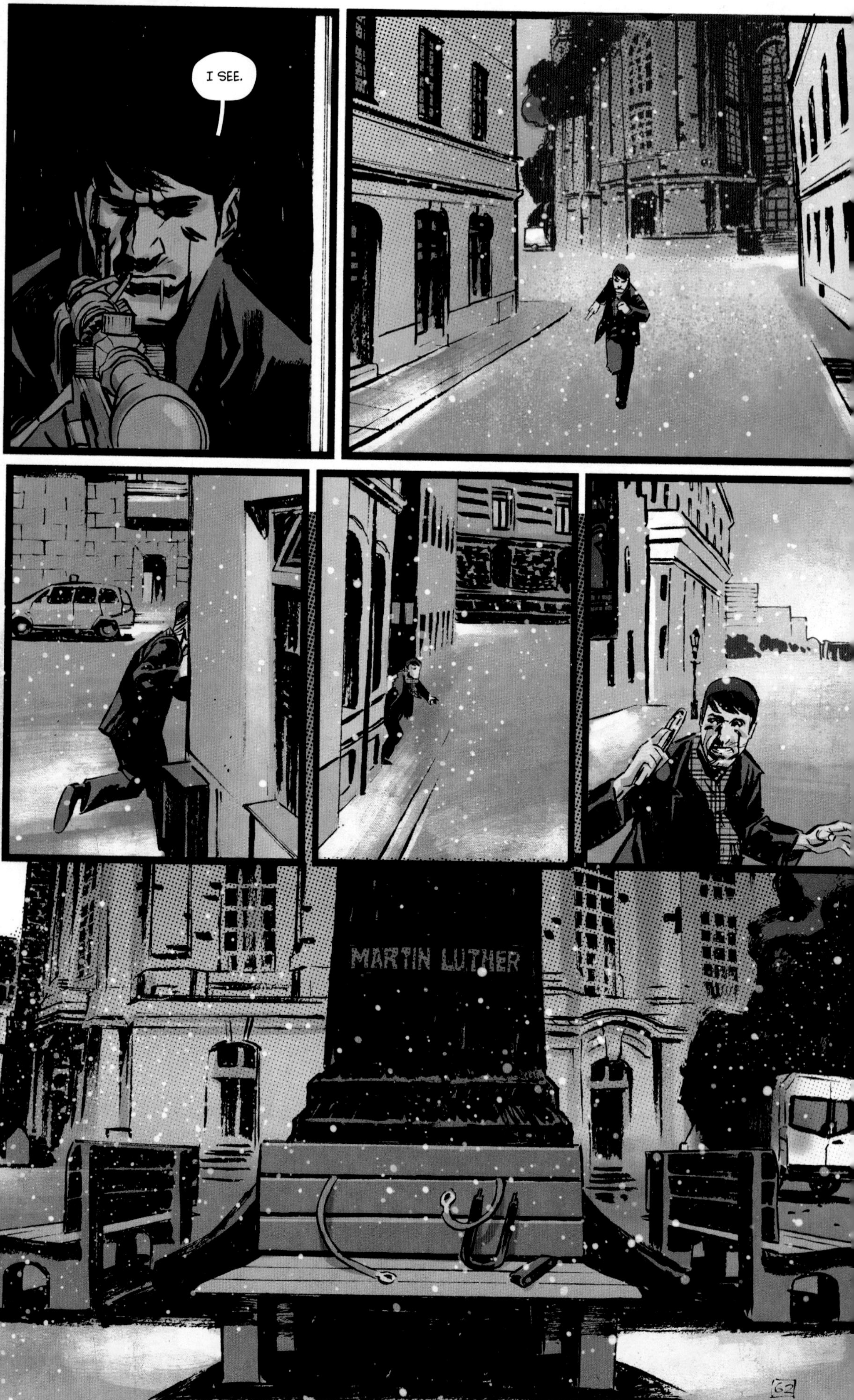
I SEE.
MARTIN LUTHER

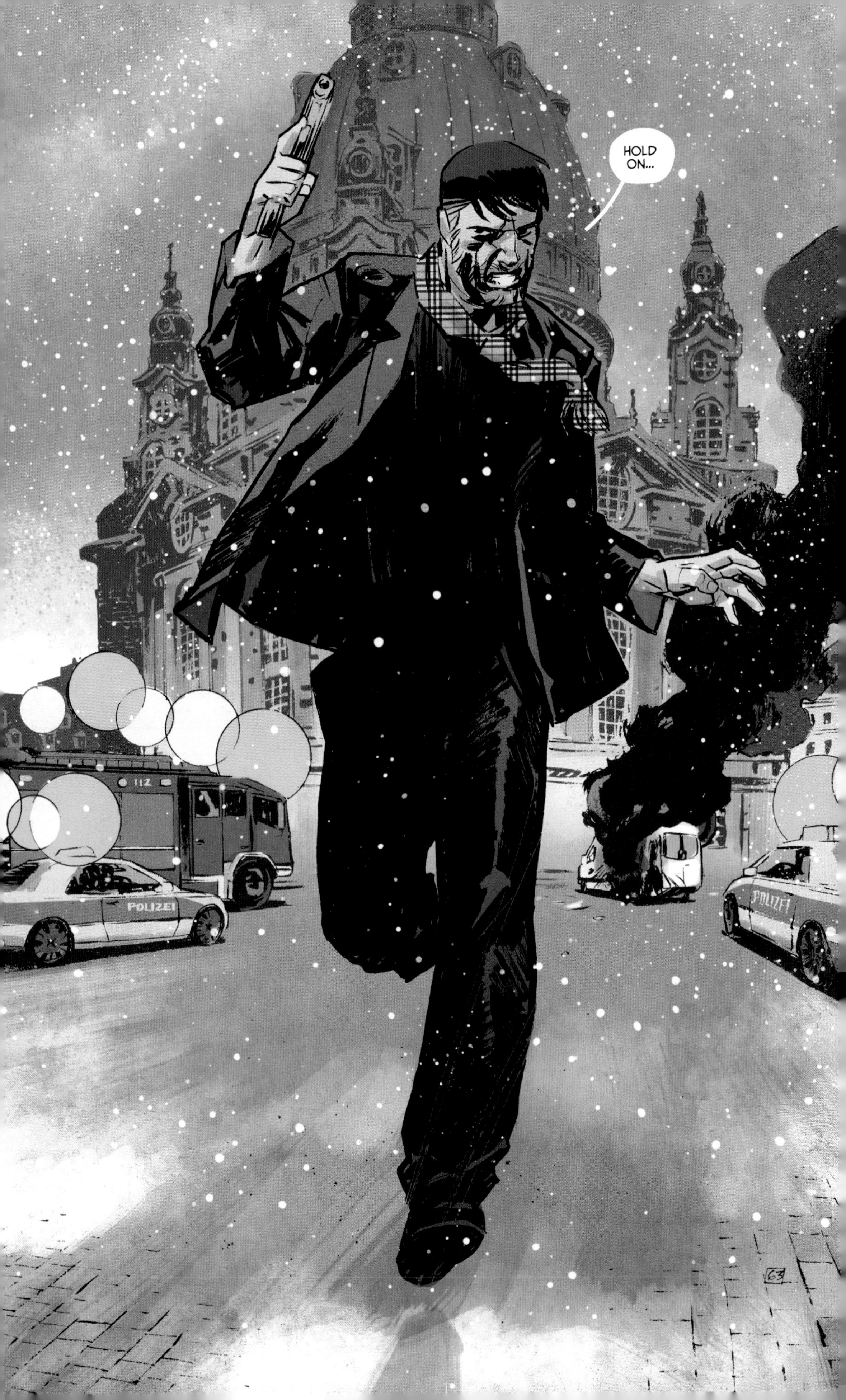
HOLD ON...
112
POLIZEI
POLIZEI

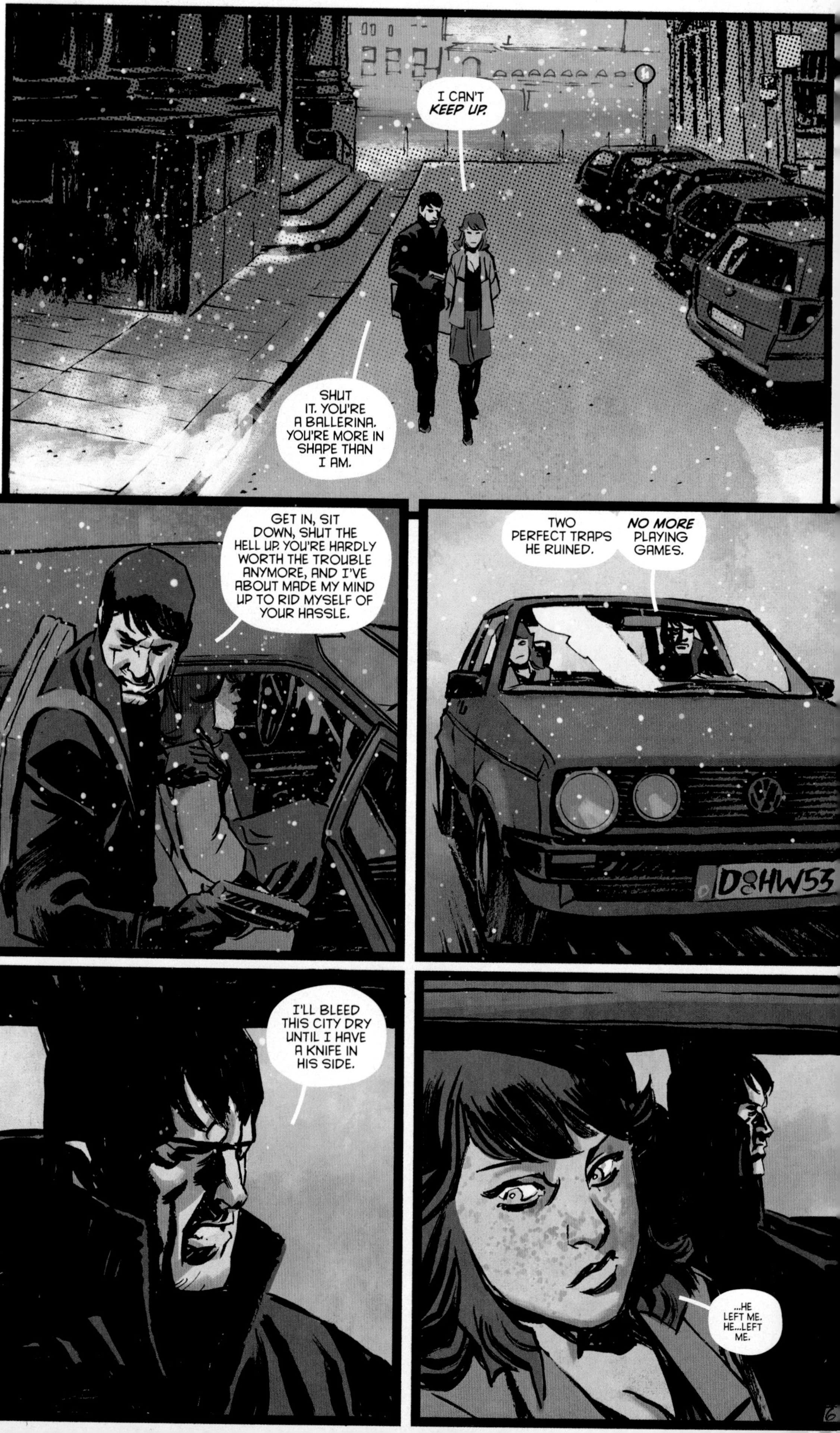
I CAN'T KEEP UP.
SHUT IT. YOU'RE A BALLERINA. YOU'RE MORE IN SHAPE THAN I AM.
GET IN, SIT DOWN, SHUT THE HELL UP. YOU'RE HARDLY WORTH THE TROUBLE ANYMORE, AND I'VE ABOUT MADE MY MIND UP TO RID MYSELF OF YOUR HASSLE.
TWO PERFECT TRAPS HE RUINED.
NO MORE PLAYING GAMES.
D HW53
I'LL BLEED THIS CITY DRY UNTIL I HAVE A KNIFE IN HIS SIDE.
...HE LEFT ME. HE...LEFT ME.

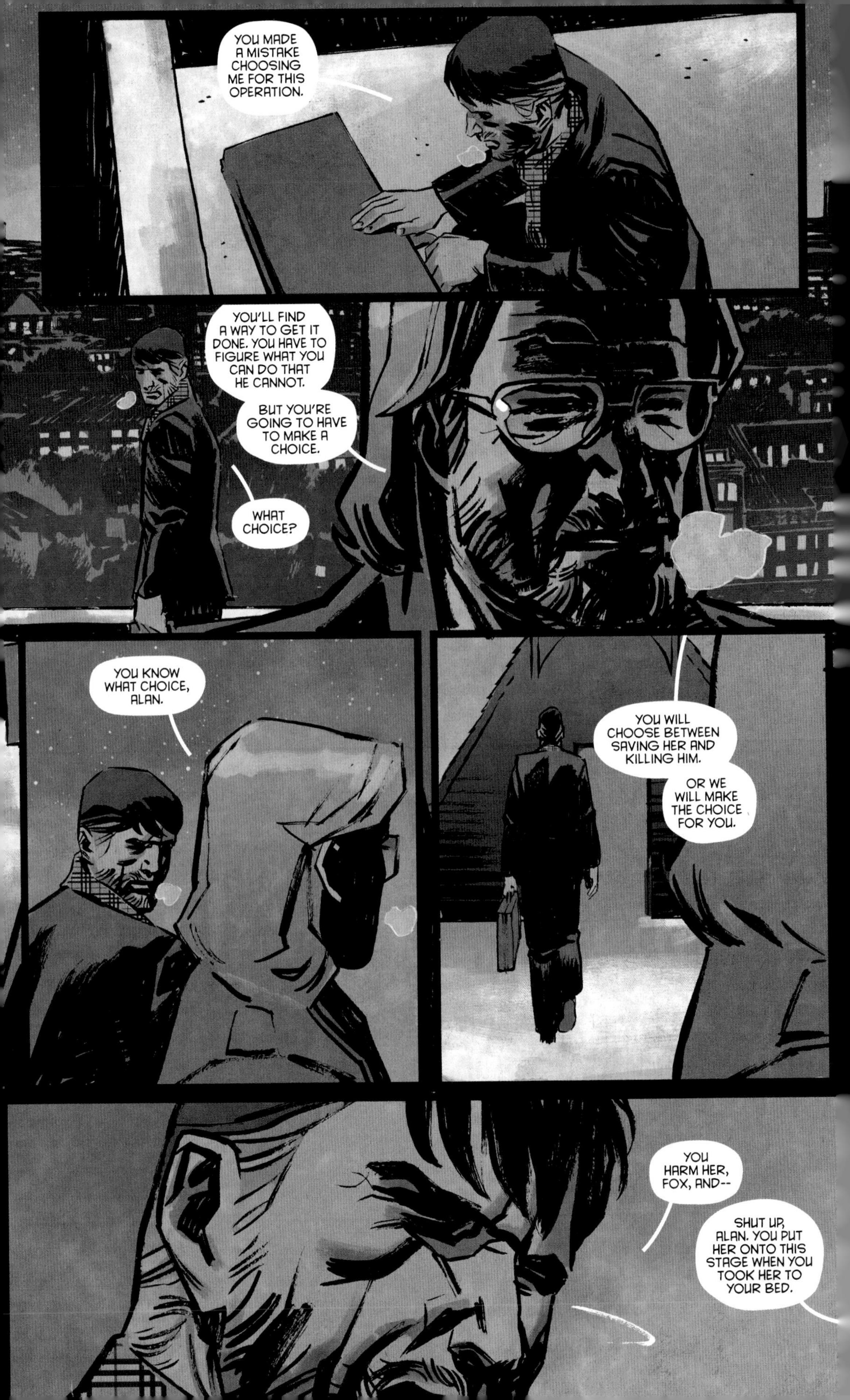
YOU MADE A MISTAKE CHOOSING ME FOR THIS OPERATION.
YOU'LL FIND A WAY TO GET IT DONE. YOU HAVE TO FIGURE WHAT YOU CAN DO THAT HE CANNOT.
BUT YOU'RE GOING TO HAVE TO MAKE A CHOICE.
WHAT CHOICE?
YOU KNOW WHAT CHOICE, ALAN.
YOU WILL CHOOSE BETWEEN SAVING HER AND KILLING HIM.
OR WE WILL MAKE THE CHOICE FOR YOU.
YOU HARM HER, FOX, AND--
SHUT UP, ALAN. YOU PUT HER ONTO THIS STAGE WHEN YOU TOOK HER TO YOUR BED.

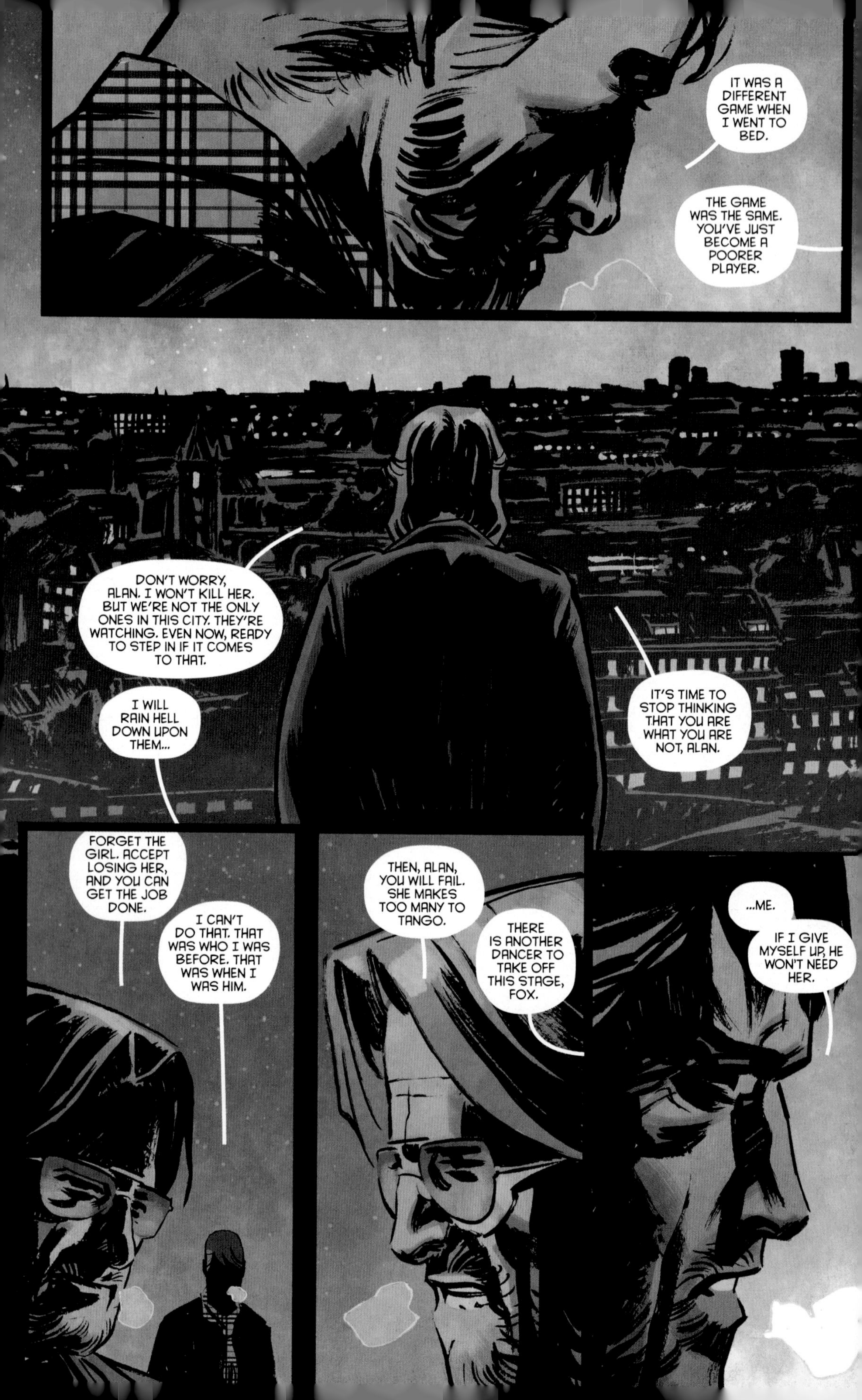
IT WAS A DIFFERENT GAME WHEN I WENT TO BED.
THE GAME WAS THE SAME. YOU'VE JUST BECOME A POORER PLAYER.
DON'T WORRY, ALAN. I WON'T KILL HER. BUT WE'RE NOT THE ONLY ONES IN THIS CITY. THEY'RE WATCHING. EVEN NOW, READY TO STEP IN IF IT COMES TO THAT.
I WILL RAIN HELL DOWN UPON THEM...
IT'S TIME TO STOP THINKING THAT YOU ARE WHAT YOU ARE NOT, ALAN.
FORGET THE GIRL. ACCEPT LOSING HER, AND YOU CAN GET THE JOB DONE.
I CAN'T DO THAT. THAT WAS WHO I WAS BEFORE. THAT WAS WHEN I WAS HIM.
THEN, ALAN, YOU WILL FAIL. SHE MAKES TOO MANY TO TANGO.
THERE IS ANOTHER DANCER TO TAKE OFF THIS STAGE, FOX.
...ME.
IF I GIVE MYSELF UP, HE WON'T NEED HER.

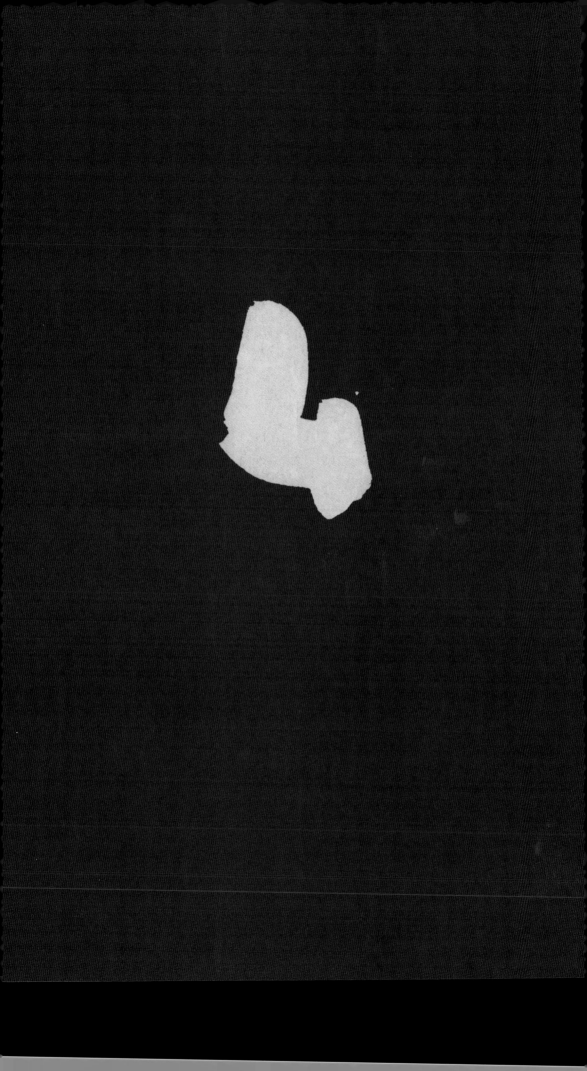

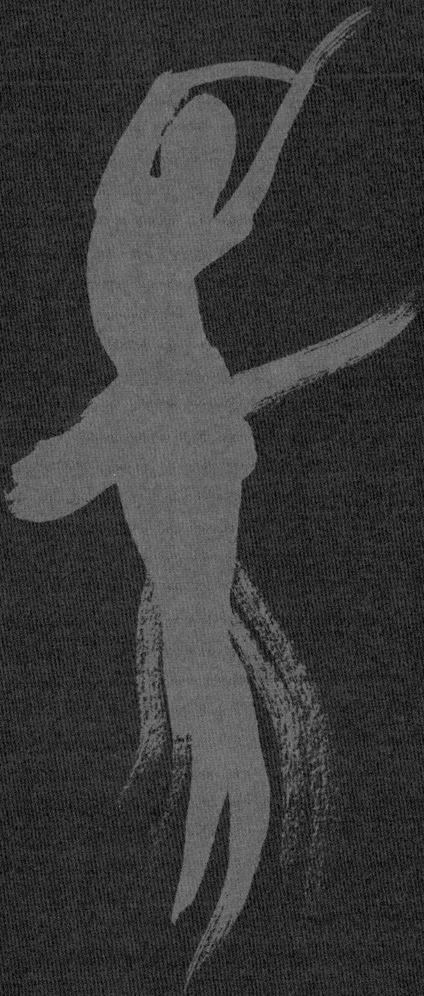

CHANGEMENT

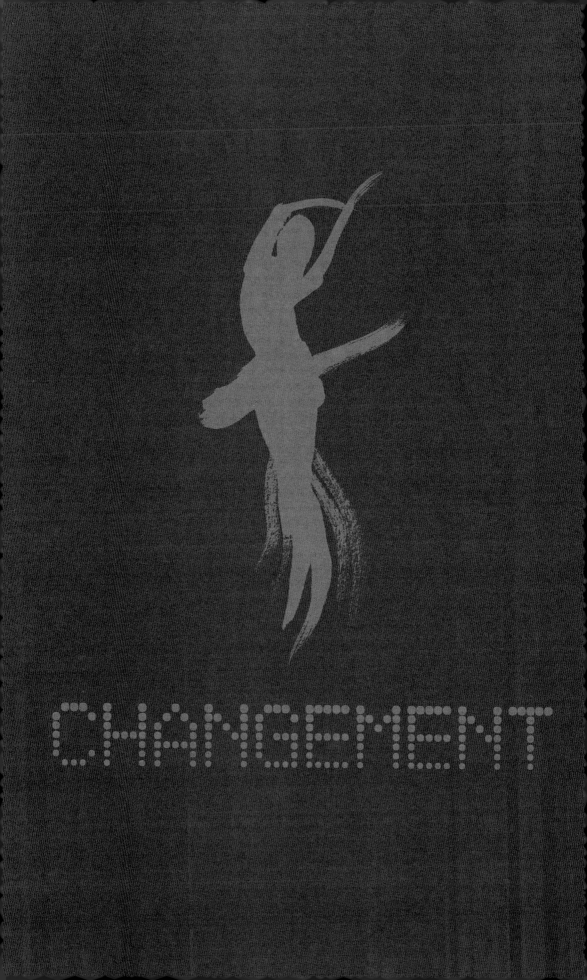

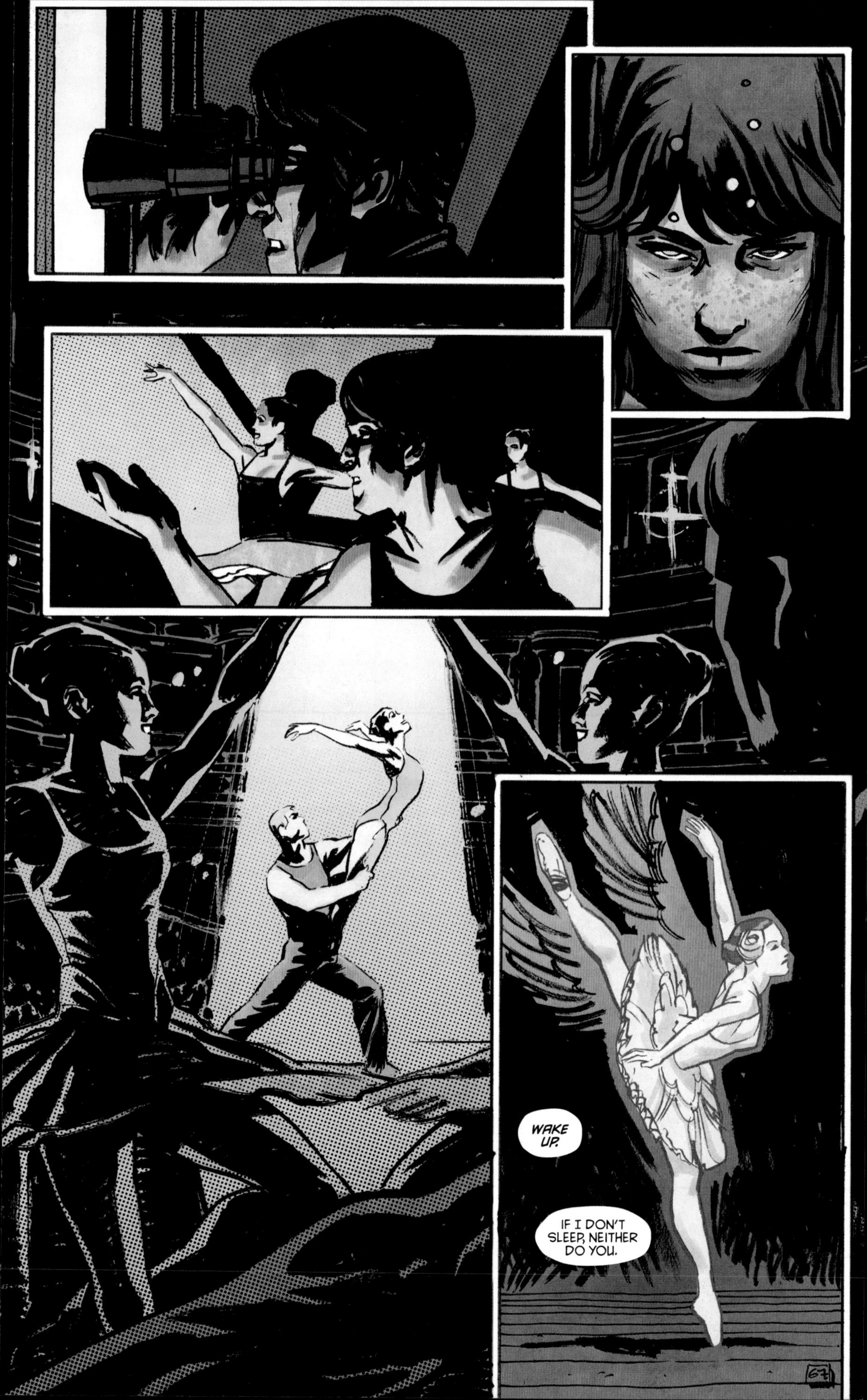
WAKE UP.
IF I DON'T SLEEP, NEITHER DO YOU.
67

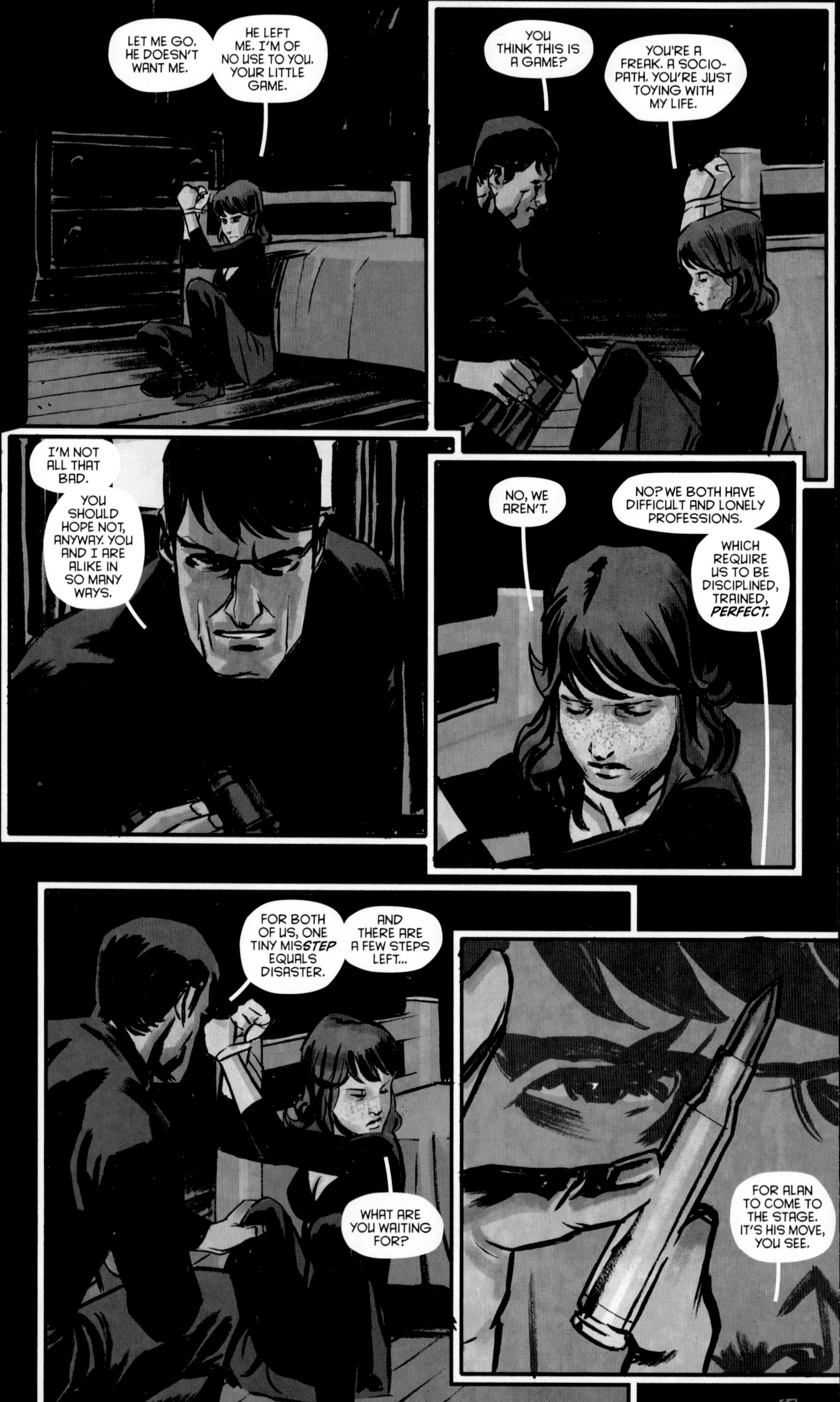
LET ME GO. HE DOESN'T WANT ME.
HE LEFT ME. I'M OF NO USE TO YOU. YOUR LITTLE GAME.
YOU THINK THIS IS A GAME?
YOU'RE A FREAK. A SOCIOPATH. YOU'RE JUST TOYING WITH MY LIFE.
I'M NOT ALL THAT BAD.
YOU SHOULD HOPE NOT, ANYWAY. YOU AND I ARE ALIKE IN SO MANY WAYS.
NO, WE AREN'T.
NO? WE BOTH HAVE DIFFICULT AND LONELY PROFESSIONS.
WHICH REQUIRE US TO BE DISCIPLINED, TRAINED, PERFECT.
FOR BOTH OF US, ONE TINY MISSTEP EQUALS DISASTER.
AND THERE ARE A FEW STEPS LEFT...
WHAT ARE YOU WAITING FOR?
FOR ALAN TO COME TO THE STAGE. IT'S HIS MOVE, YOU SEE.

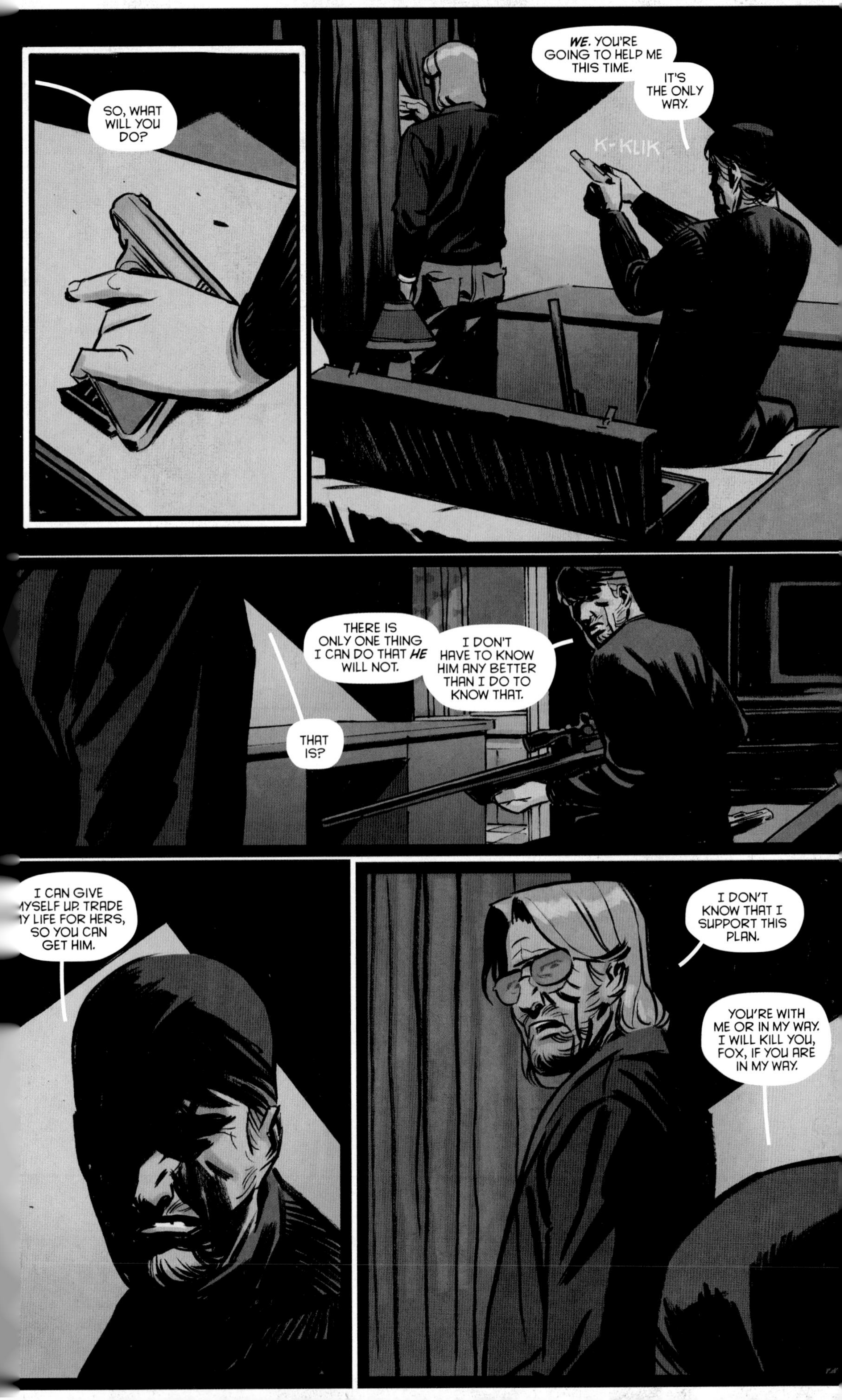
SO, WHAT WILL YOU DO?
WE. YOU'RE GOING TO HELP ME THIS TIME.
IT'S THE ONLY WAY.
K-KLIK
THAT IS?
THERE IS ONLY ONE THING I CAN DO THAT HE WILL NOT.
I DON'T HAVE TO KNOW HIM ANY BETTER THAN I DO TO KNOW THAT.
I CAN GIVE MYSELF UP. TRADE MY LIFE FOR HERS, SO YOU CAN GET HIM.
I DON'T KNOW THAT I SUPPORT THIS PLAN.
YOU'RE WITH ME OR IN MY WAY. I WILL KILL YOU, FOX, IF YOU ARE IN MY WAY.

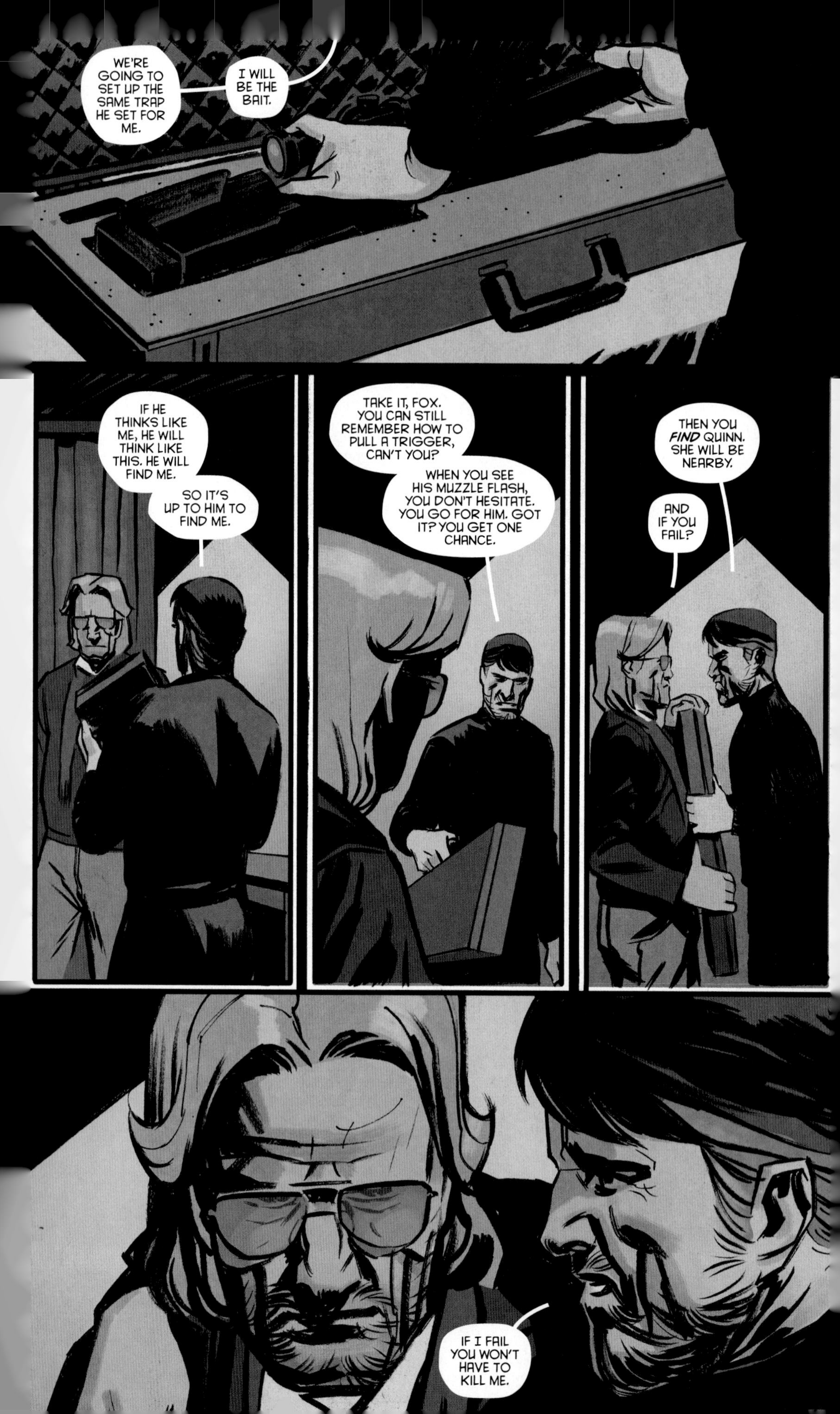
WE'RE GOING TO SET UP THE SAME TRAP HE SET FOR ME.
I WILL BE THE BAIT.
IF HE THINKS LIKE ME, HE WILL THINK LIKE THIS. HE WILL FIND ME.
SO IT'S UP TO HIM TO FIND ME.
TAKE IT, FOX. YOU CAN STILL REMEMBER HOW TO PULL A TRIGGER, CAN'T YOU?
WHEN YOU SEE HIS MUZZLE FLASH, YOU DON'T HESITATE. YOU GO FOR HIM. GOT IT? YOU GET ONE CHANCE.
THEN YOU *FIND* QUINN. SHE WILL BE NEARBY.
AND IF YOU FAIL?
IF I FAIL YOU WON'T HAVE TO KILL ME.

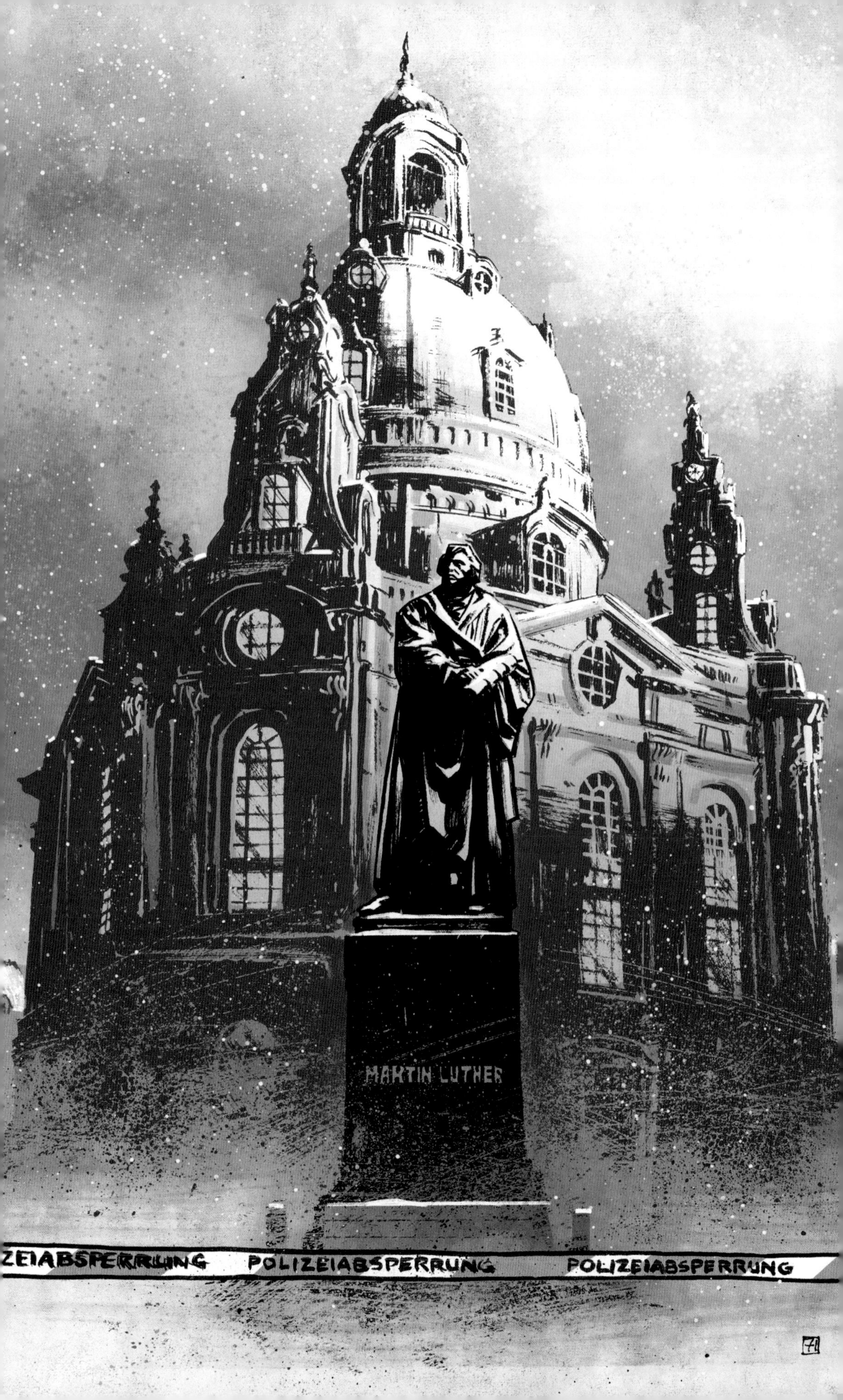
MARTIN LUTHER
ZEIABSPERRUNG
POLIZEIABSPERRUNG
POLIZEIABSPERRUNG

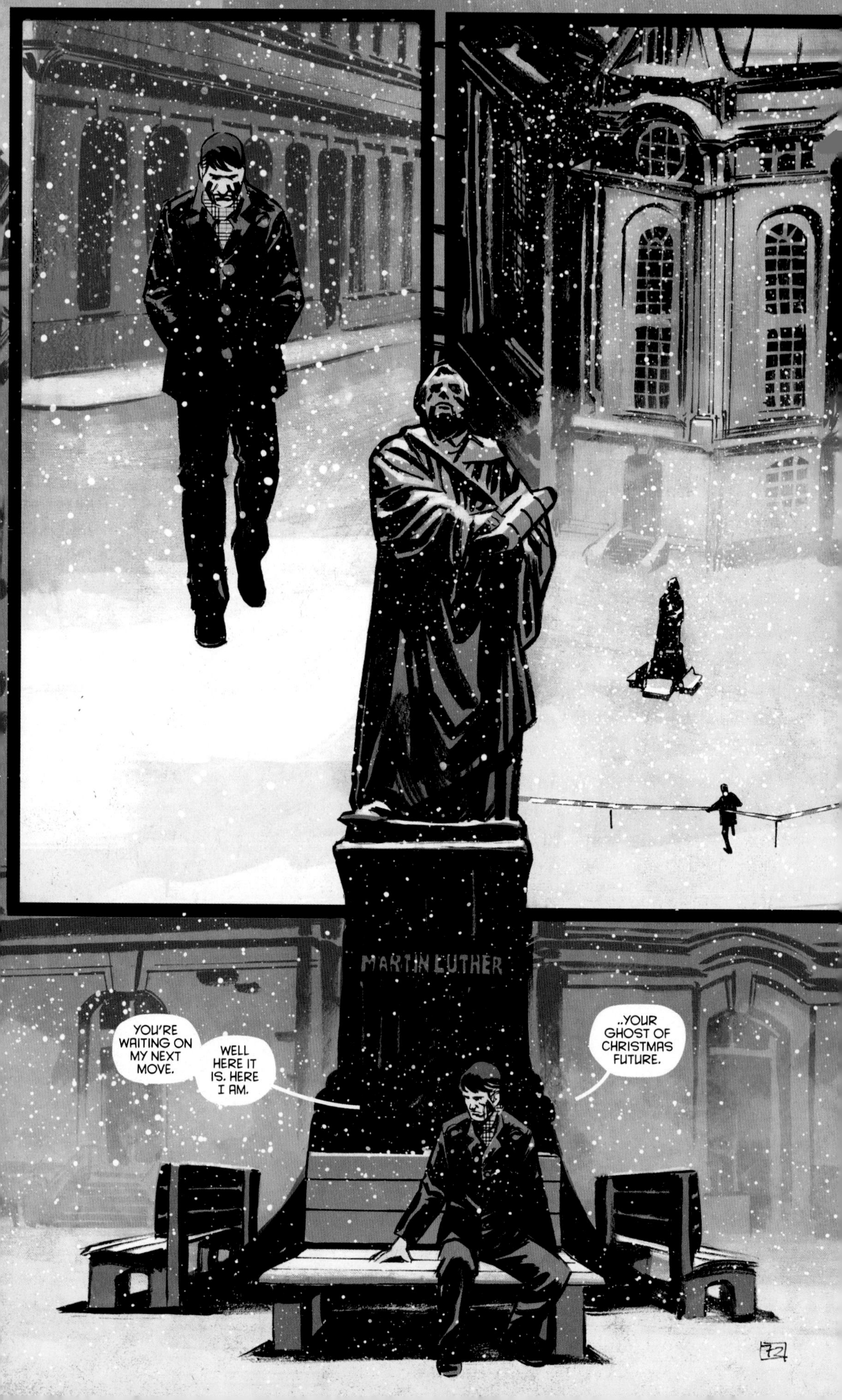

MARTIN LUTHER
YOU'RE WAITING ON MY NEXT MOVE.
WELL HERE IT IS. HERE I AM.
..YOUR GHOST OF CHRISTMAS FUTURE.

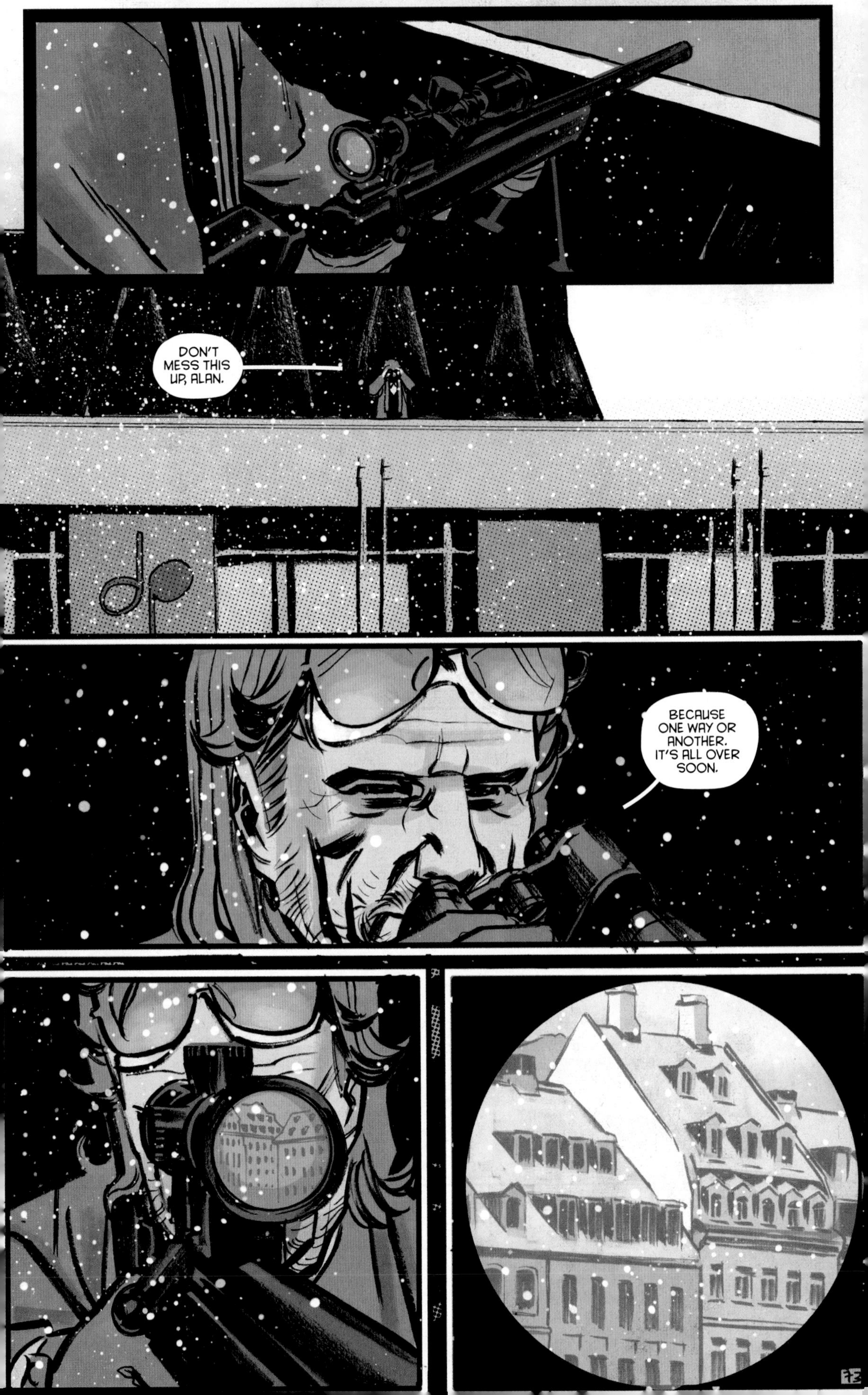
DON'T MESS THIS UP, ALAN.
BECAUSE ONE WAY OR ANOTHER. IT'S ALL OVER SOON.

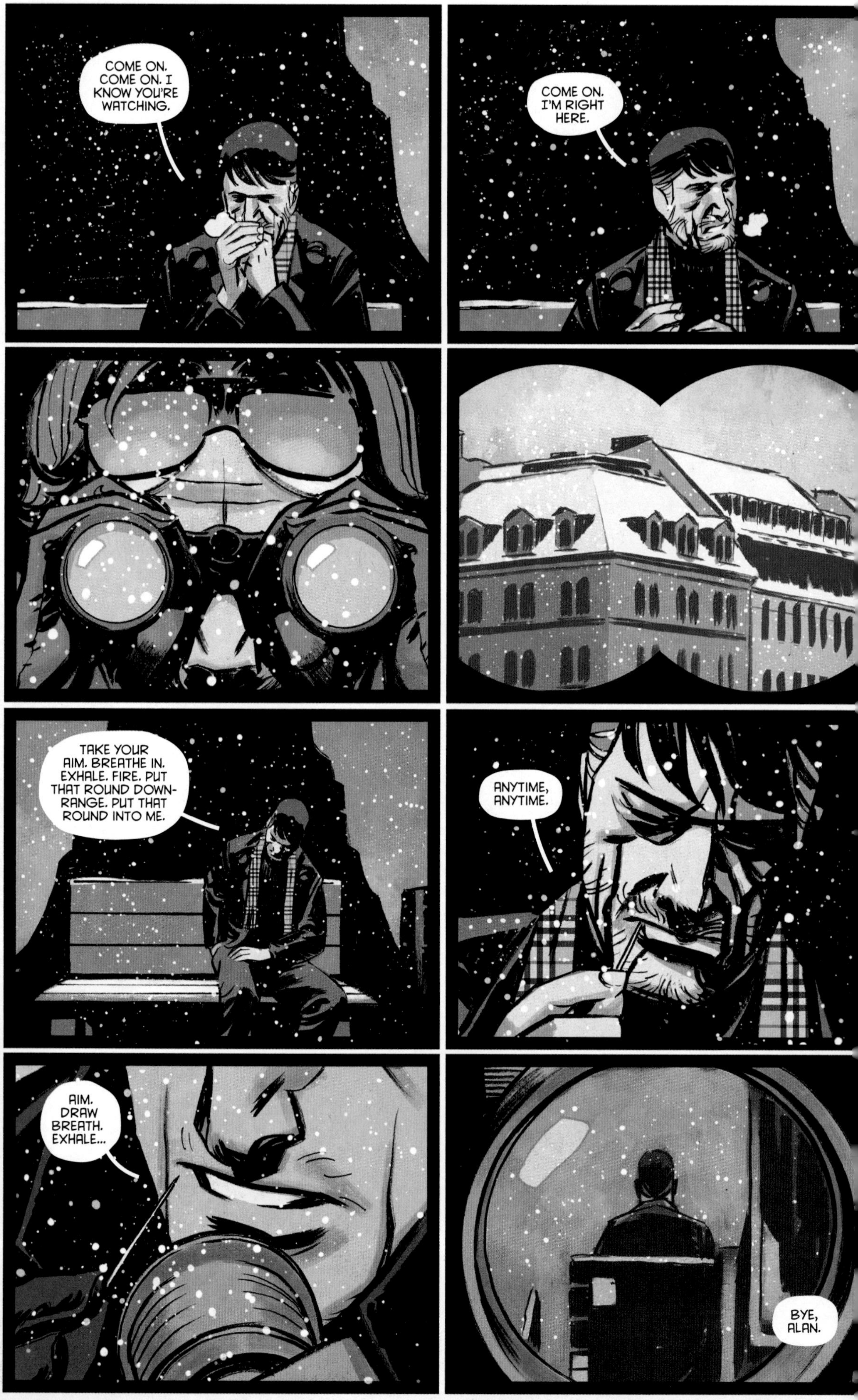

COME ON. COME ON. I KNOW YOU'RE WATCHING.
COME ON. I'M RIGHT HERE.
TAKE YOUR AIM. BREATHE IN. EXHALE. FIRE. PUT THAT ROUND DOWN-RANGE. PUT THAT ROUND INTO ME.
ANYTIME, ANYTIME.
AIM. DRAW BREATH. EXHALE...
BYE, ALAN.

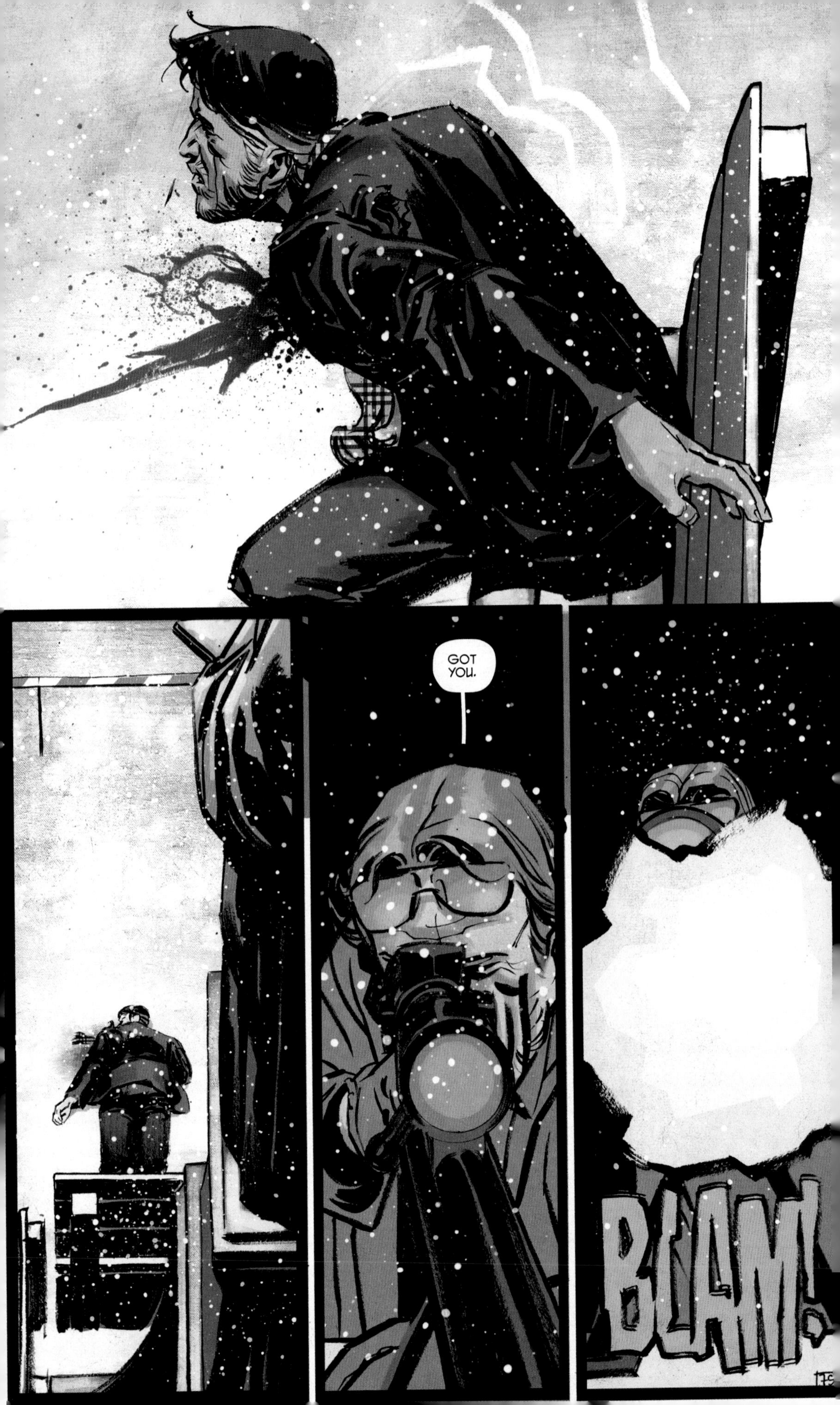
GOT YOU.
BLAM!

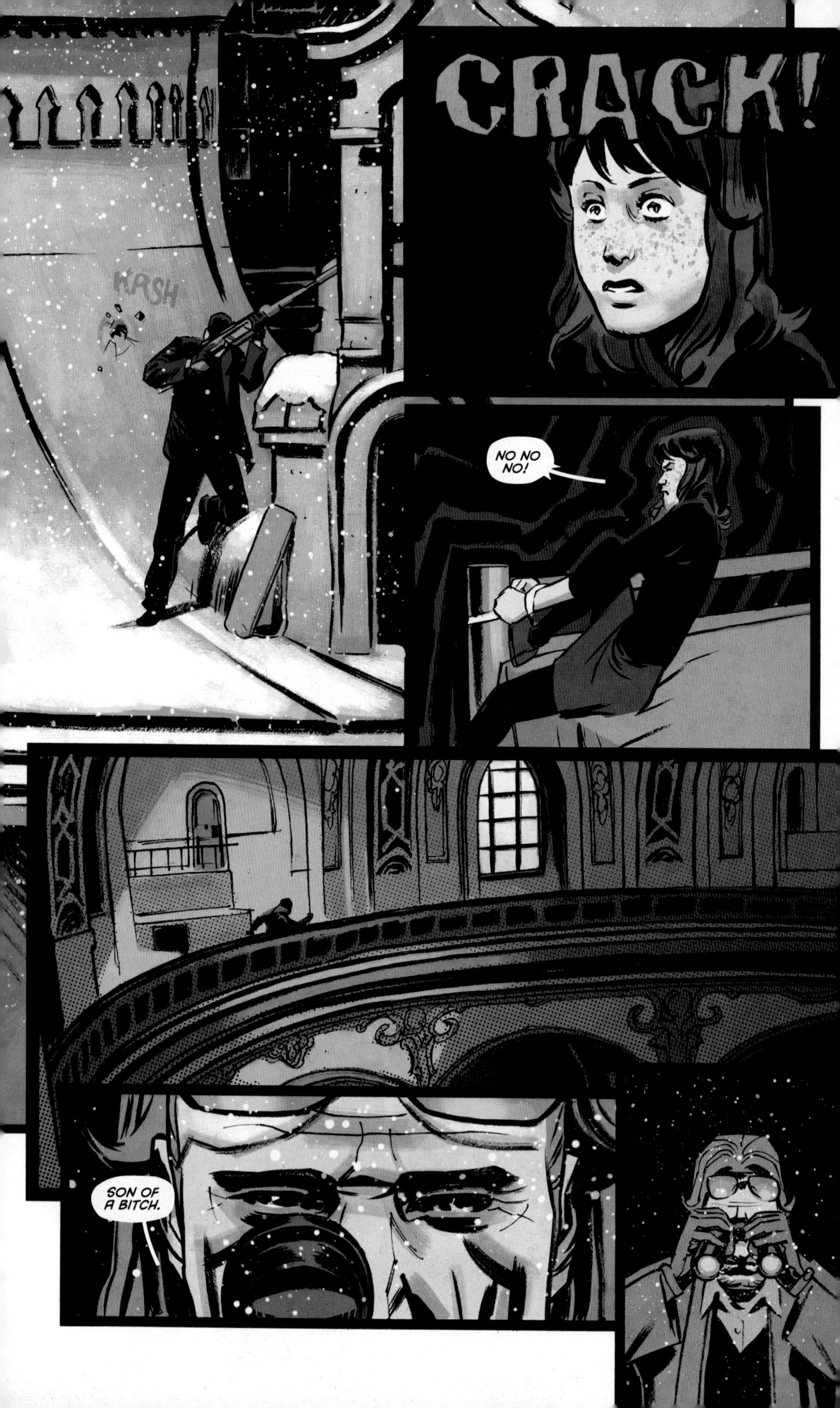
KRSH
CRACK!
NO NO NO!
SON OF A BITCH.

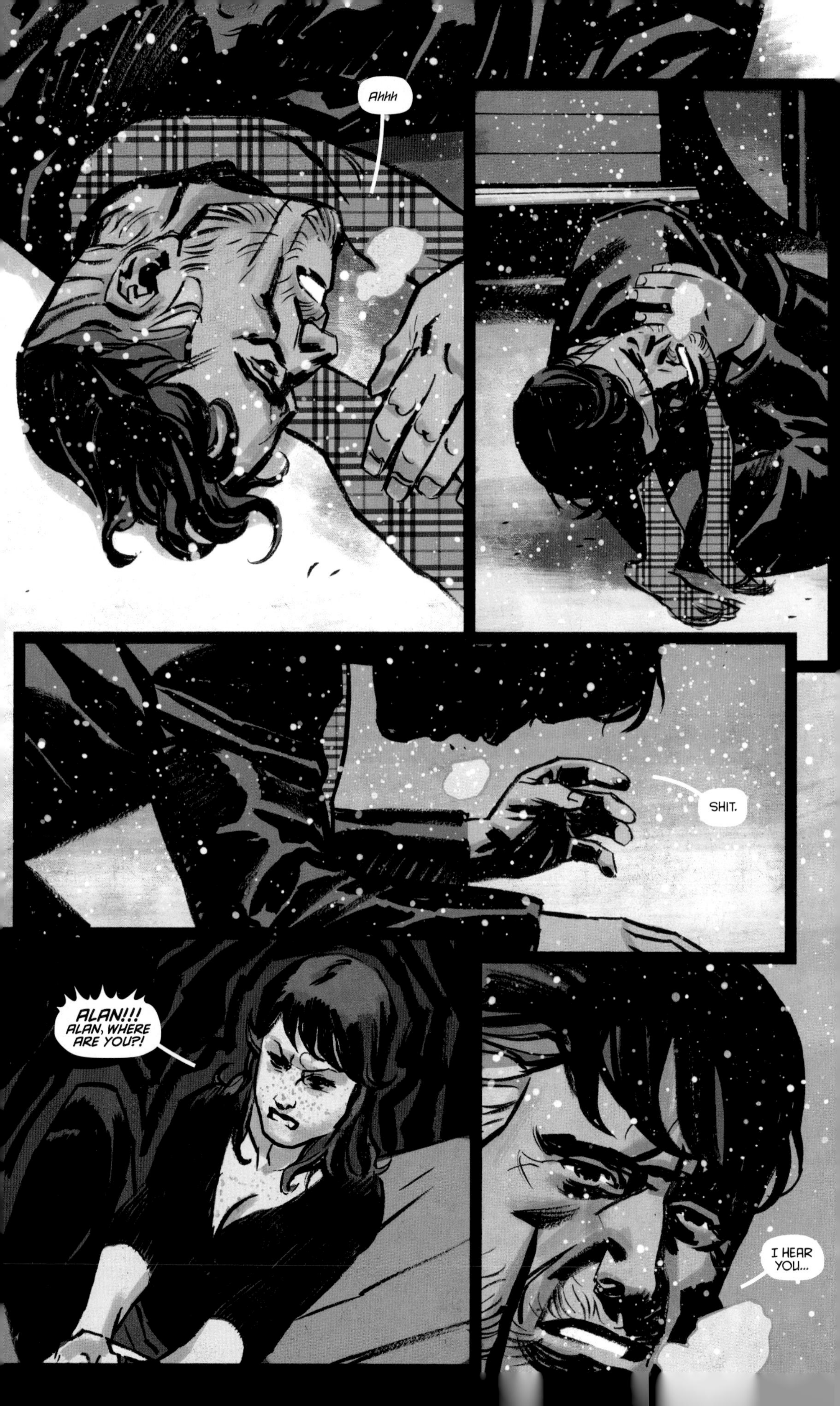
Ahhh
SHIT.
ALAN!!! ALAN, WHERE ARE YOU?!
I HEAR YOU...

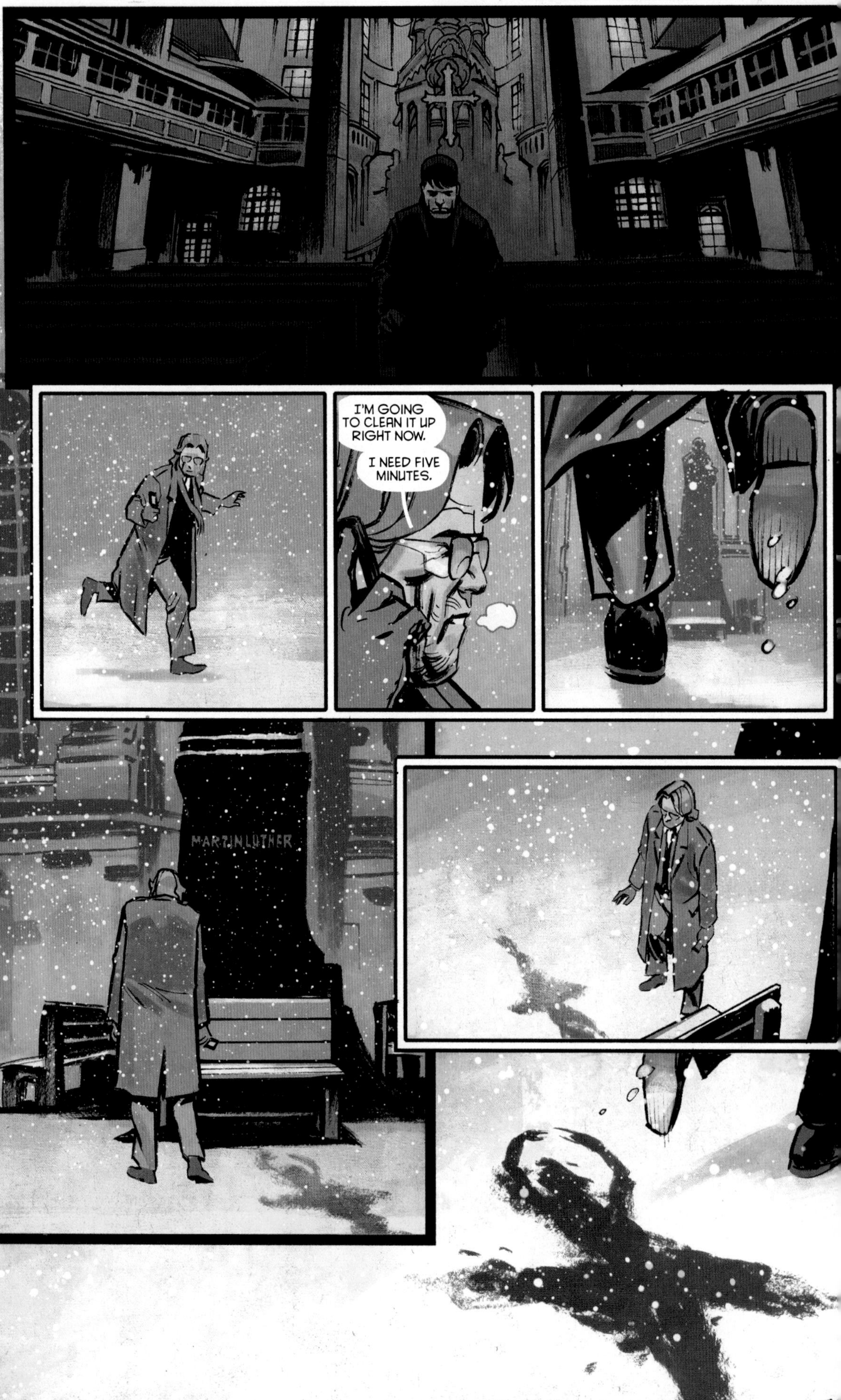

I'M GOING TO CLEAN IT UP RIGHT NOW.
I NEED FIVE MINUTES.
MARTIN LUTHER

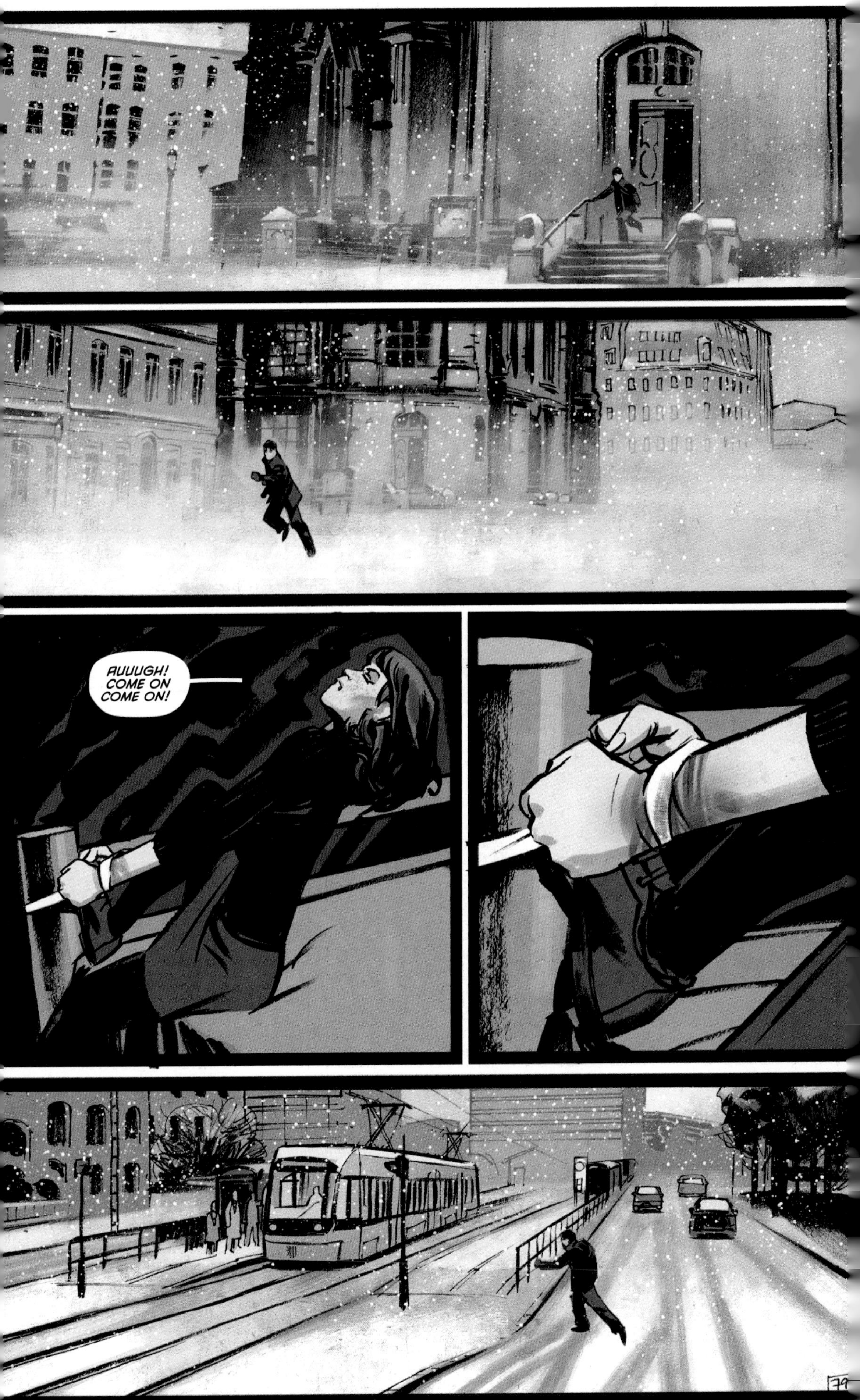
AUUUGH! COME ON COME ON!

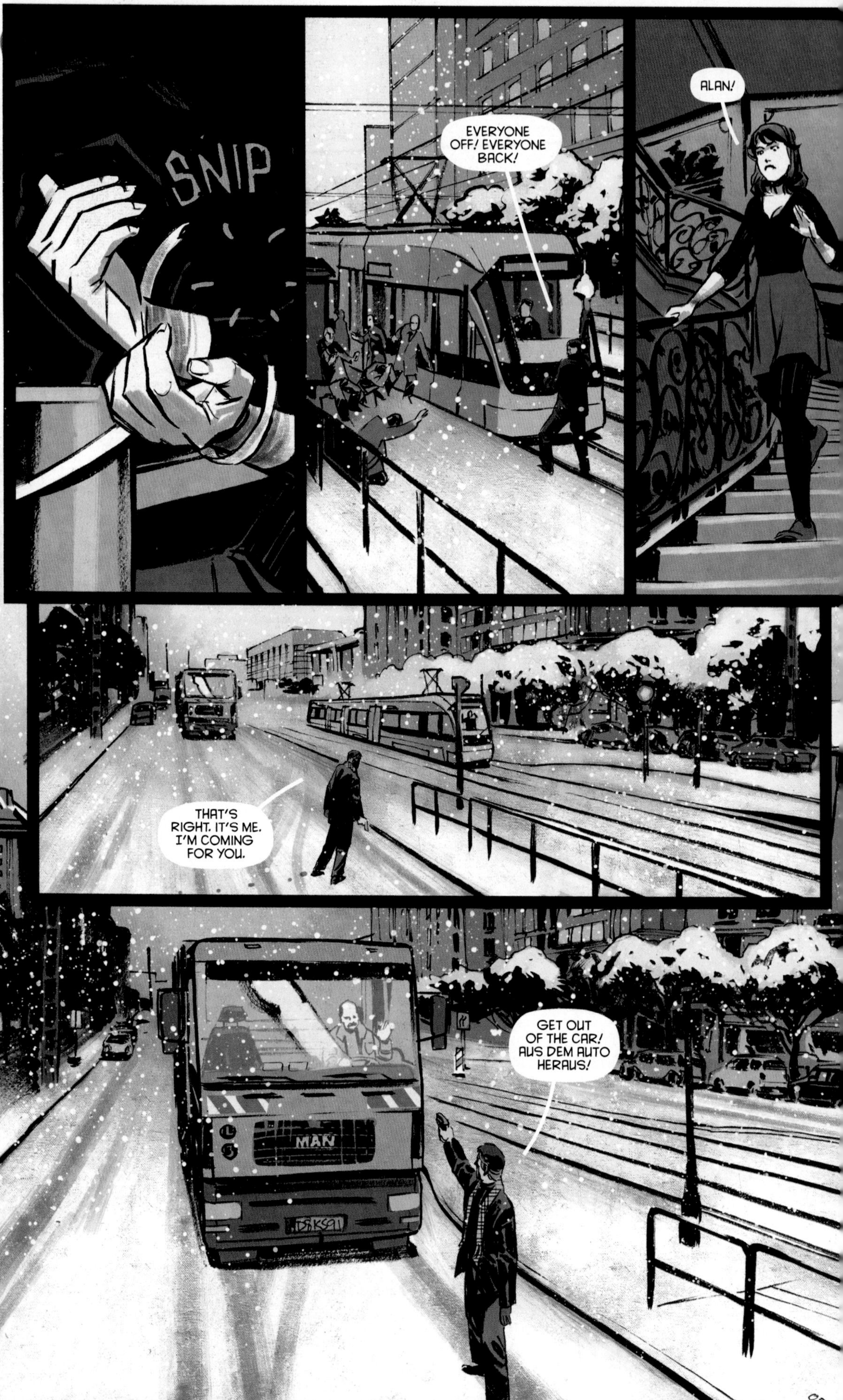
SNIP
EVERYONE OFF! EVERYONE BACK!
ALAN!
THAT'S RIGHT. IT'S ME. I'M COMING FOR YOU.
MAN
GET OUT OF THE CAR! AUS DEM AUTO HERAUS!

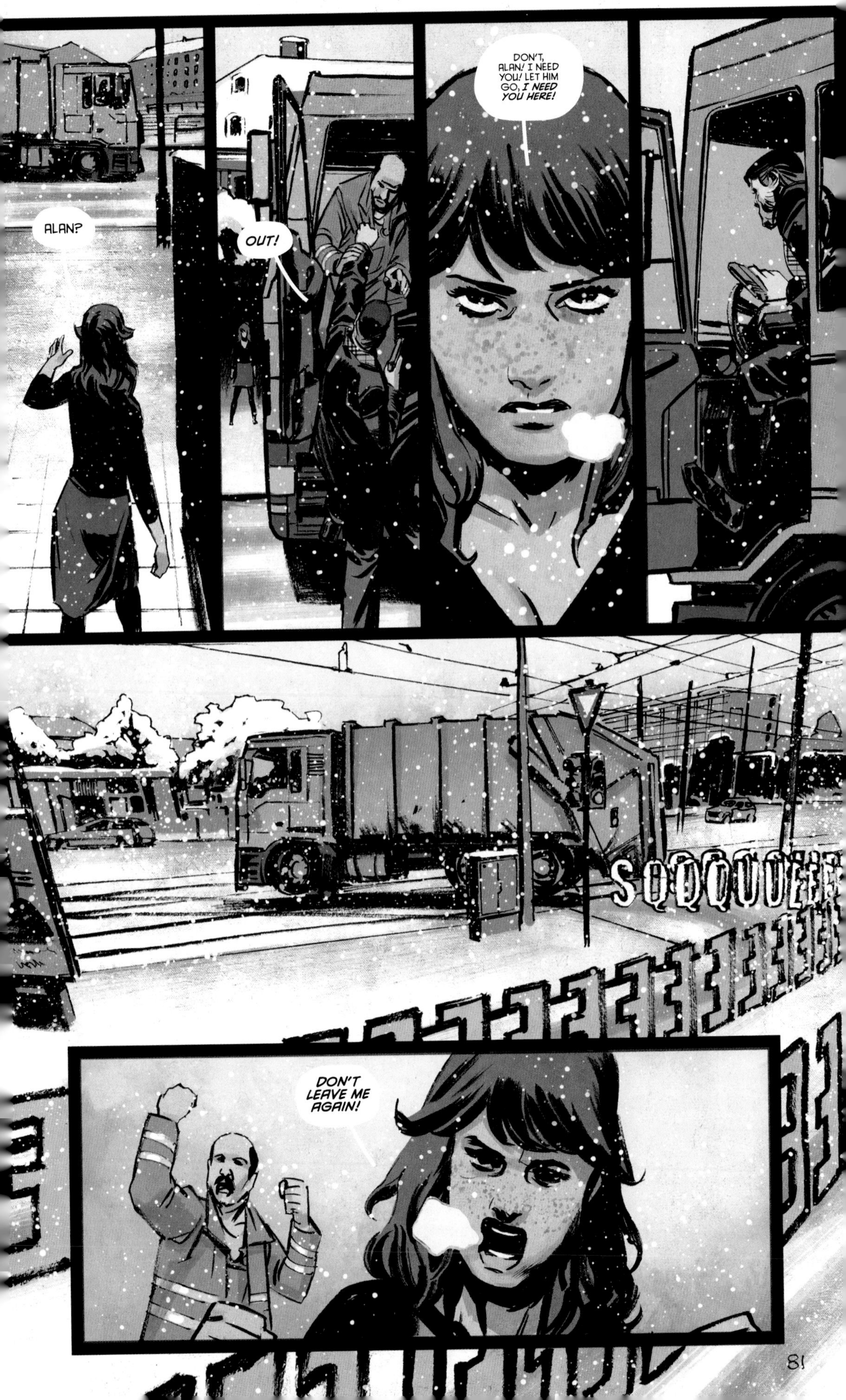

ALAN?
OUT!
DON'T, ALAN! I NEED YOU! LET HIM GO, I NEED YOU HERE!
SQQQUEEE
DON'T LEAVE ME AGAIN!

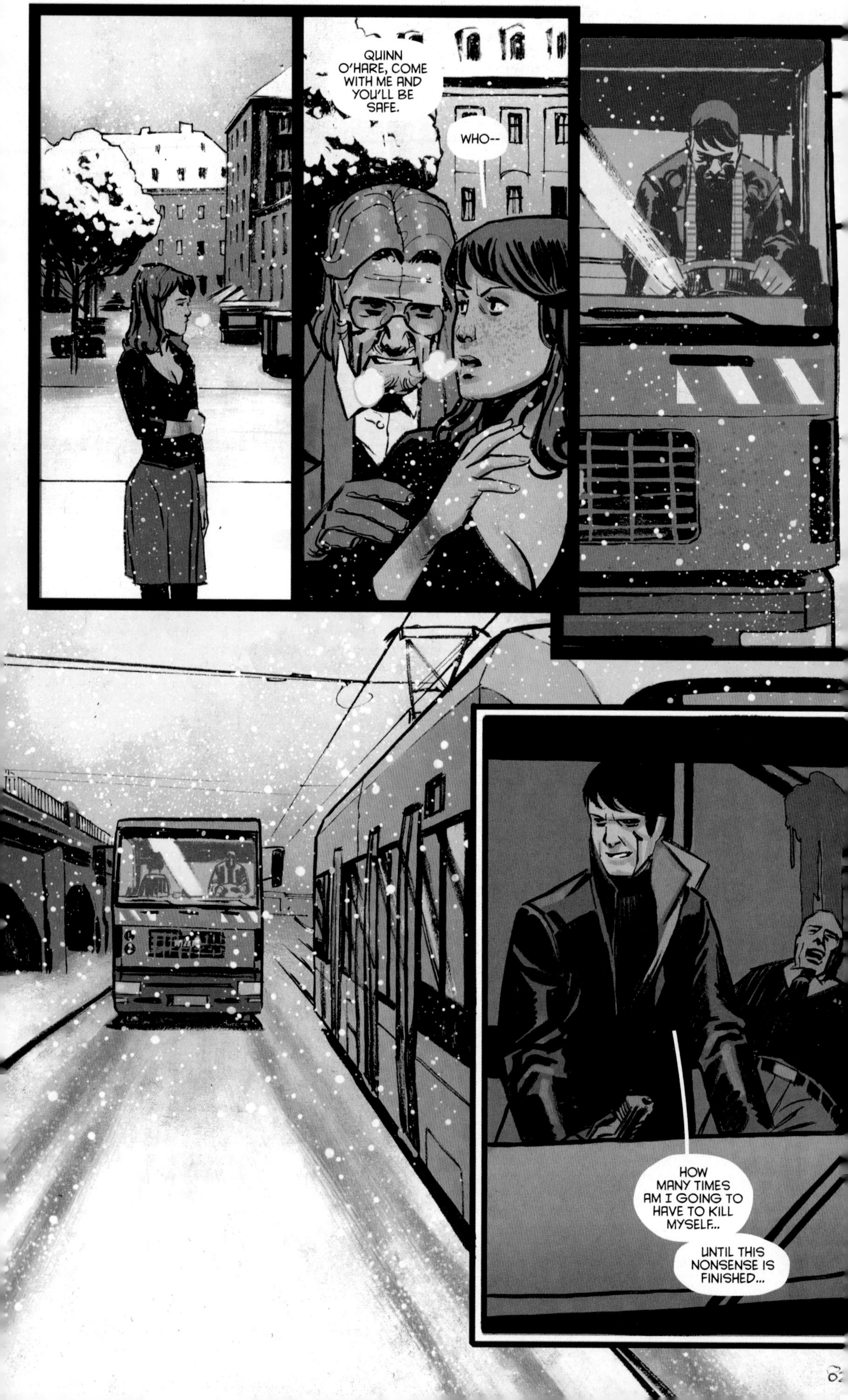
QUINN O'HARE, COME WITH ME AND YOU'LL BE SAFE.
WHO--
HOW MANY TIMES AM I GOING TO HAVE TO KILL MYSELF...
UNTIL THIS NONSENSE IS FINISHED...

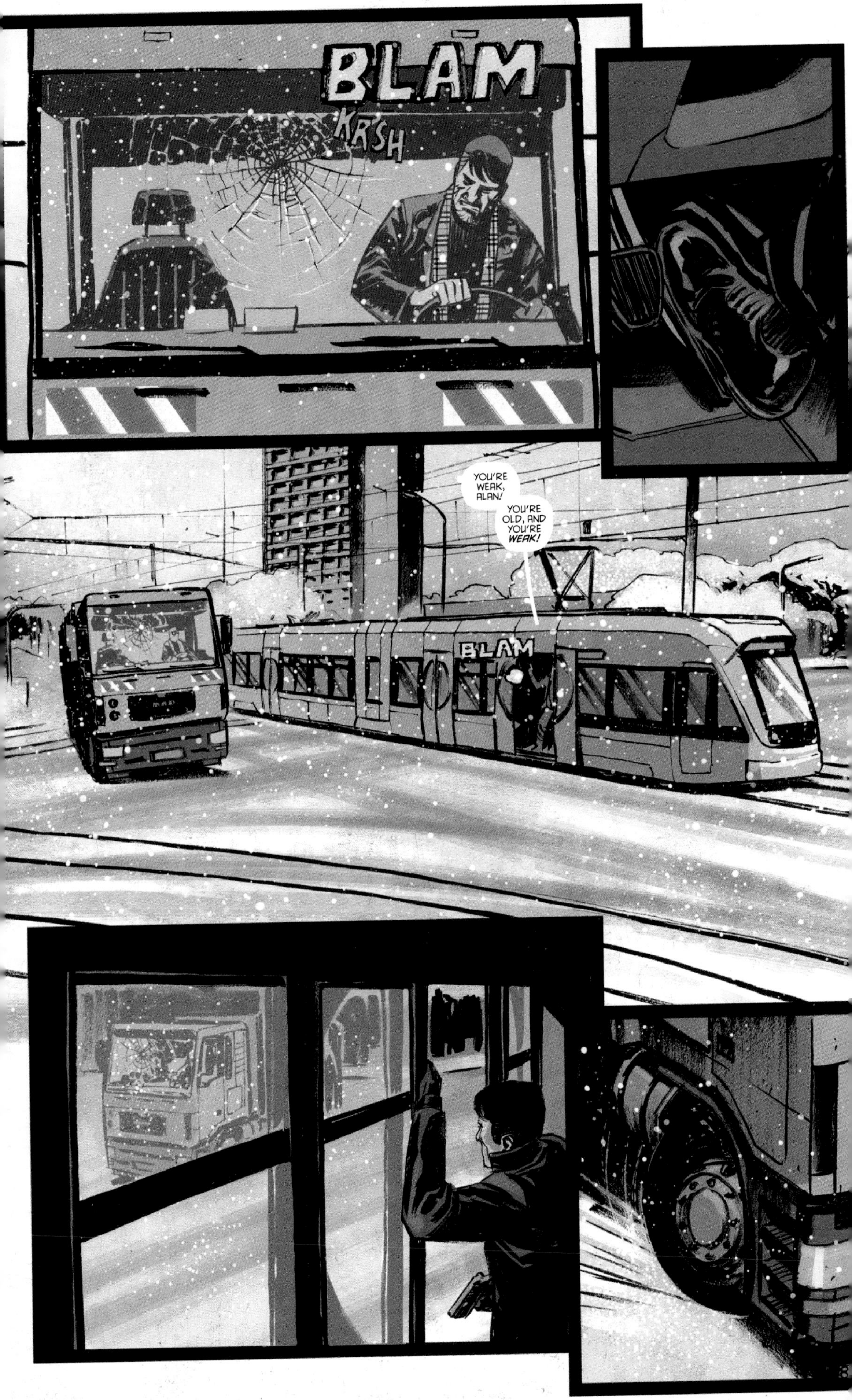
BLAM
KRSH
YOU'RE WEAK, ALAN!
YOU'RE OLD, AND YOU'RE WEAK!
BLAM

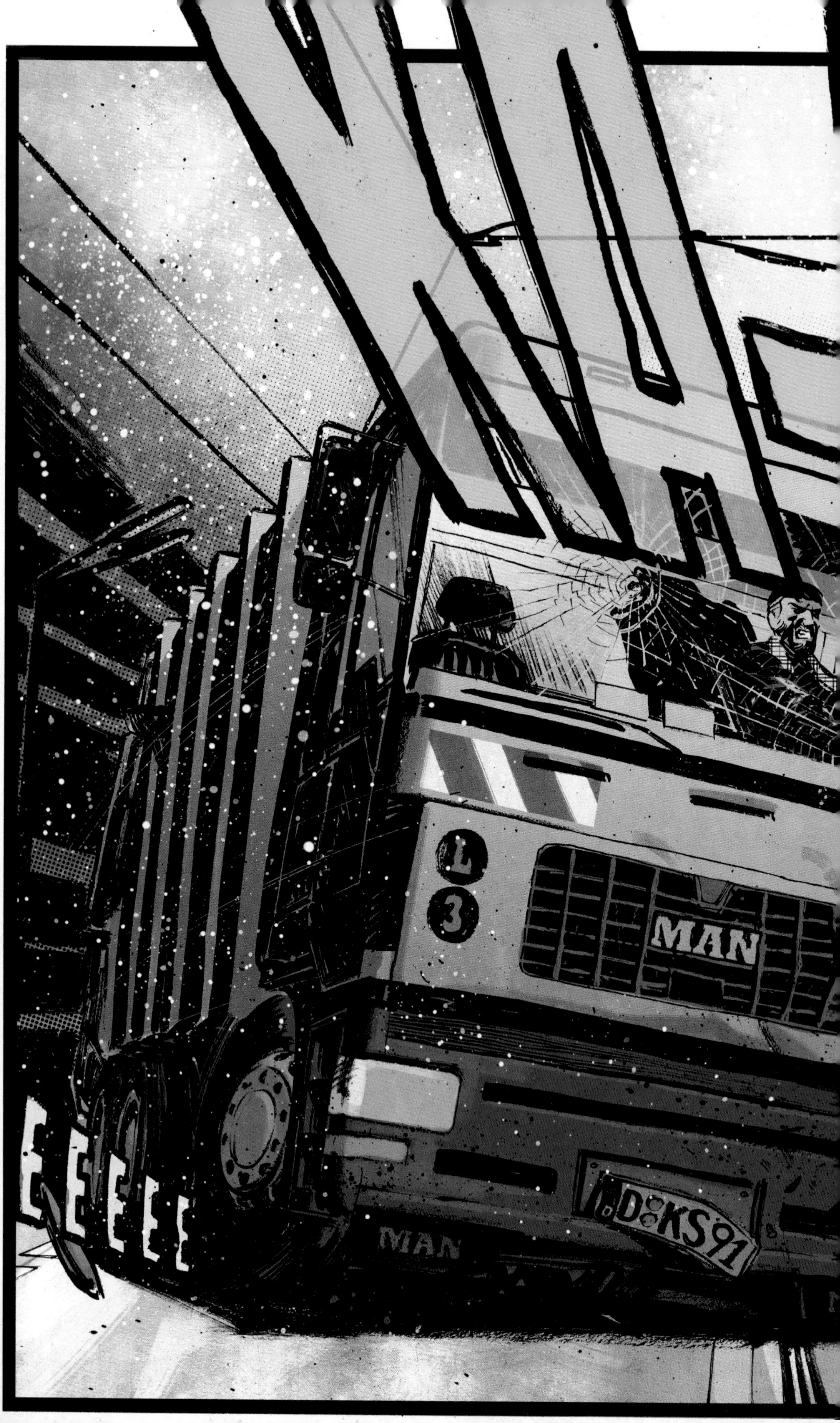
EEEEE
L
3
MAN
D KS 91
MAN

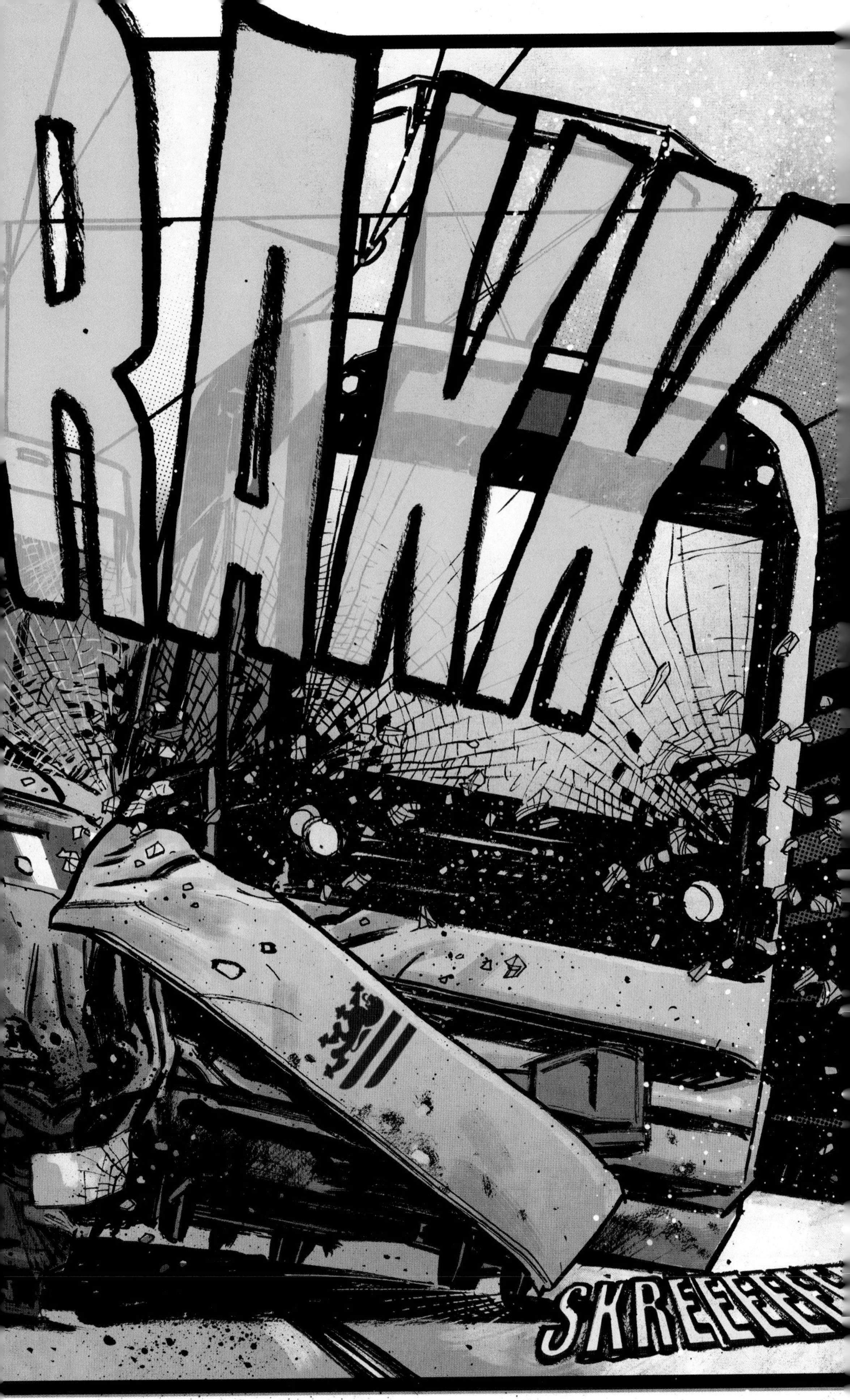
SKREEEEE

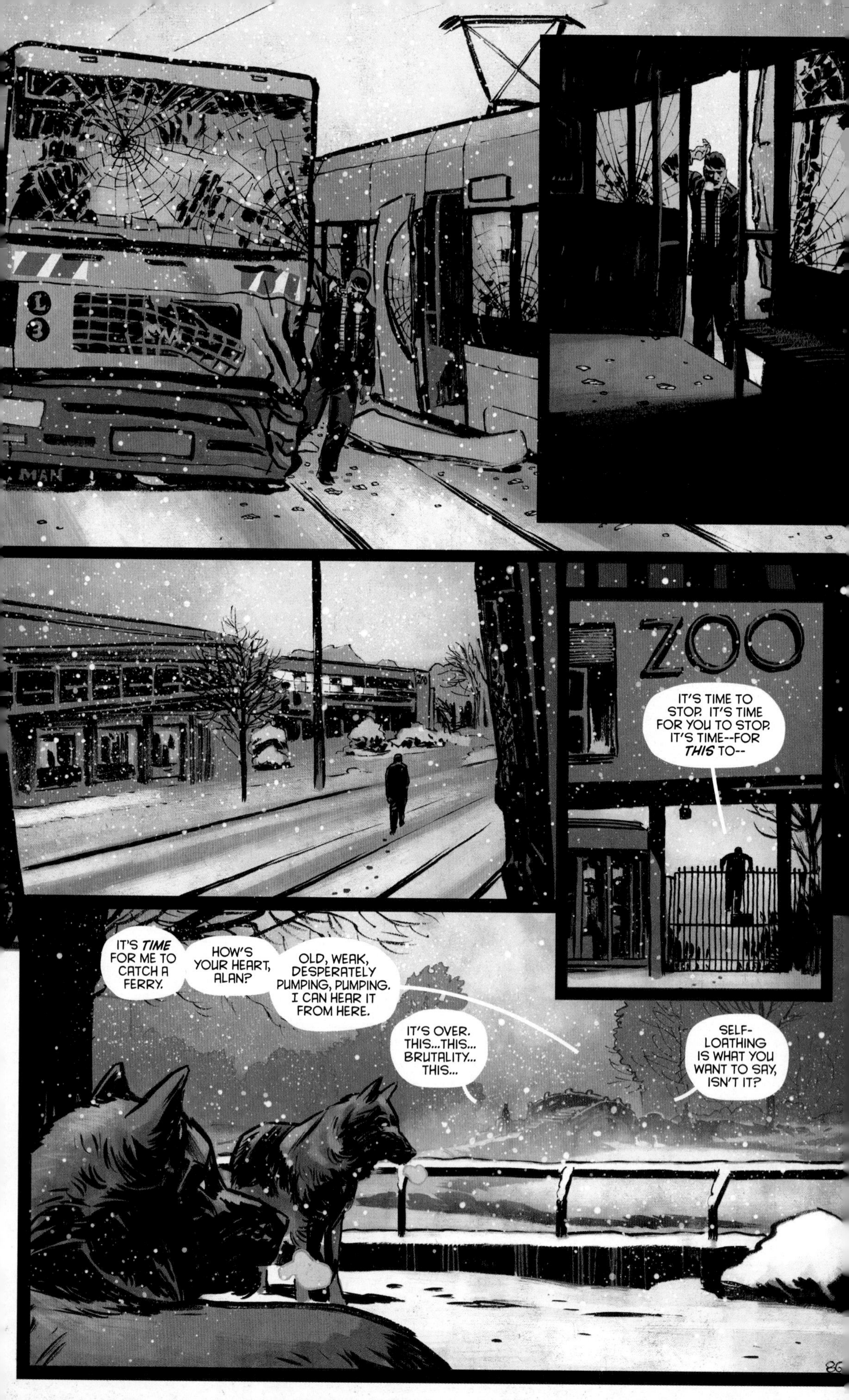

MAN
ZOO
IT'S TIME TO STOP. IT'S TIME FOR YOU TO STOP. IT'S TIME--FOR *THIS* TO--
IT'S *TIME* FOR ME TO CATCH A FERRY.
HOW'S YOUR HEART, ALAN?
OLD, WEAK, DESPERATELY PUMPING, PUMPING. I CAN HEAR IT FROM HERE.
IT'S OVER. THIS...THIS... BRUTALITY... THIS...
SELF-LOATHING IS WHAT YOU WANT TO SAY, ISN'T IT?

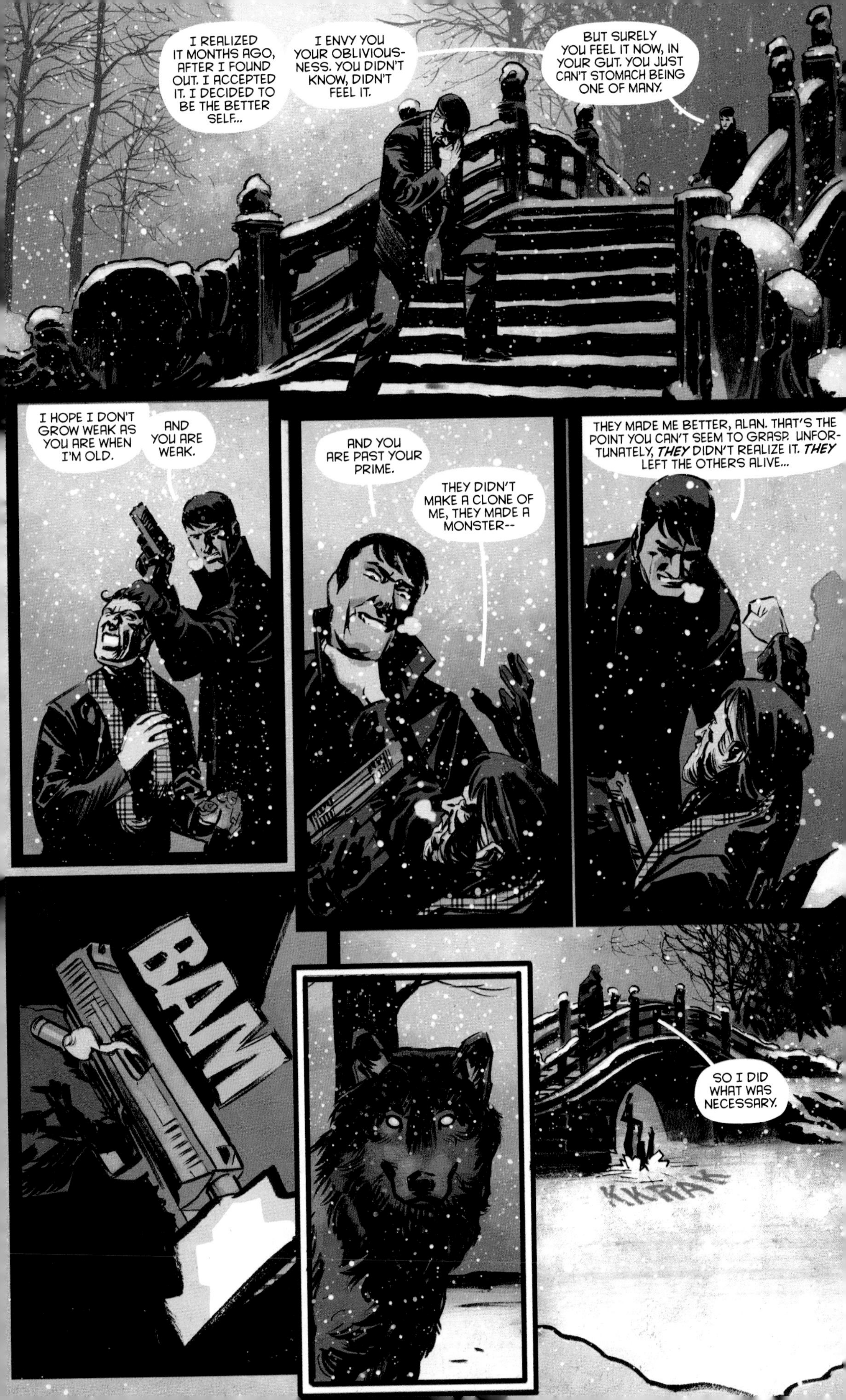
I REALIZED IT MONTHS AGO, AFTER I FOUND OUT. I ACCEPTED IT. I DECIDED TO BE THE BETTER SELF...
I ENVY YOU YOUR OBLIVIOUSNESS. YOU DIDN'T KNOW, DIDN'T FEEL IT.
BUT SURELY YOU FEEL IT NOW, IN YOUR GUT. YOU JUST CAN'T STOMACH BEING ONE OF MANY.
I HOPE I DON'T GROW WEAK AS YOU ARE WHEN I'M OLD.
AND YOU ARE WEAK.
AND YOU ARE PAST YOUR PRIME.
THEY DIDN'T MAKE A CLONE OF ME, THEY MADE A MONSTER--
THEY MADE ME BETTER, ALAN. THAT'S THE POINT YOU CAN'T SEEM TO GRASP. UNFORTUNATELY, *THEY* DIDN'T REALIZE IT. *THEY* LEFT THE OTHERS ALIVE...
BAM
SO I DID WHAT WAS NECESSARY.
KKRAK

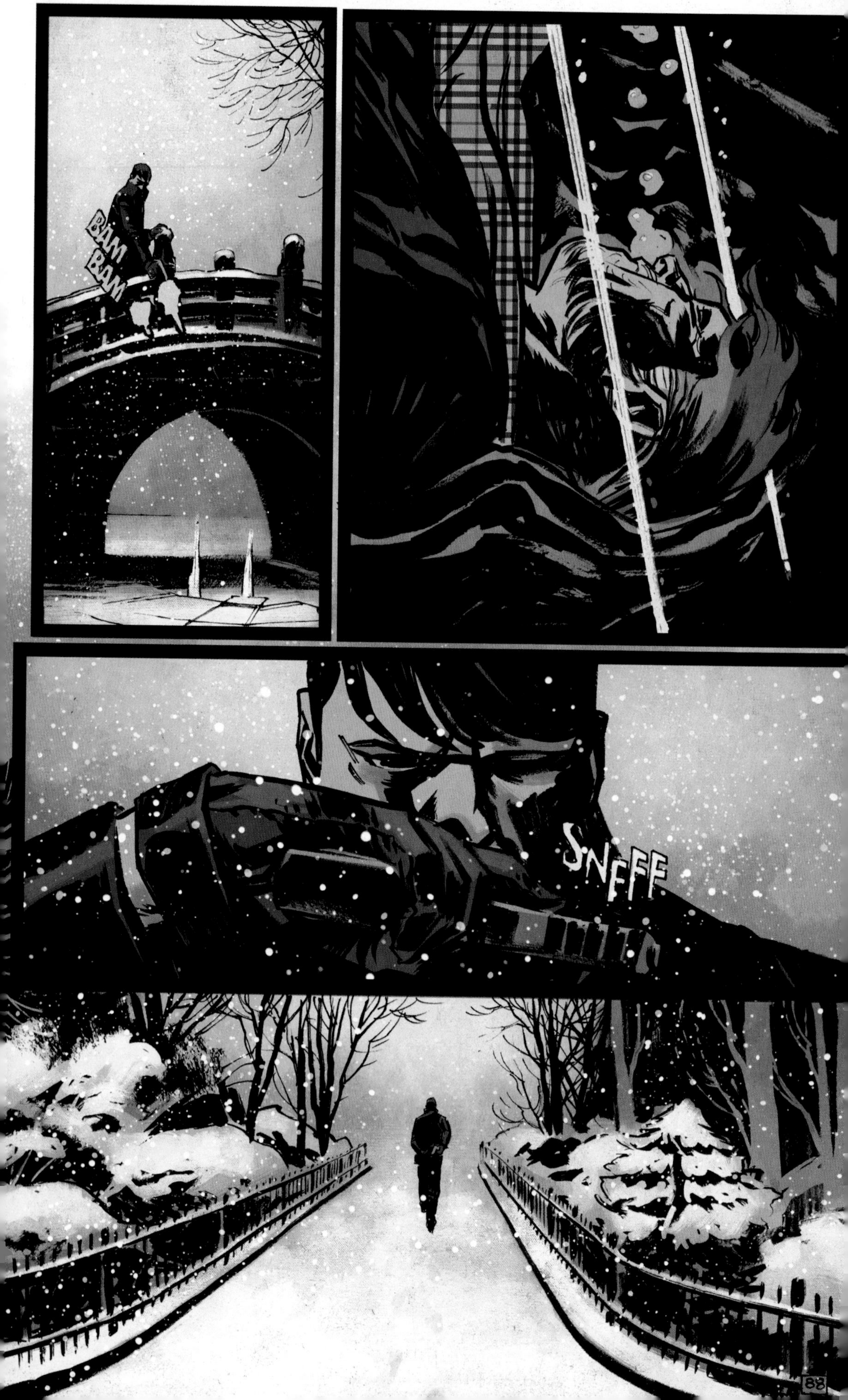
BAM
BAM
SNFFF

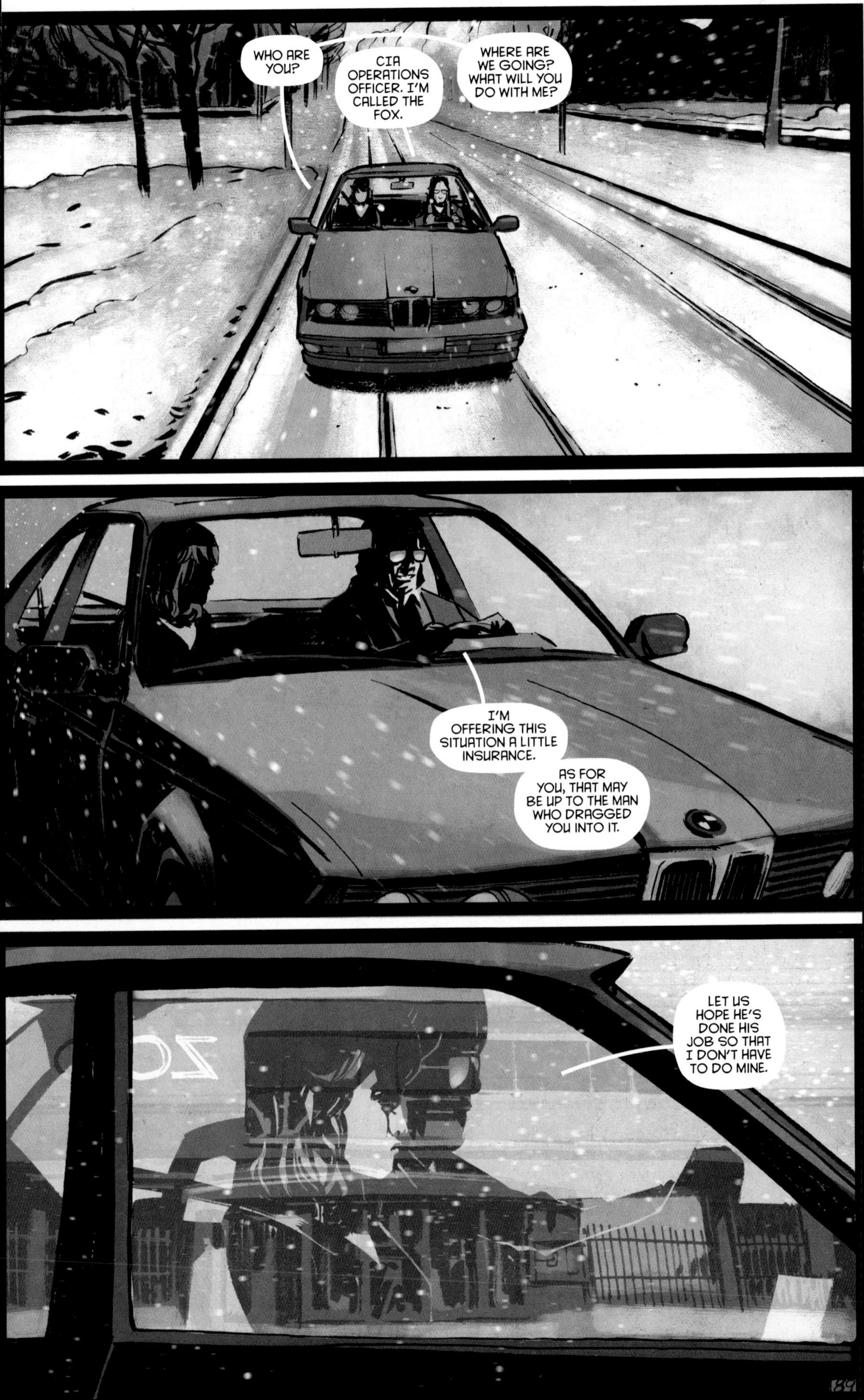
WHO ARE YOU?
CIA OPERATIONS OFFICER. I'M CALLED THE FOX.
WHERE ARE WE GOING? WHAT WILL YOU DO WITH ME?
I'M OFFERING THIS SITUATION A LITTLE INSURANCE.
AS FOR YOU, THAT MAY BE UP TO THE MAN WHO DRAGGED YOU INTO IT.
LET US HOPE HE'S DONE HIS JOB SO THAT I DON'T HAVE TO DO MINE.

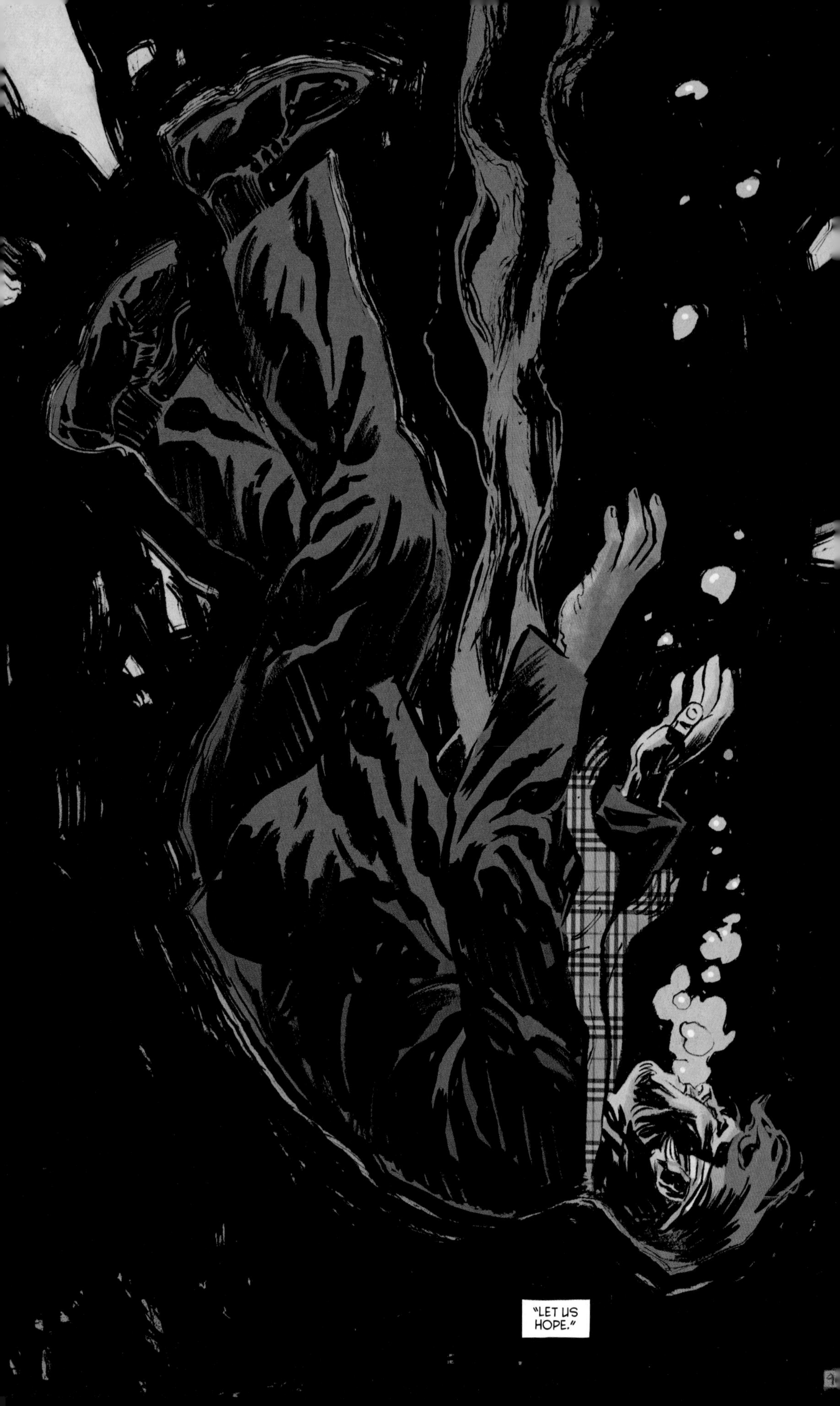
"LET US
HOPE."

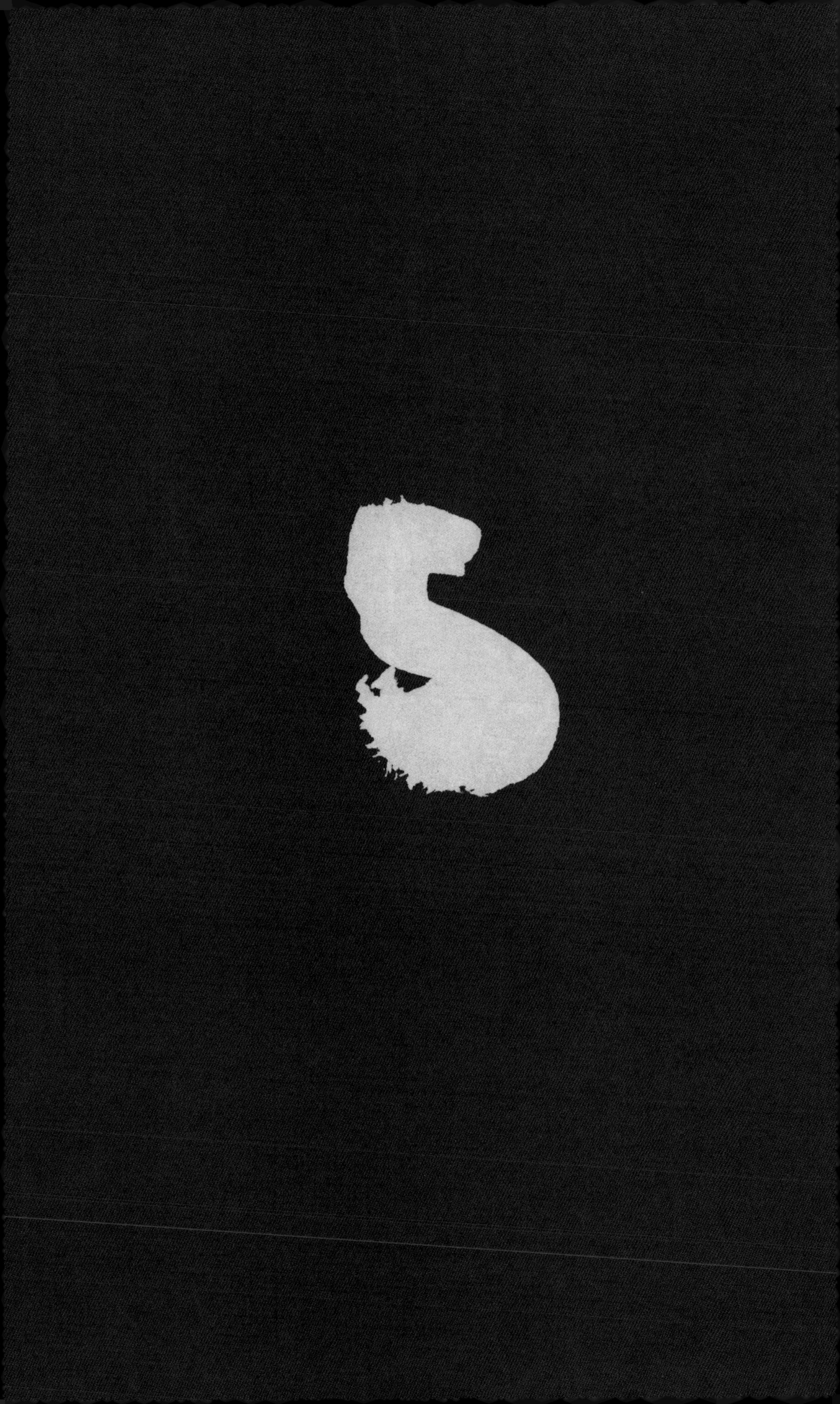

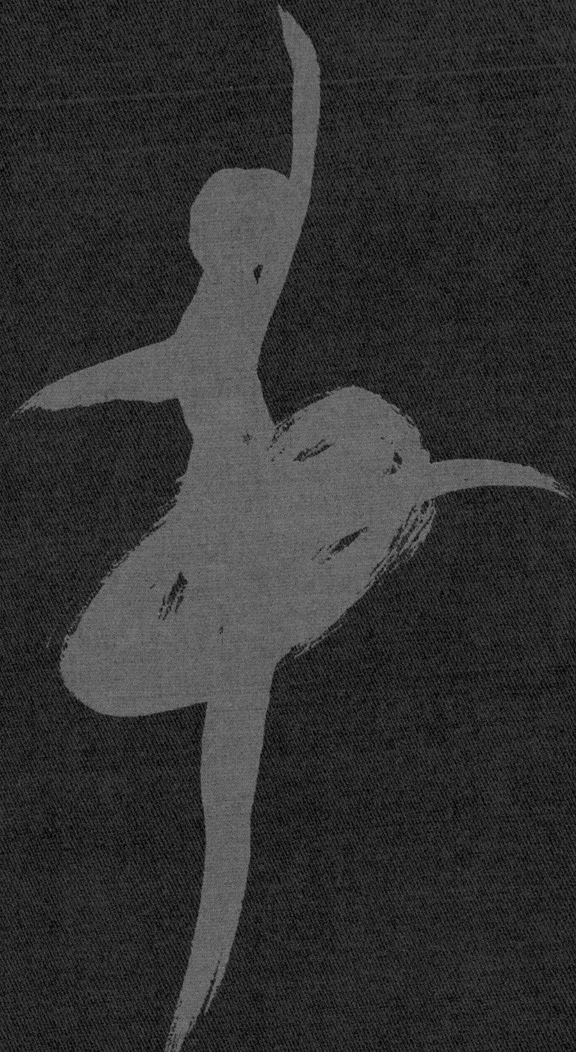

CODA

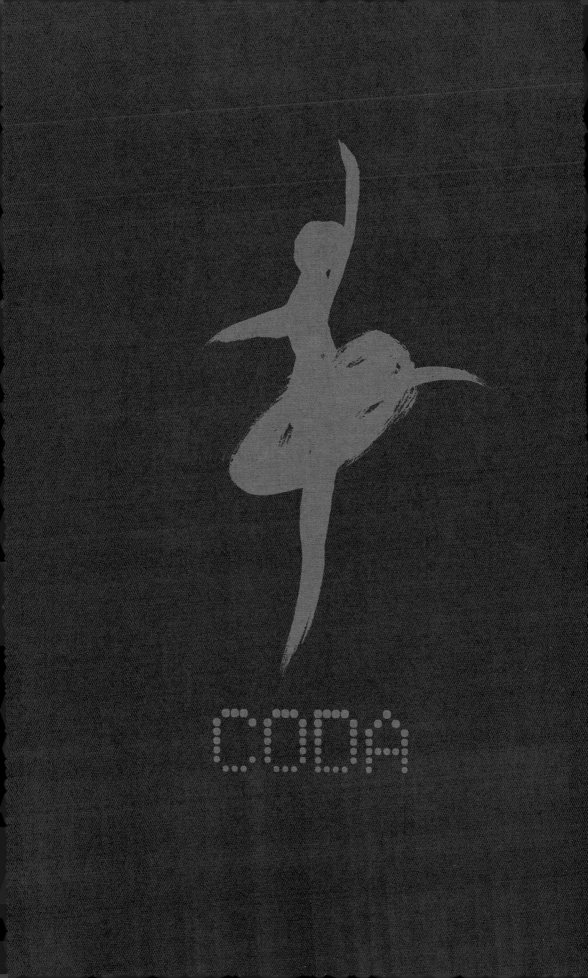

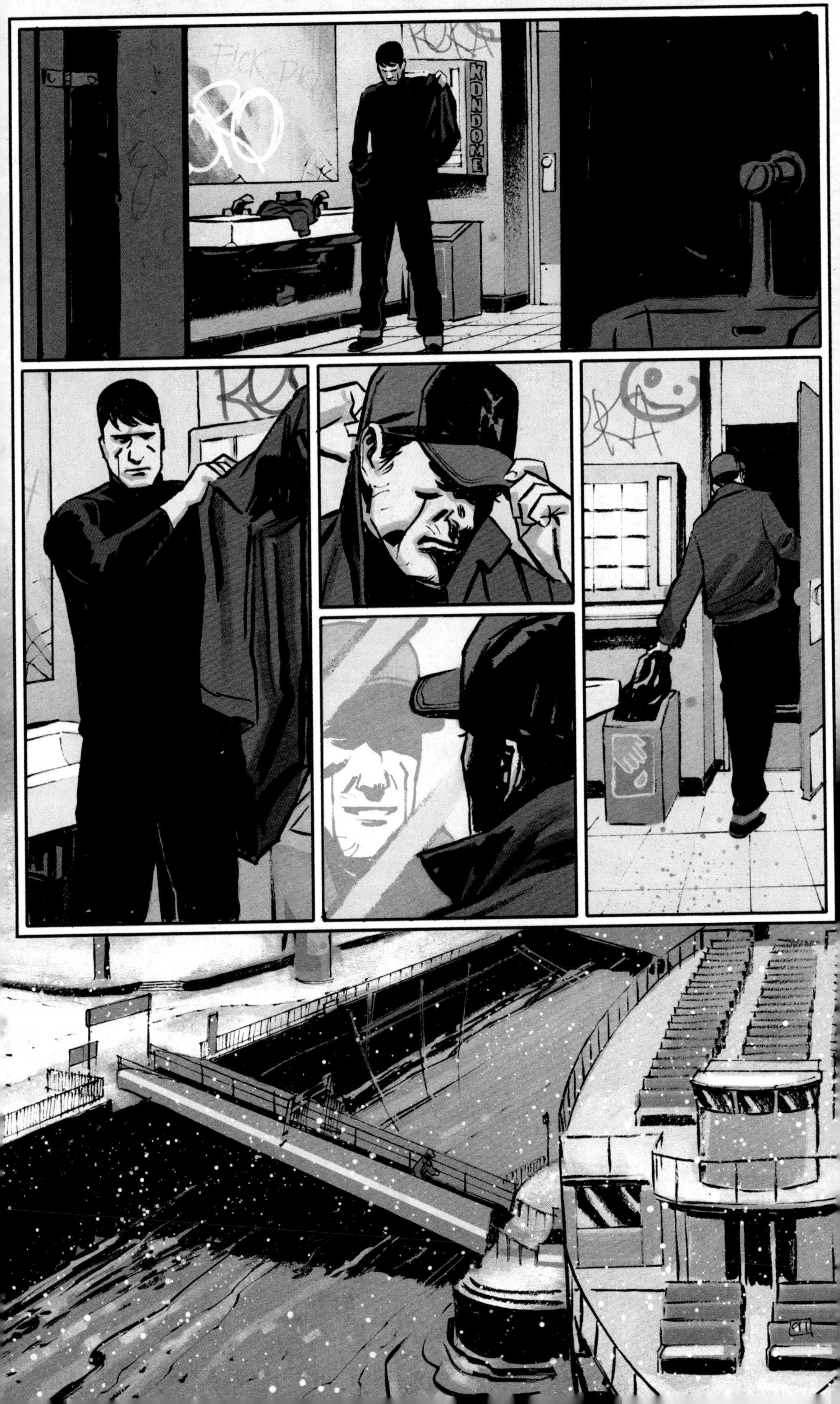
KONDOME

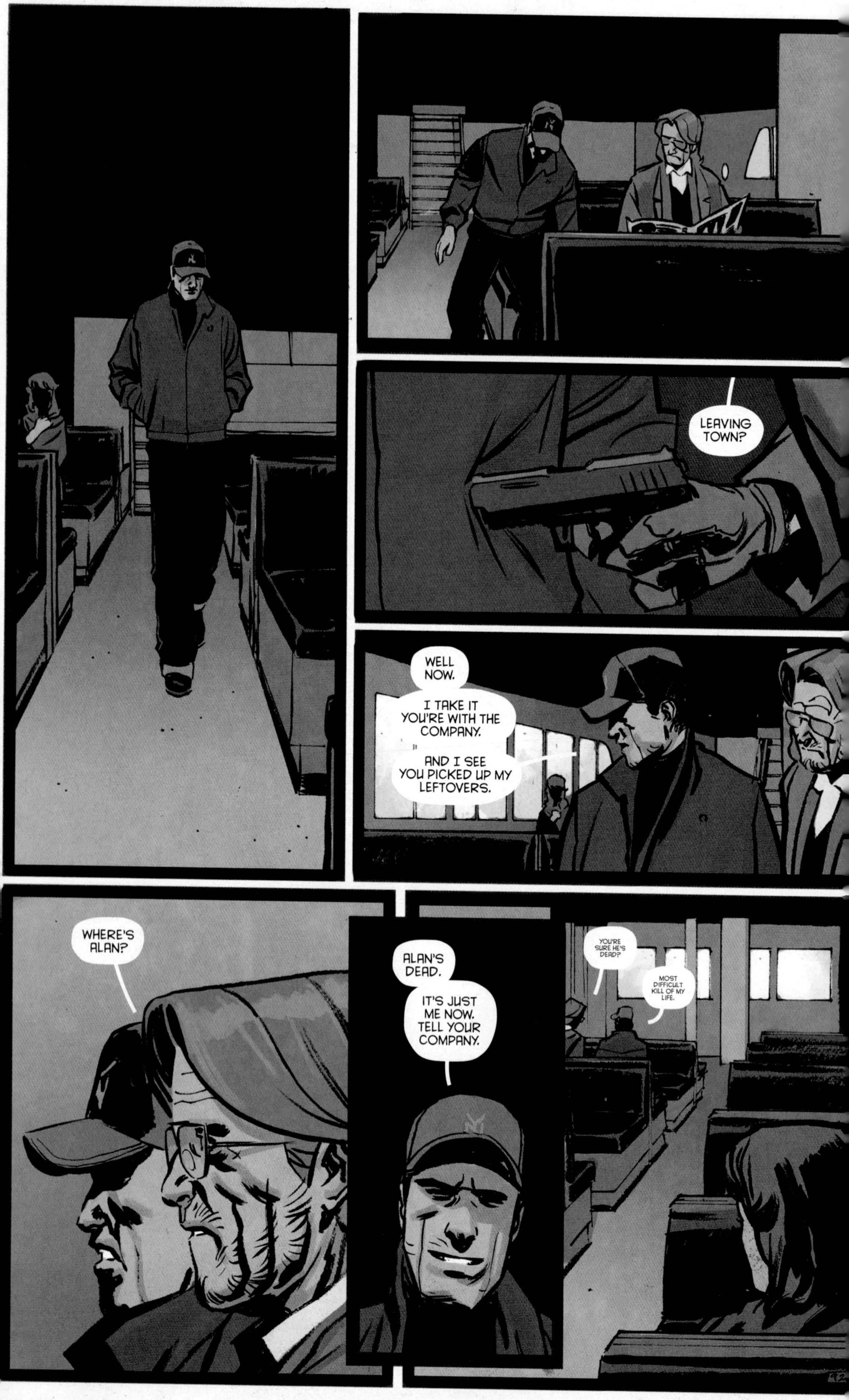

LEAVING TOWN?
WELL NOW.
I TAKE IT YOU'RE WITH THE COMPANY.
AND I SEE YOU PICKED UP MY LEFTOVERS.
WHERE'S ALAN?
ALAN'S DEAD.
IT'S JUST ME NOW. TELL YOUR COMPANY.
YOU'RE SURE HE'S DEAD?
MOST DIFFICULT KILL OF MY LIFE.

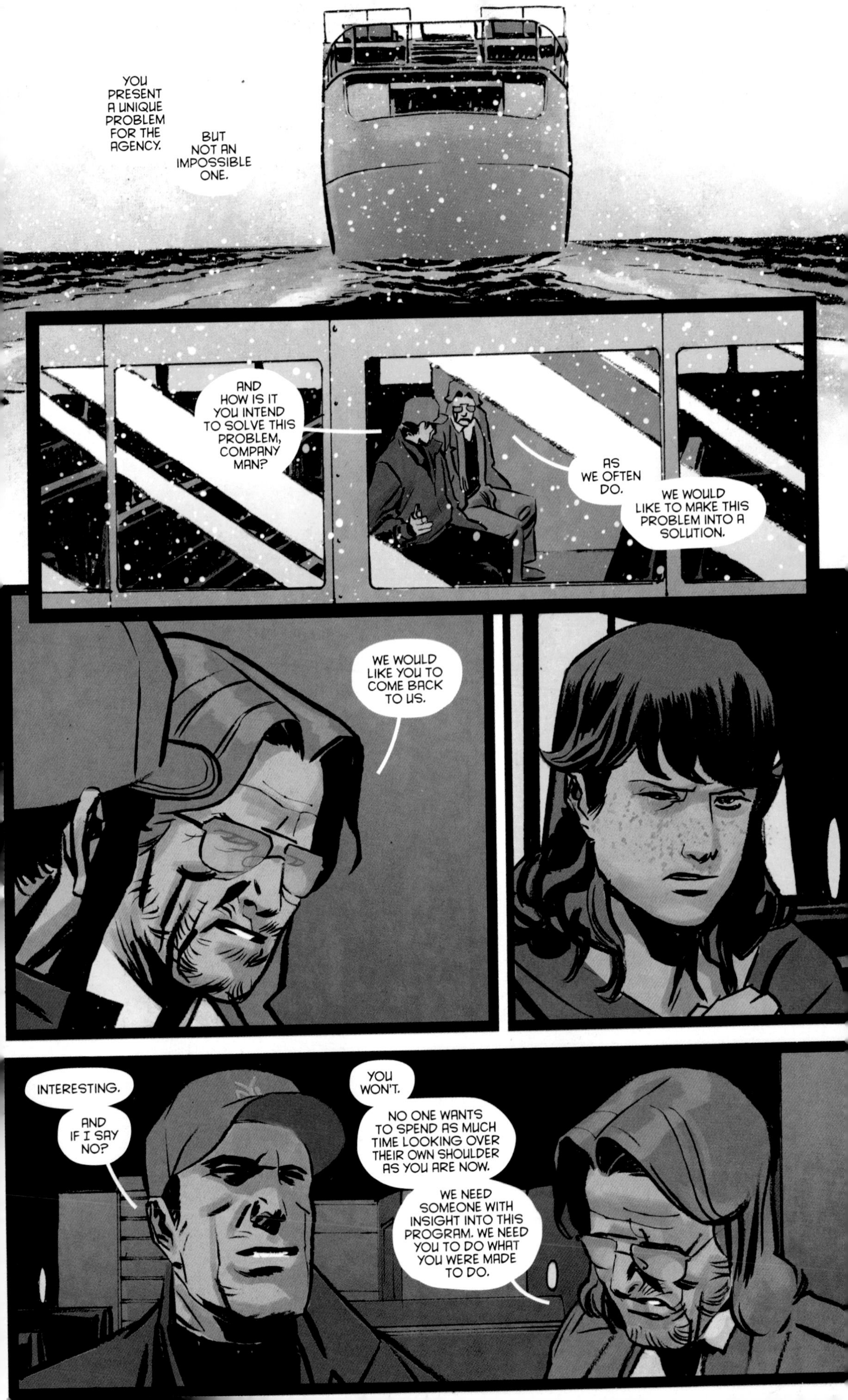
YOU PRESENT A UNIQUE PROBLEM FOR THE AGENCY.
BUT NOT AN IMPOSSIBLE ONE.
AND HOW IS IT YOU INTEND TO SOLVE THIS PROBLEM, COMPANY MAN?
AS WE OFTEN DO.
WE WOULD LIKE TO MAKE THIS PROBLEM INTO A SOLUTION.
WE WOULD LIKE YOU TO COME BACK TO US.
INTERESTING.
AND IF I SAY NO?
YOU WON'T.
NO ONE WANTS TO SPEND AS MUCH TIME LOOKING OVER THEIR OWN SHOULDER AS YOU ARE NOW.
WE NEED SOMEONE WITH INSIGHT INTO THIS PROGRAM. WE NEED YOU TO DO WHAT YOU WERE MADE TO DO.

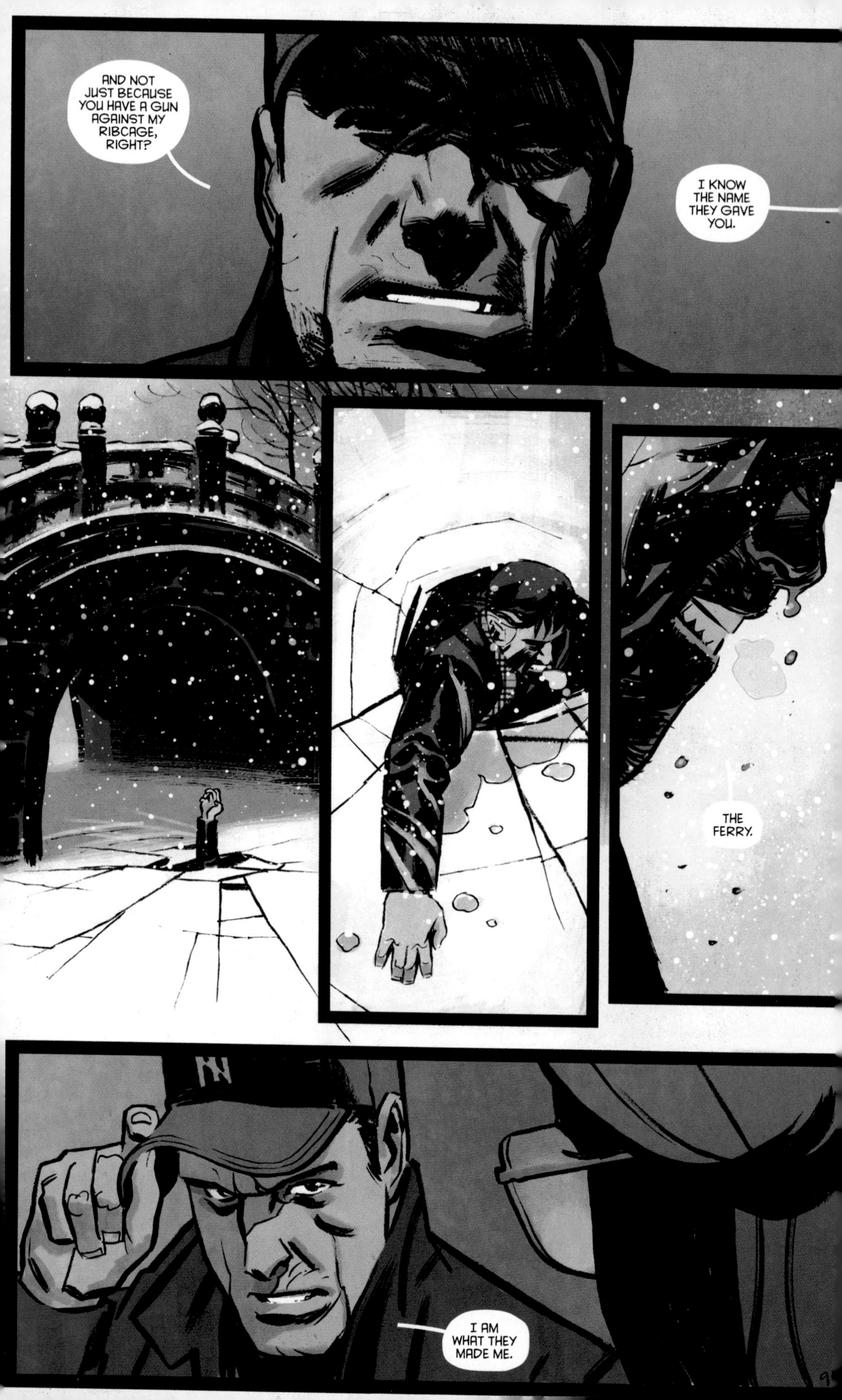
AND NOT JUST BECAUSE YOU HAVE A GUN AGAINST MY RIBCAGE, RIGHT?
I KNOW THE NAME THEY GAVE YOU.
THE FERRY.
I AM WHAT THEY MADE ME.

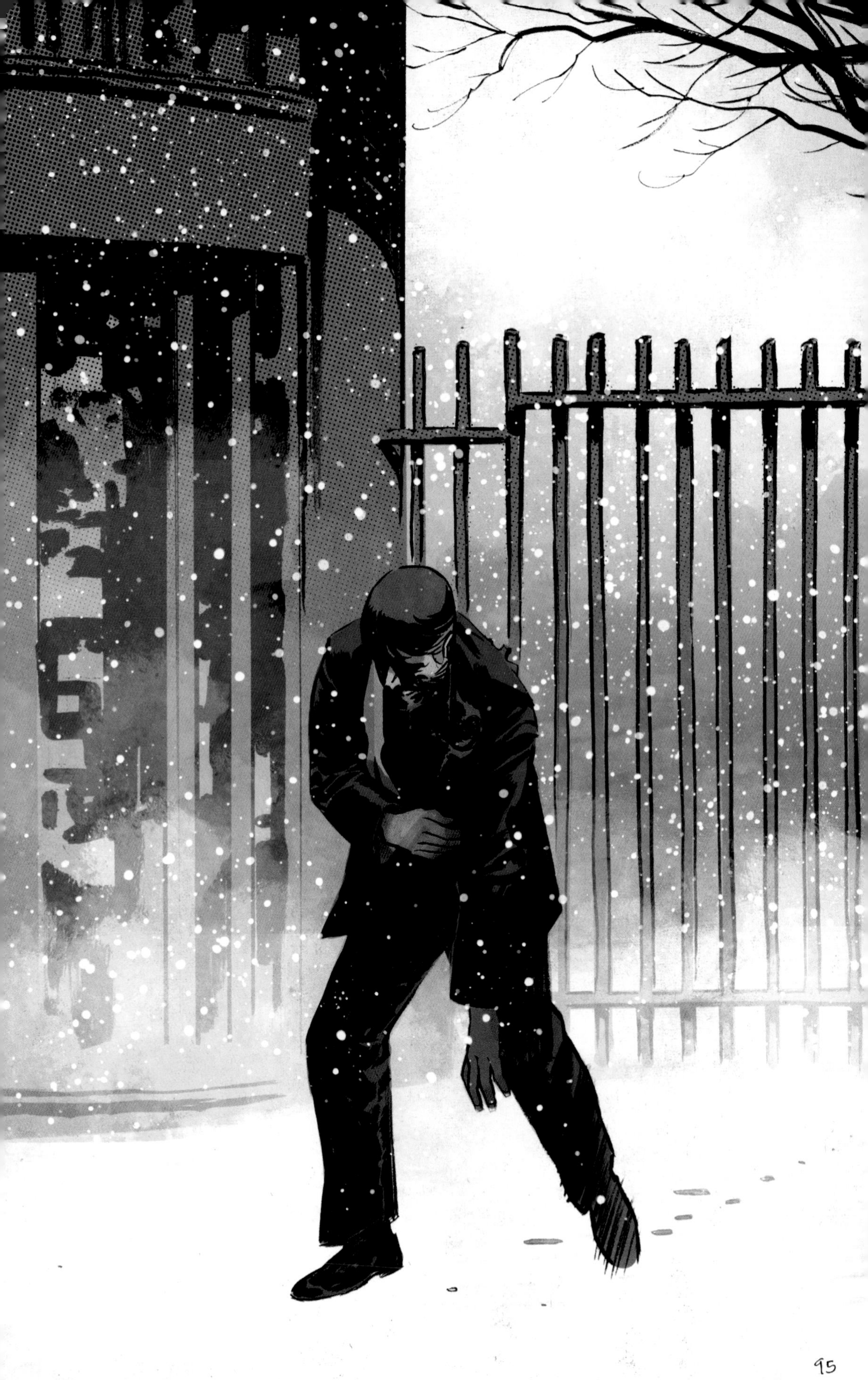

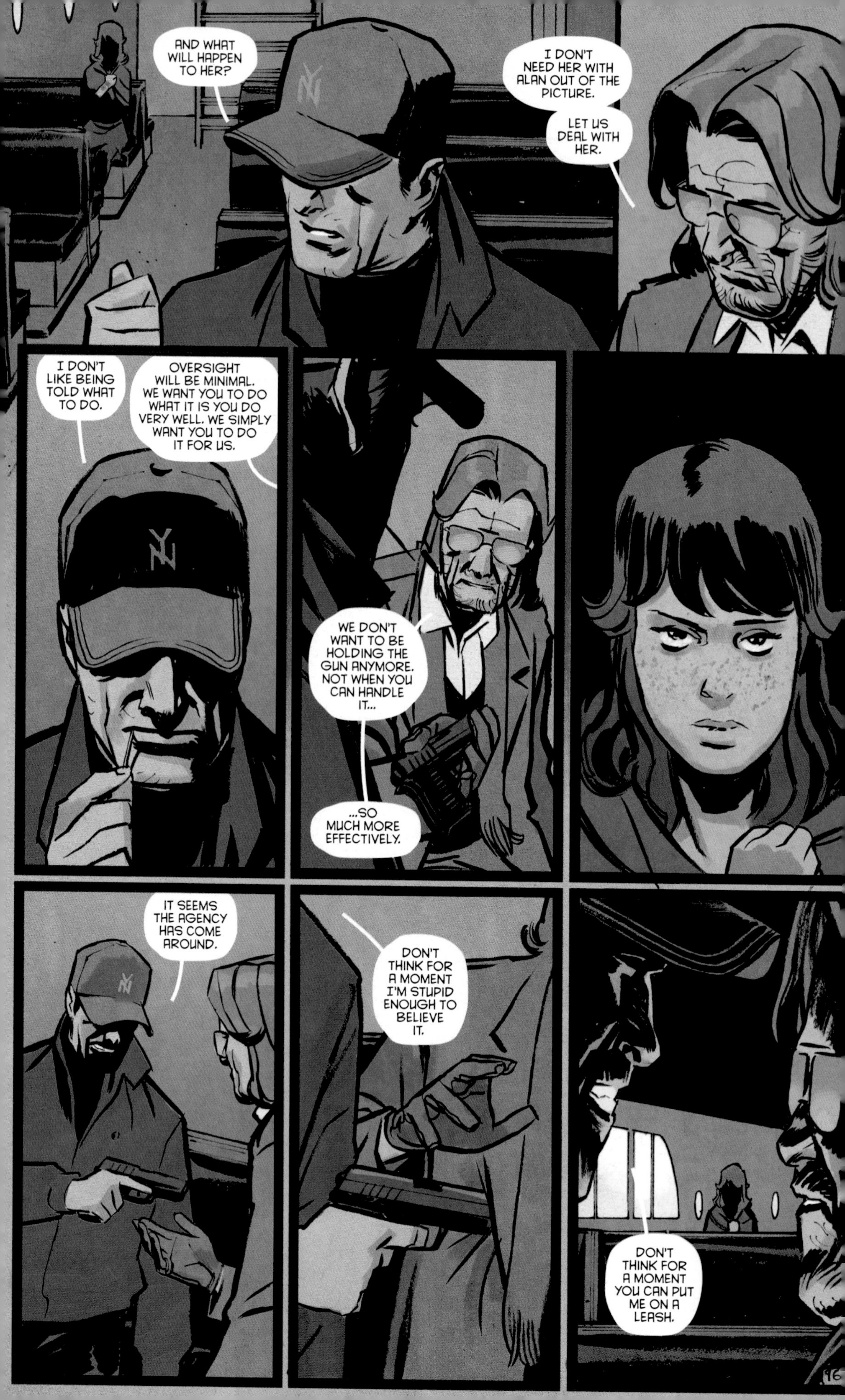
AND WHAT WILL HAPPEN TO HER?
I DON'T NEED HER WITH ALAN OUT OF THE PICTURE.
LET US DEAL WITH HER.
I DON'T LIKE BEING TOLD WHAT TO DO.
OVERSIGHT WILL BE MINIMAL. WE WANT YOU TO DO WHAT IT IS YOU DO VERY WELL. WE SIMPLY WANT YOU TO DO IT FOR US.
WE DON'T WANT TO BE HOLDING THE GUN ANYMORE. NOT WHEN YOU CAN HANDLE IT...
...SO MUCH MORE EFFECTIVELY.
IT SEEMS THE AGENCY HAS COME AROUND.
DON'T THINK FOR A MOMENT I'M STUPID ENOUGH TO BELIEVE IT.
DON'T THINK FOR A MOMENT YOU CAN PUT ME ON A LEASH.

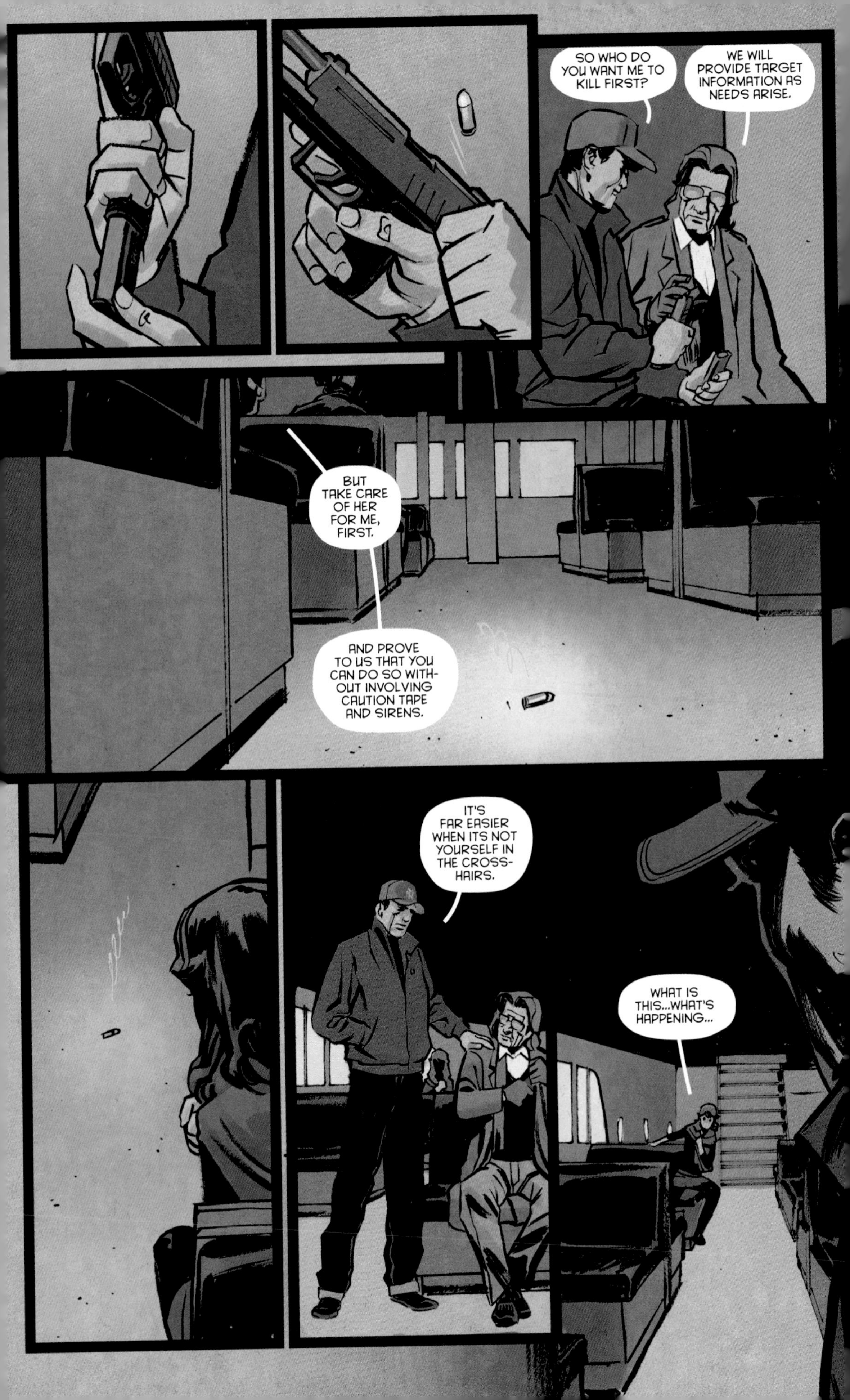
SO WHO DO YOU WANT ME TO KILL FIRST?
WE WILL PROVIDE TARGET INFORMATION AS NEEDS ARISE.
BUT TAKE CARE OF HER FOR ME, FIRST.
AND PROVE TO US THAT YOU CAN DO SO WITH-OUT INVOLVING CAUTION TAPE AND SIRENS.
IT'S FAR EASIER WHEN ITS NOT YOURSELF IN THE CROSS-HAIRS.
WHAT IS THIS...WHAT'S HAPPENING...

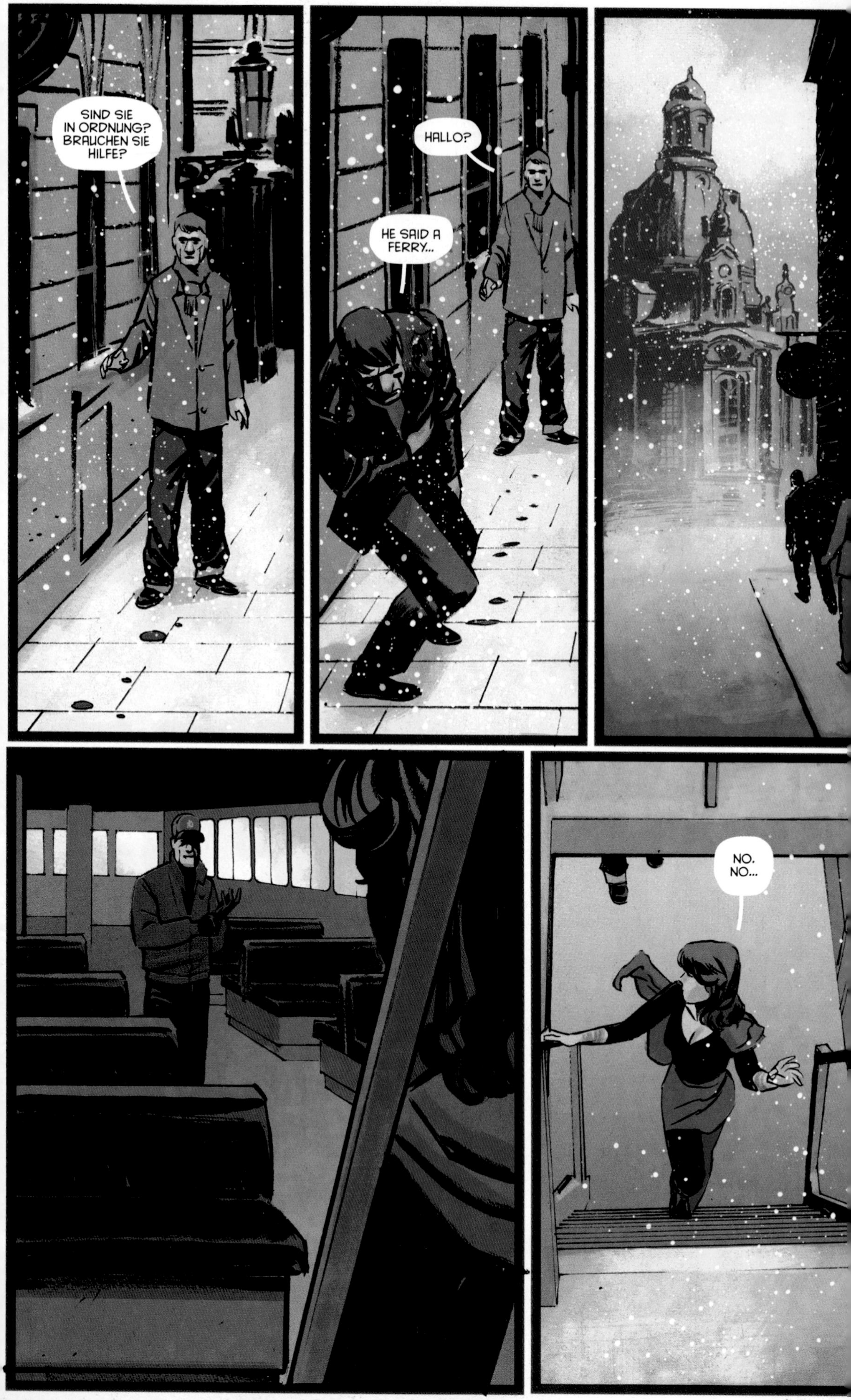
SIND SIE IN ORDNUNG? BRAUCHEN SIE HILFE?
HALLO?
HE SAID A FERRY...
NO. NO...

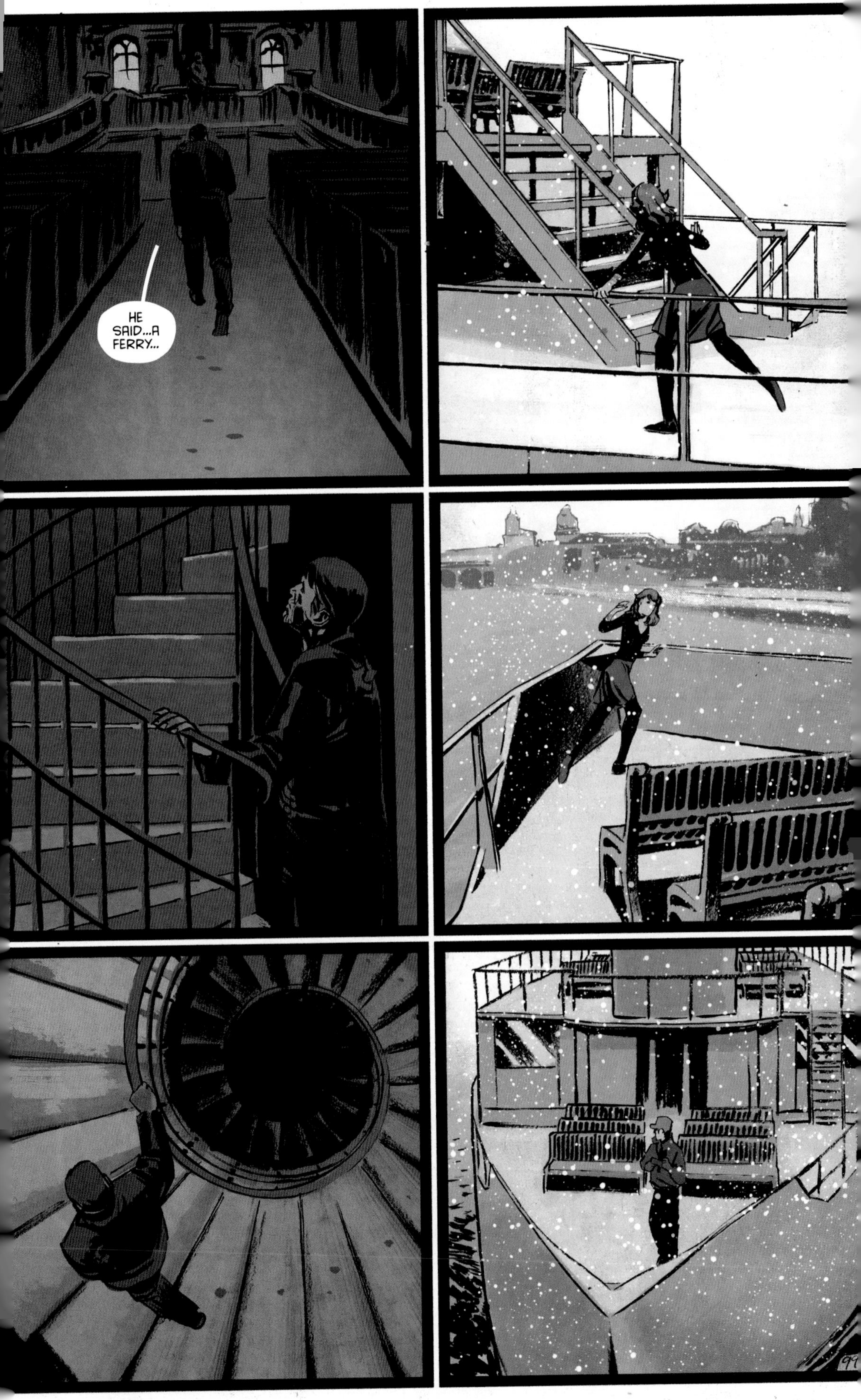
HE SAID...A FERRY...

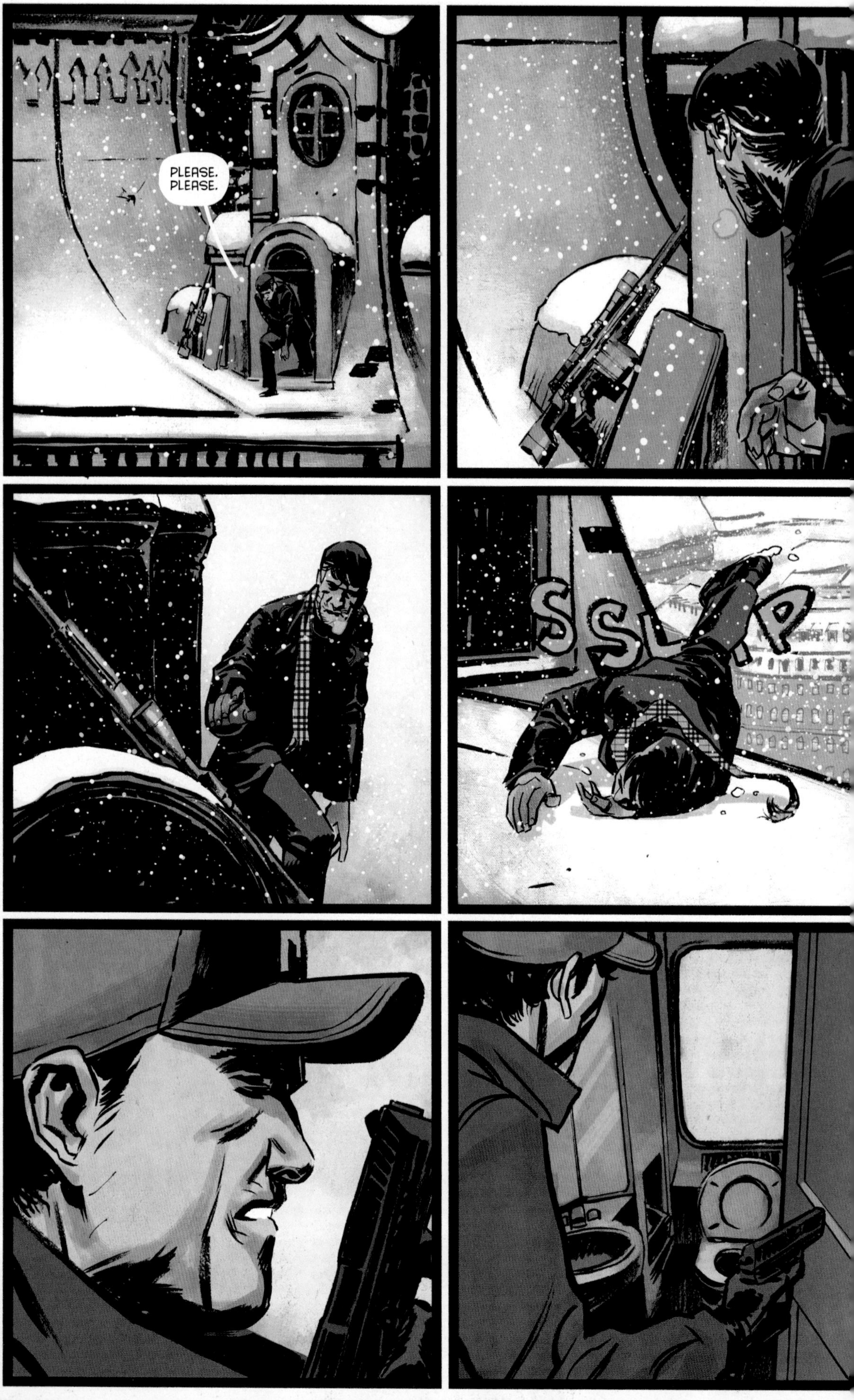
PLEASE.
PLEASE.
SSLAP

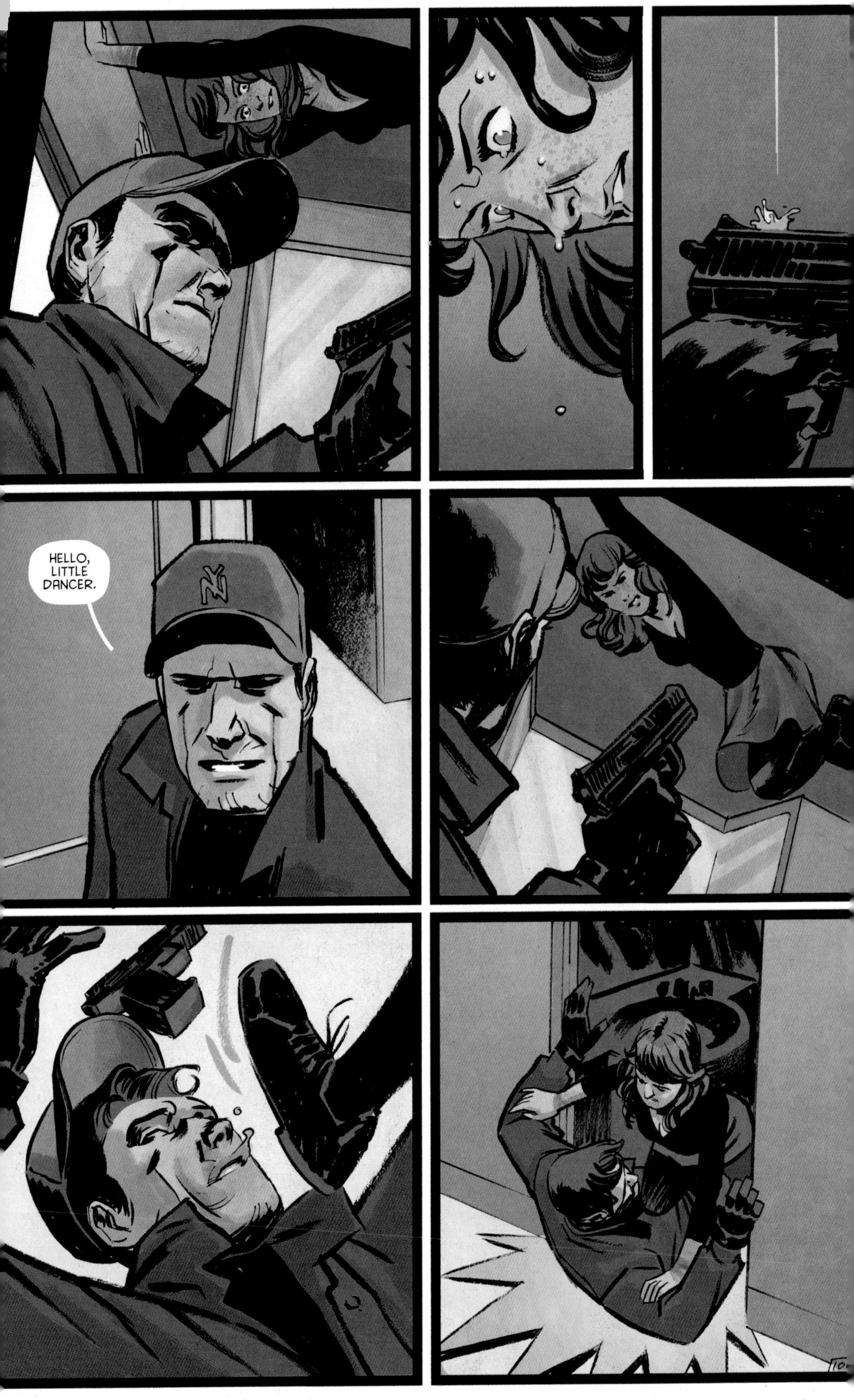
HELLO, LITTLE DANCER.

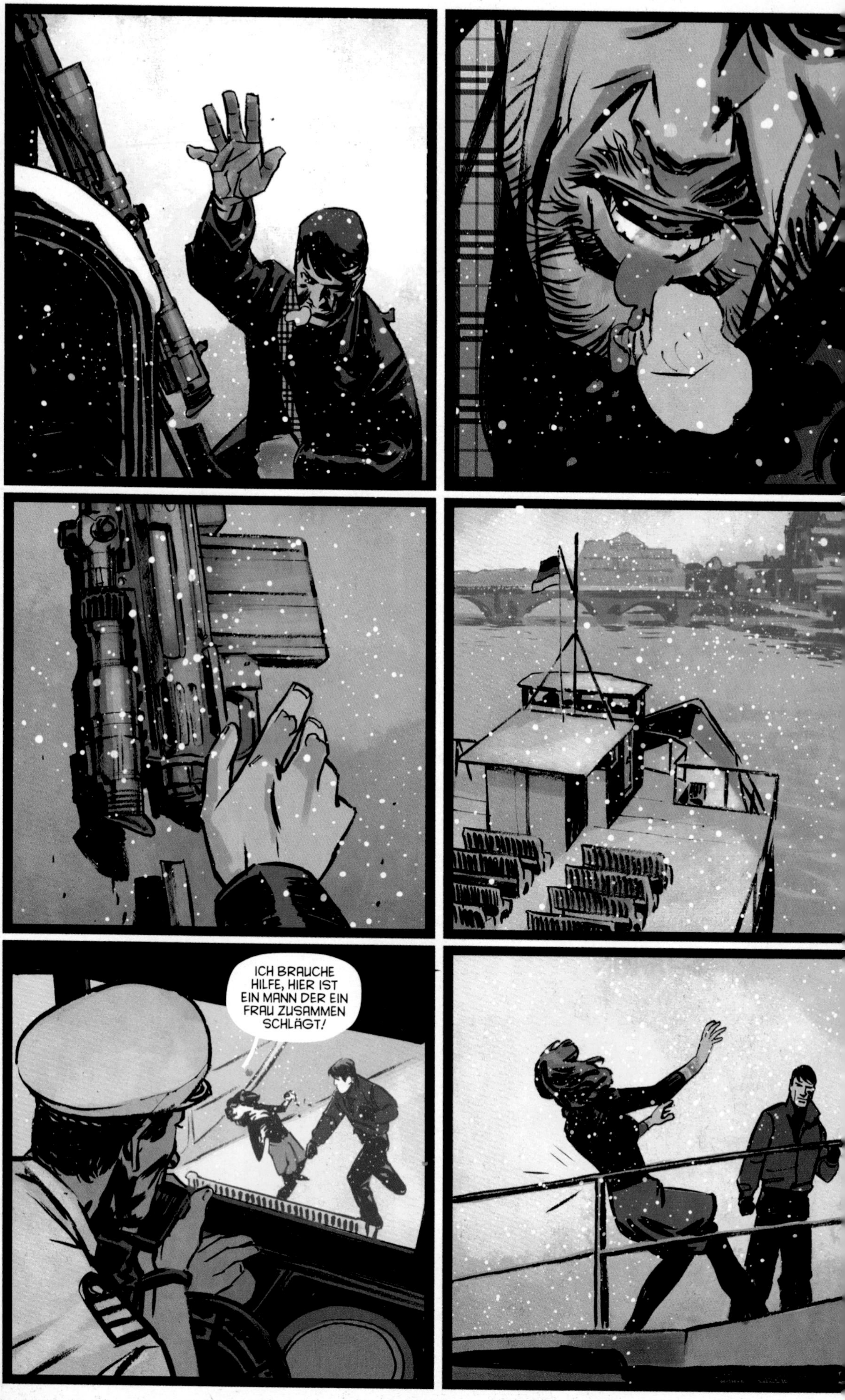
ICH BRAUCHE HILFE, HIER IST EIN MANN DER EIN FRAU ZUSAMMEN SCHLÄGT!

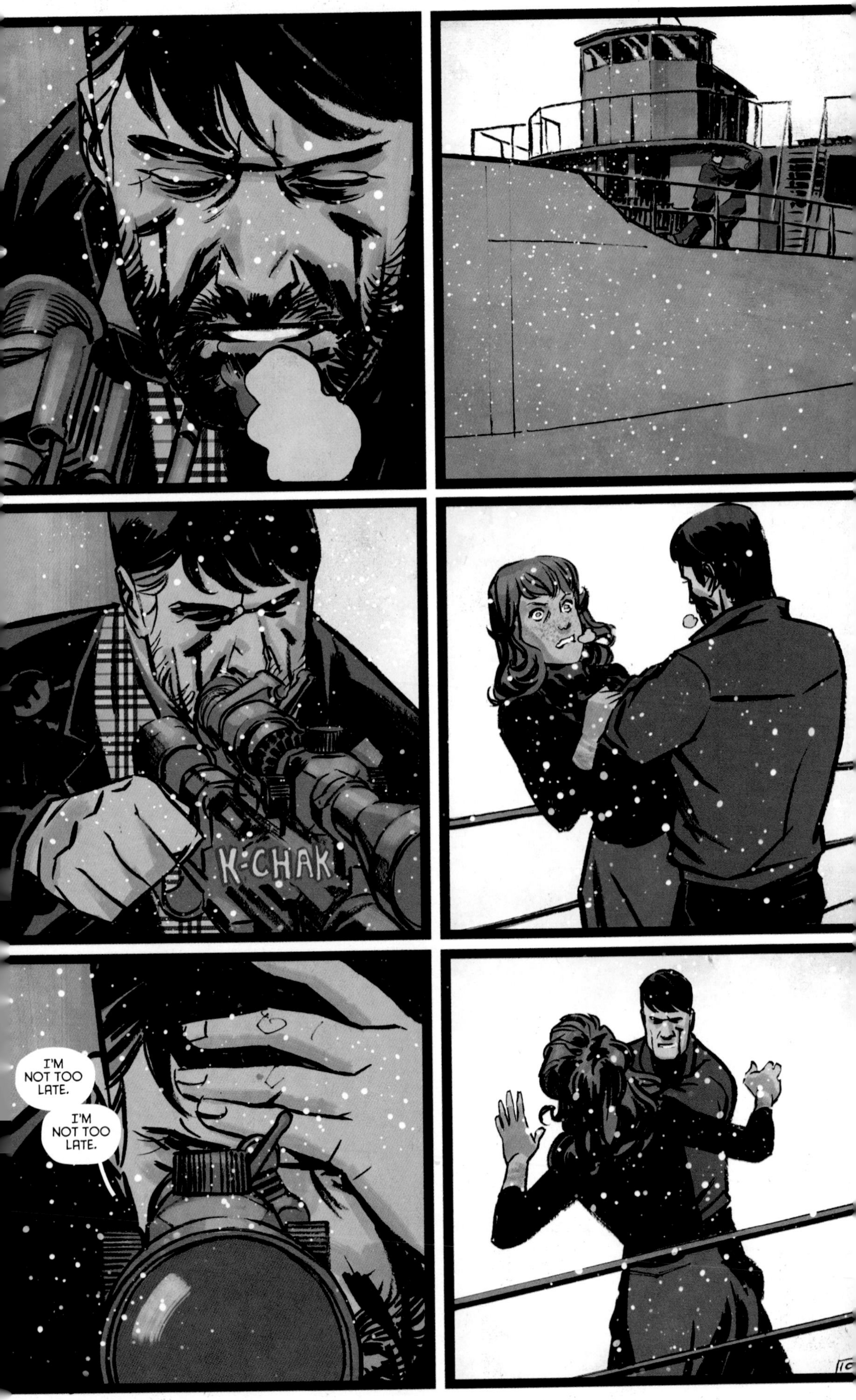
K-CHAK
I'M NOT TOO LATE.
I'M NOT TOO LATE.

IT'S TIME FOR YOU TO DIE.

NO!

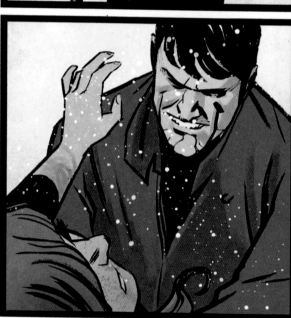

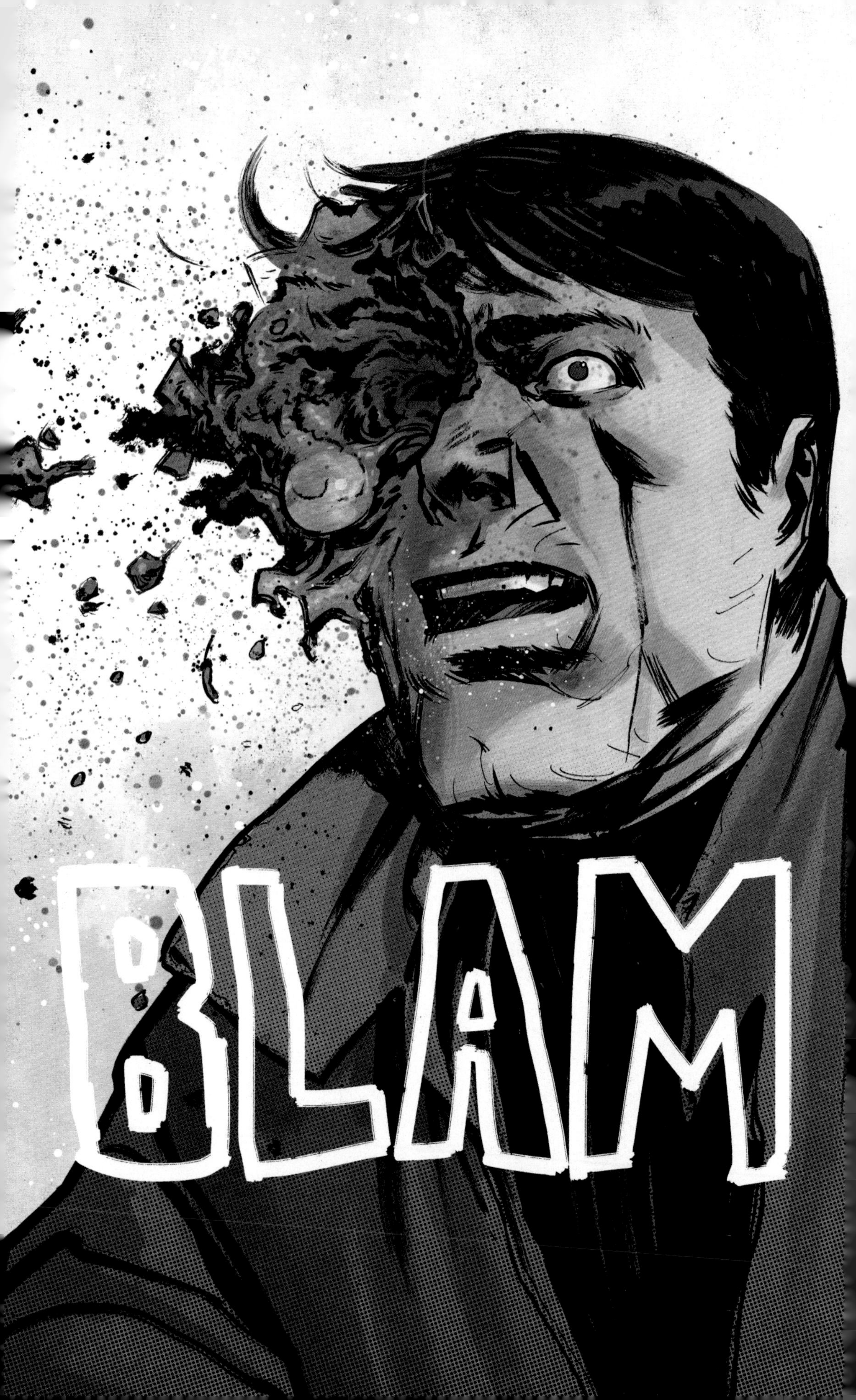
BLAM

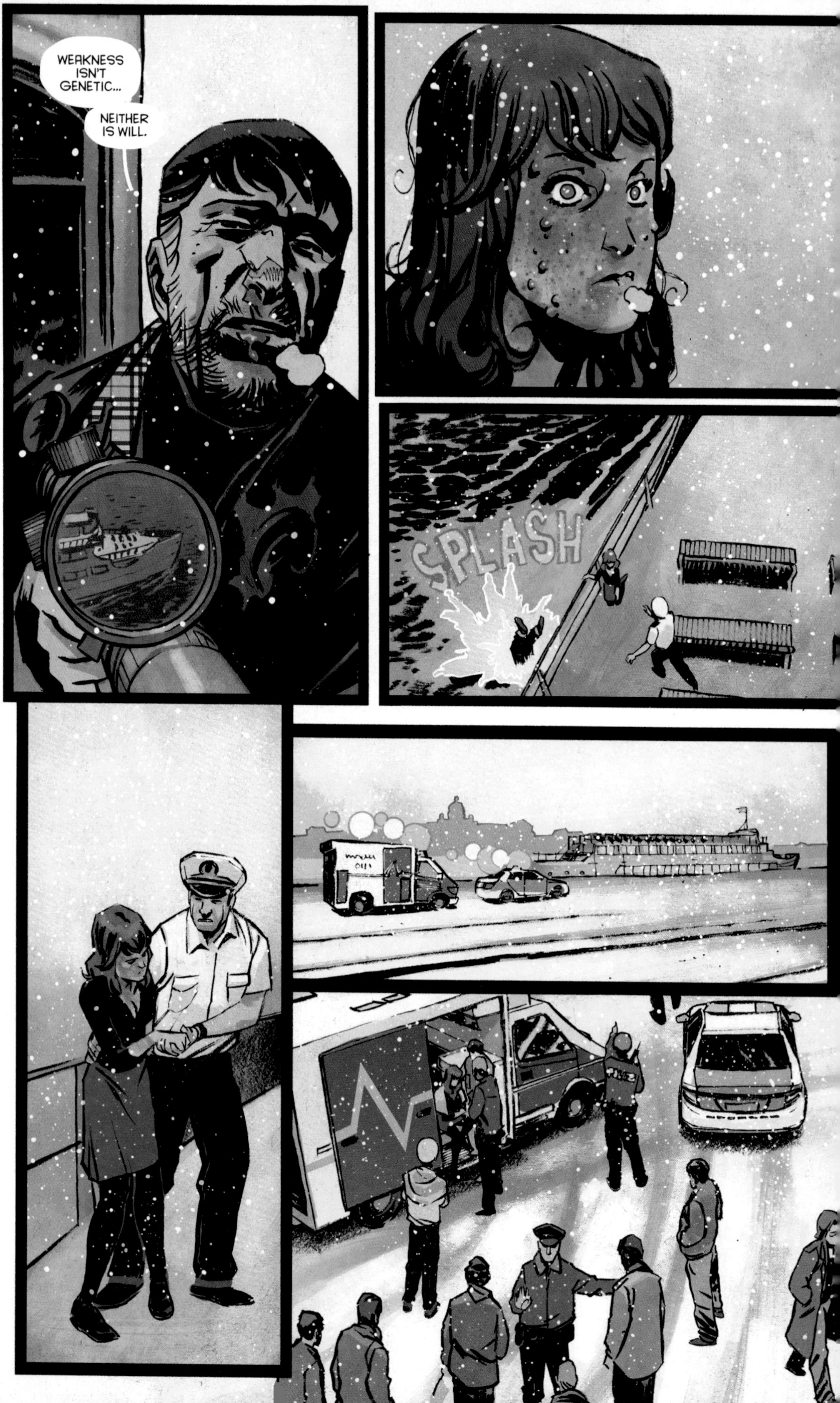
WEAKNESS ISN'T GENETIC...
NEITHER IS WILL.
SPLASH

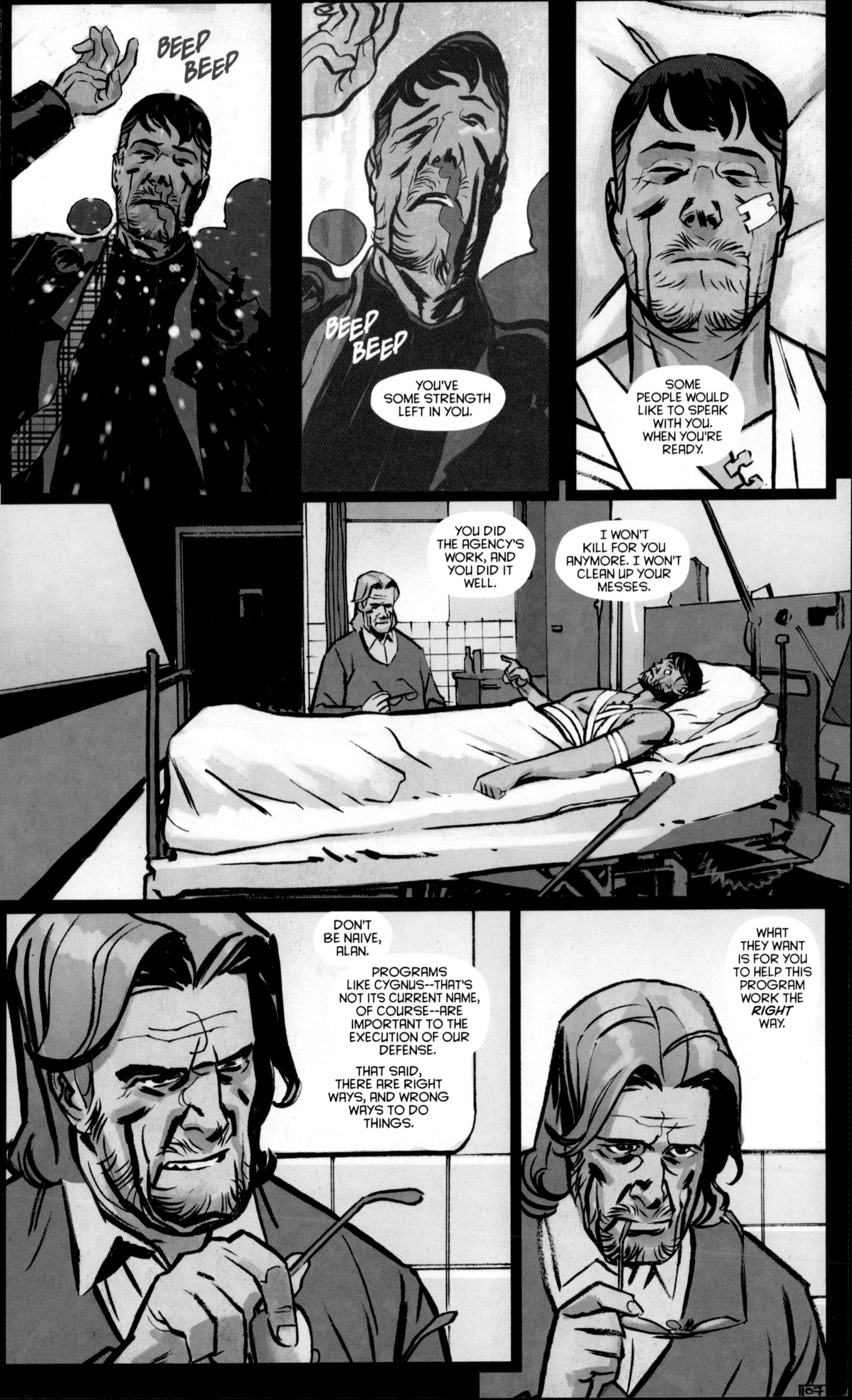
BEEP BEEP
BEEP BEEP
YOU'VE SOME STRENGTH LEFT IN YOU.
SOME PEOPLE WOULD LIKE TO SPEAK WITH YOU. WHEN YOU'RE READY.
YOU DID THE AGENCY'S WORK, AND YOU DID IT WELL.
I WON'T KILL FOR YOU ANYMORE. I WON'T CLEAN UP YOUR MESSES.
DON'T BE NAIVE, ALAN.
PROGRAMS LIKE CYGNUS--THAT'S NOT ITS CURRENT NAME, OF COURSE--ARE IMPORTANT TO THE EXECUTION OF OUR DEFENSE.
THAT SAID, THERE ARE RIGHT WAYS, AND WRONG WAYS TO DO THINGS.
WHAT THEY WANT IS FOR YOU TO HELP THIS PROGRAM WORK THE *RIGHT* WAY.

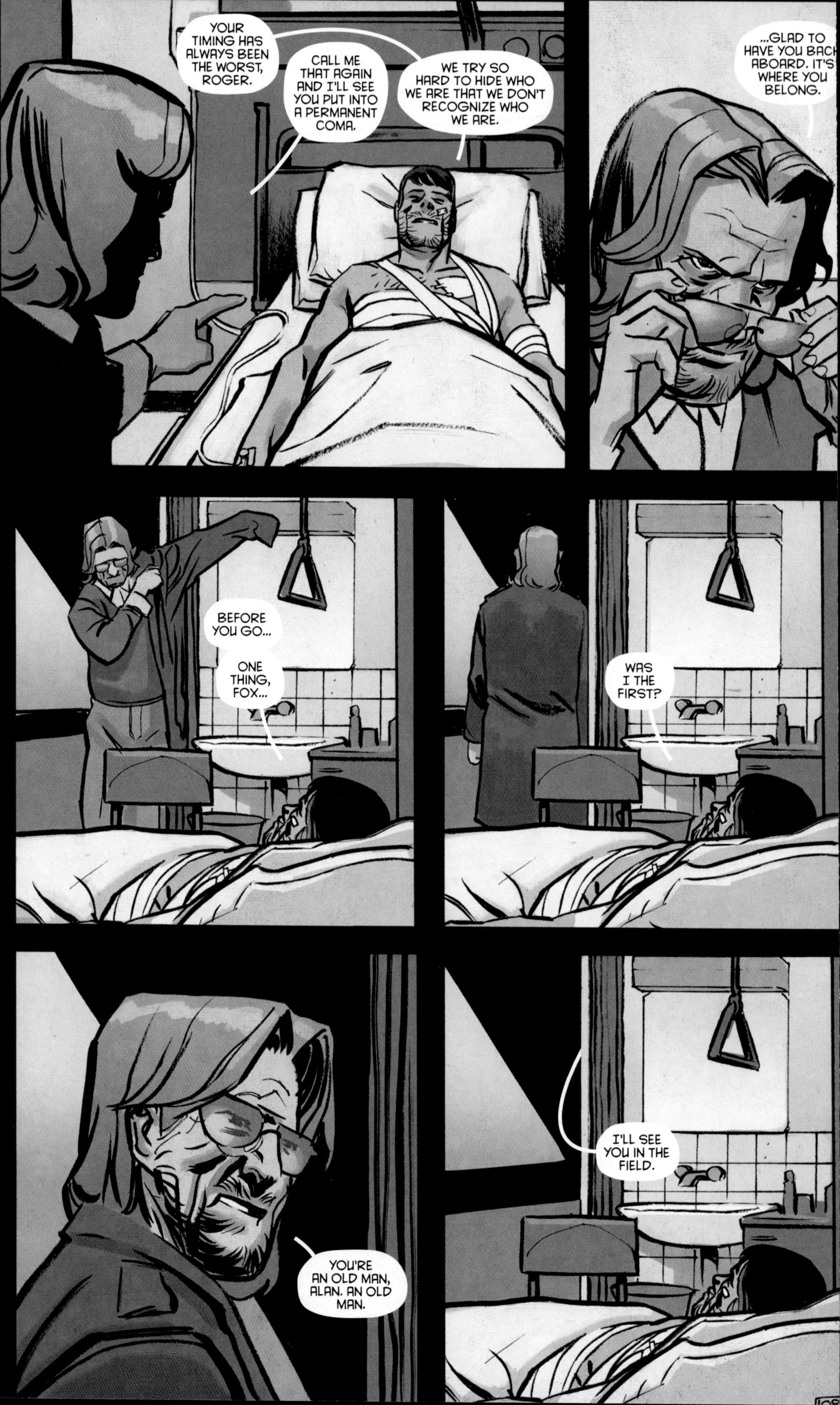
YOUR TIMING HAS ALWAYS BEEN THE WORST, ROGER.
CALL ME THAT AGAIN AND I'LL SEE YOU PUT INTO A PERMANENT COMA.
WE TRY SO HARD TO HIDE WHO WE ARE THAT WE DON'T RECOGNIZE WHO WE ARE.
...GLAD TO HAVE YOU BACK ABOARD. IT'S WHERE YOU BELONG.
BEFORE YOU GO...
ONE THING, FOX...
WAS I THE FIRST?
YOU'RE AN OLD MAN, ALAN. AN OLD MAN.
I'LL SEE YOU IN THE FIELD.

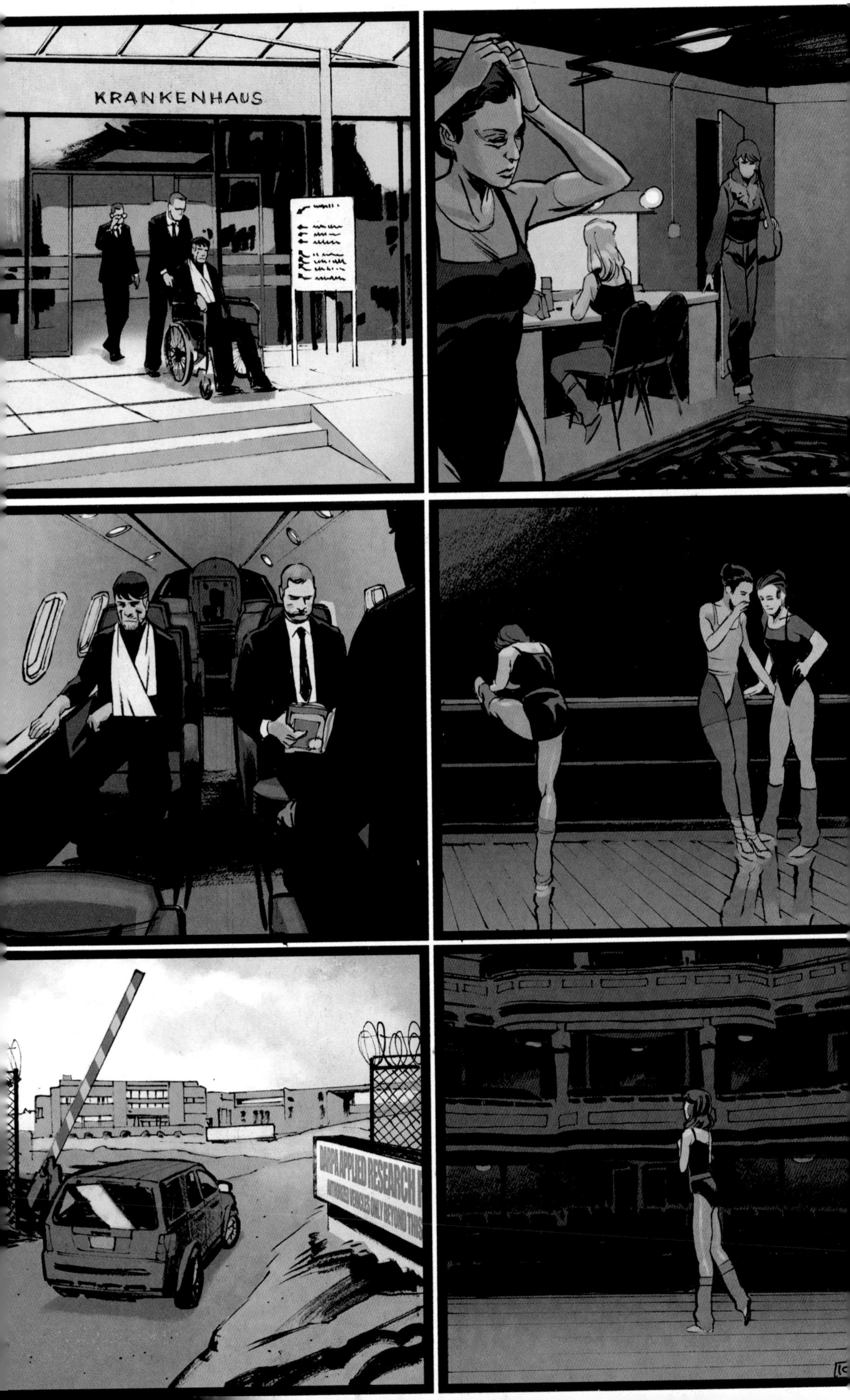
KRANKENHAUS
DARPA APPLIED RESEARCH
AUTHORIZED VEHICLES ONLY BEYOND THIS

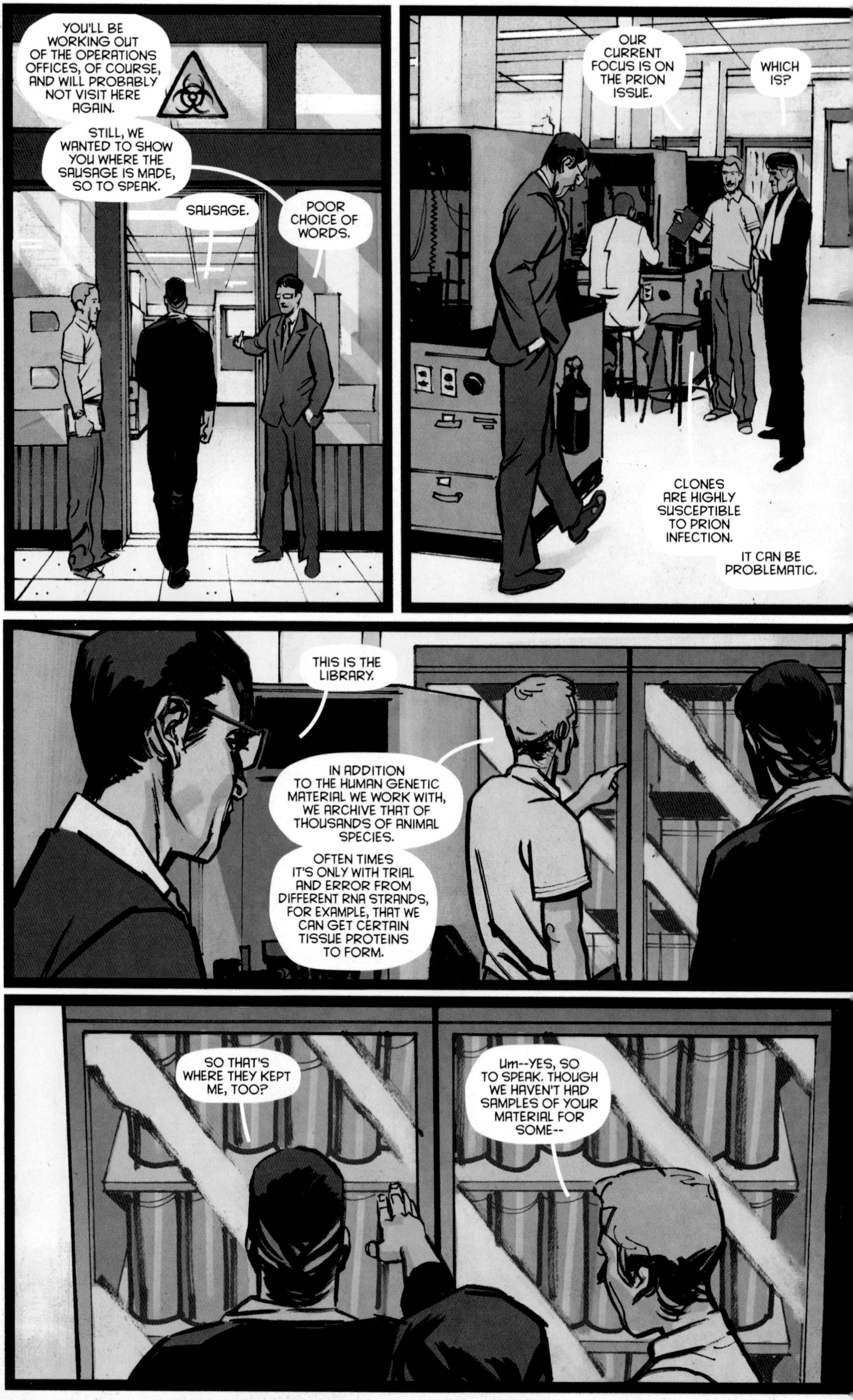
YOU'LL BE WORKING OUT OF THE OPERATIONS OFFICES, OF COURSE, AND WILL PROBABLY NOT VISIT HERE AGAIN.
STILL, WE WANTED TO SHOW YOU WHERE THE SAUSAGE IS MADE, SO TO SPEAK.
SAUSAGE.
POOR CHOICE OF WORDS.
OUR CURRENT FOCUS IS ON THE PRION ISSUE.
WHICH IS?
CLONES ARE HIGHLY SUSCEPTIBLE TO PRION INFECTION.
IT CAN BE PROBLEMATIC.
THIS IS THE LIBRARY.
IN ADDITION TO THE HUMAN GENETIC MATERIAL WE WORK WITH, WE ARCHIVE THAT OF THOUSANDS OF ANIMAL SPECIES.
OFTEN TIMES IT'S ONLY WITH TRIAL AND ERROR FROM DIFFERENT RNA STRANDS, FOR EXAMPLE, THAT WE CAN GET CERTAIN TISSUE PROTEINS TO FORM.
SO THAT'S WHERE THEY KEPT ME, TOO?
UM--YES, SO TO SPEAK. THOUGH WE HAVEN'T HAD SAMPLES OF YOUR MATERIAL FOR SOME--

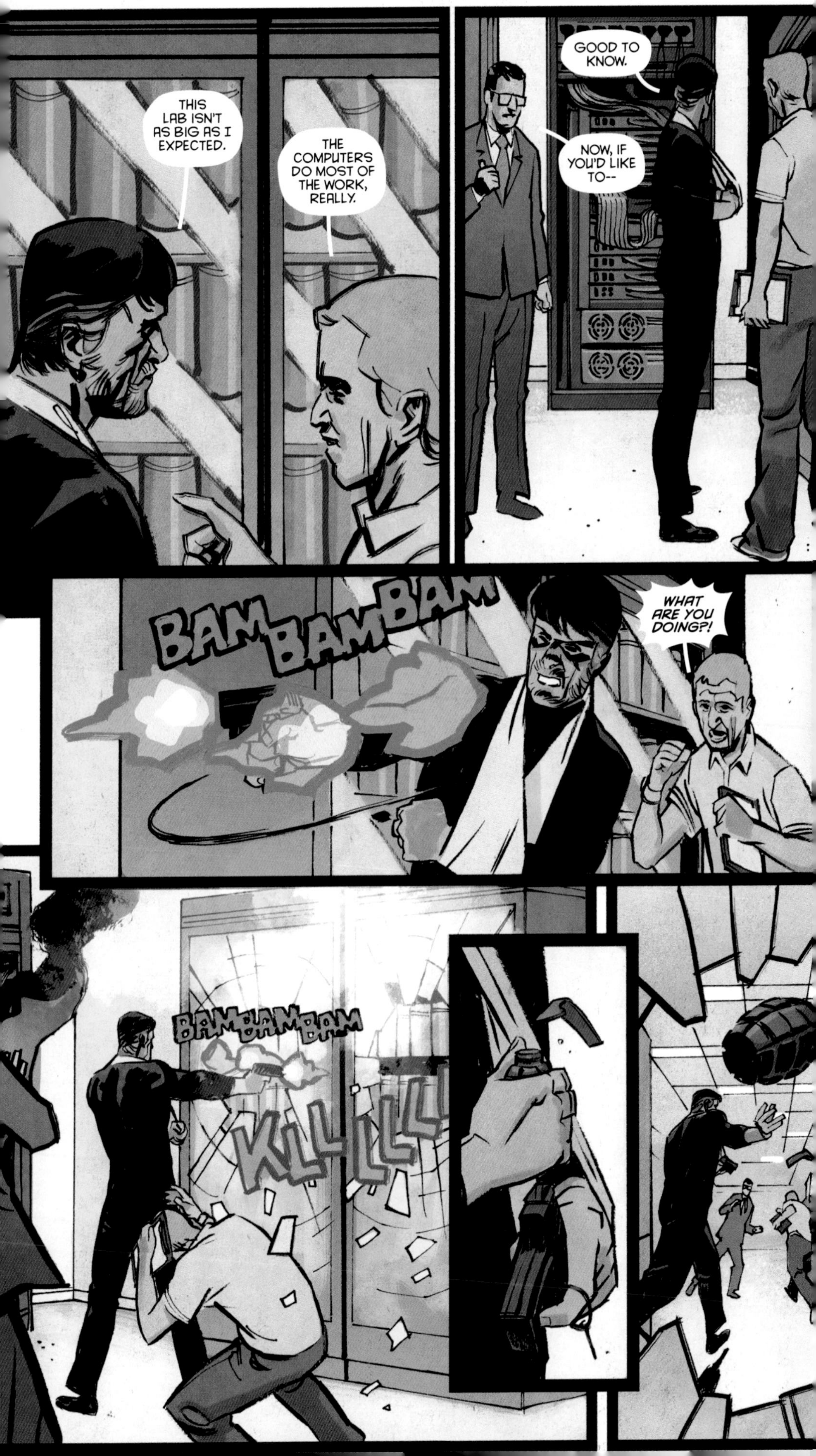
THIS LAB ISN'T AS BIG AS I EXPECTED.
THE COMPUTERS DO MOST OF THE WORK, REALLY.
GOOD TO KNOW.
NOW, IF YOU'D LIKE TO--
BAM BAM BAM
WHAT ARE YOU DOING?!
BAMBAMBAM
KLLLLL

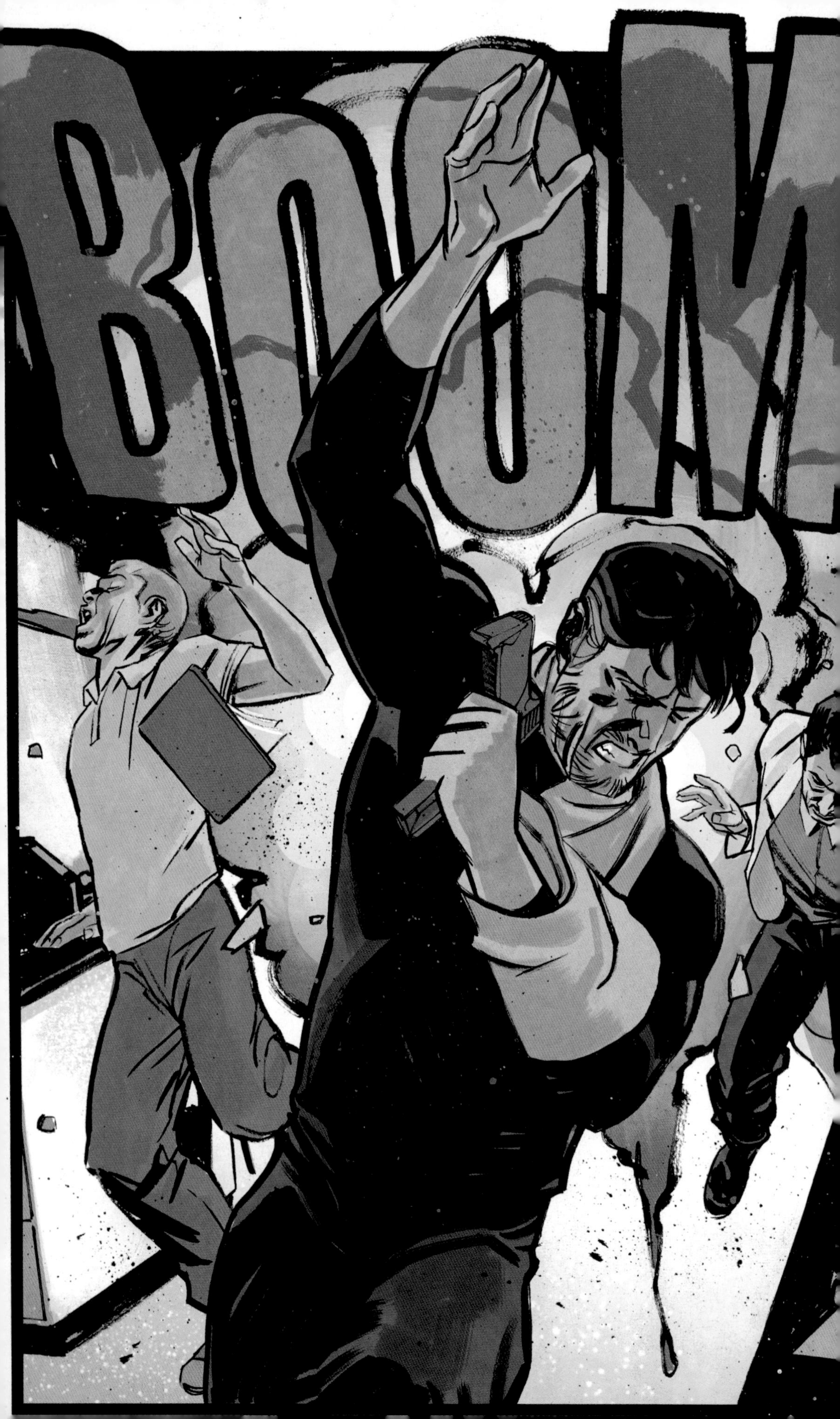
BOOM

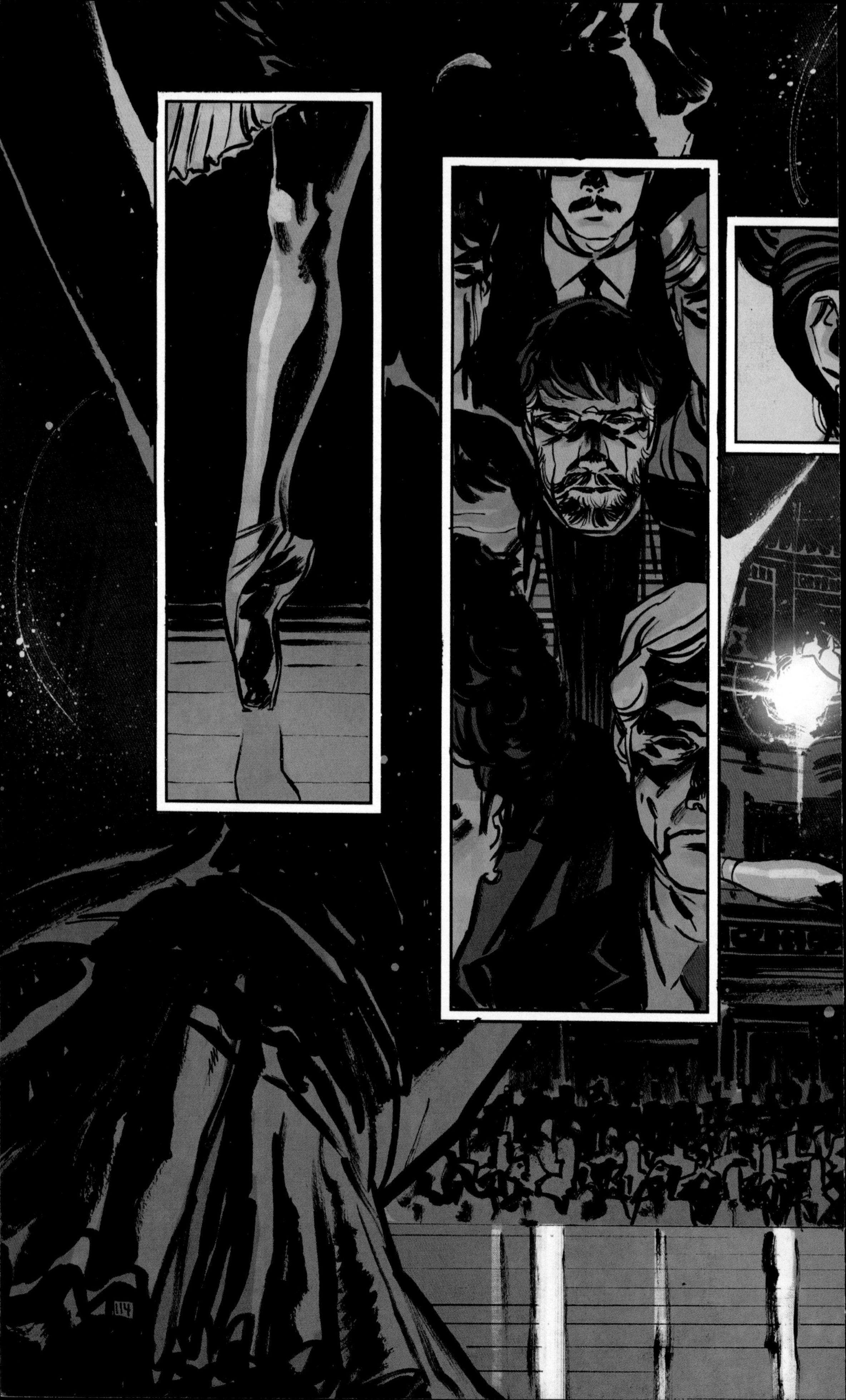

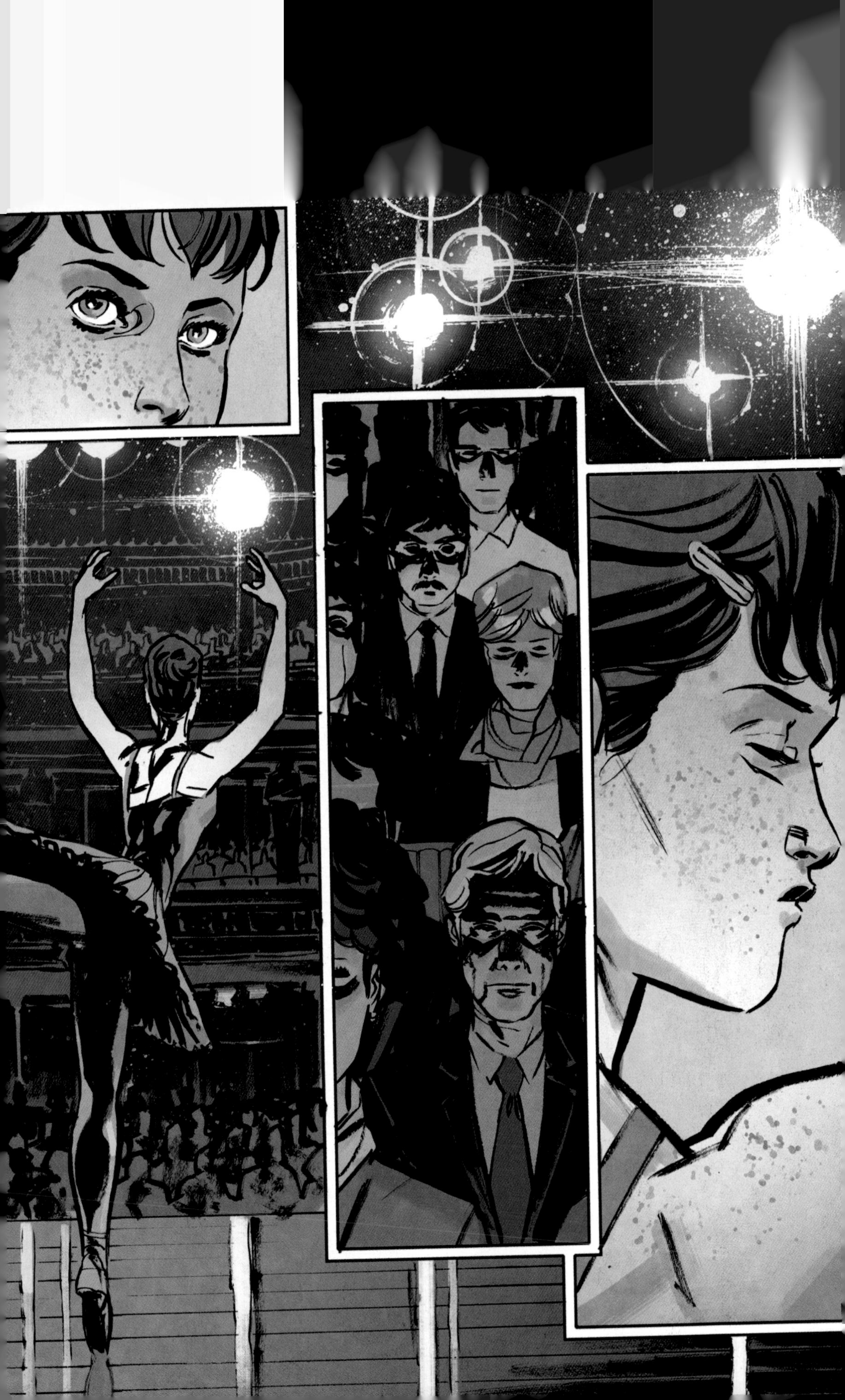

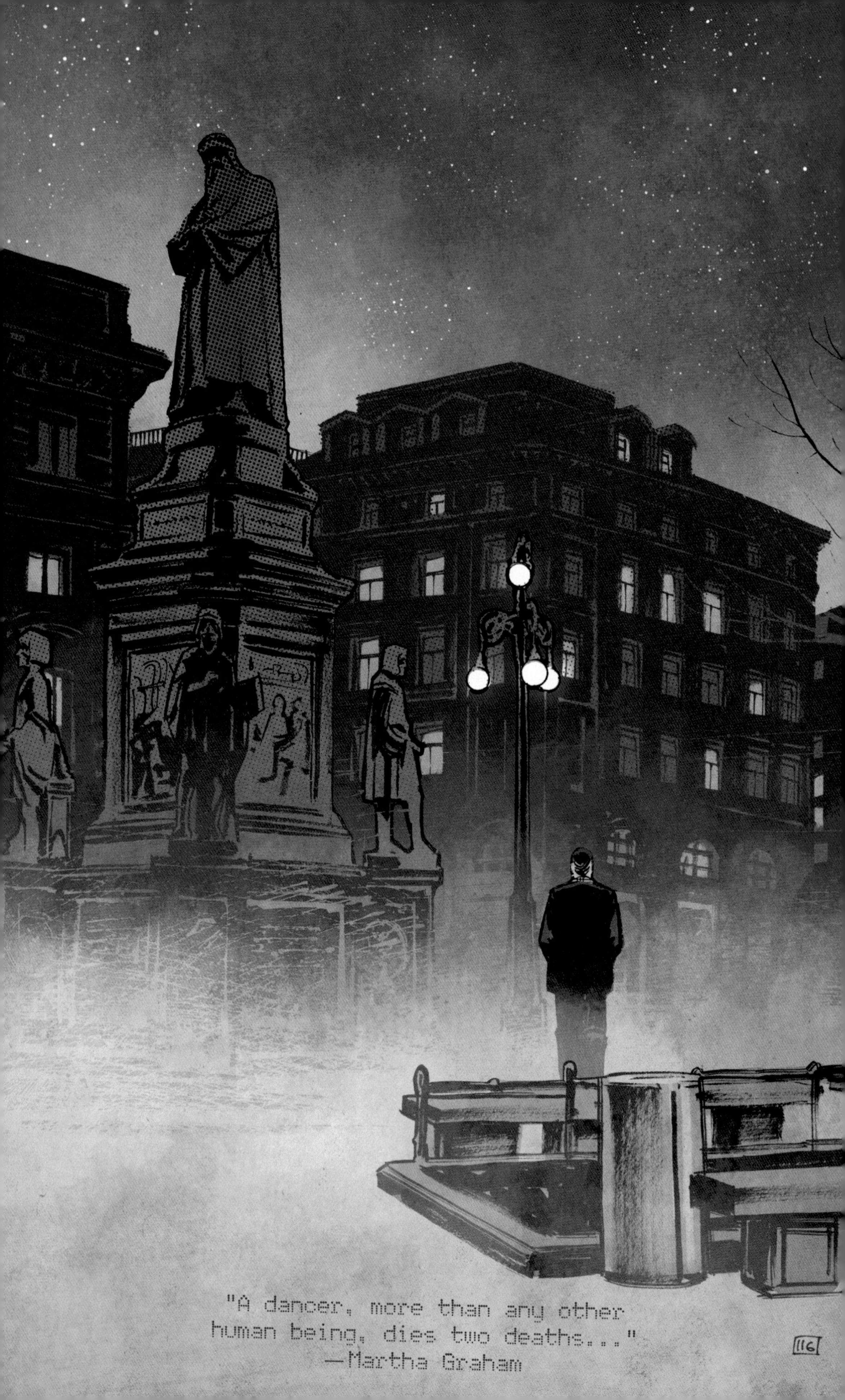
"A dancer, more than any other human being, dies two deaths..."
—Martha Graham

ORIGINAL SERIES
COVERS

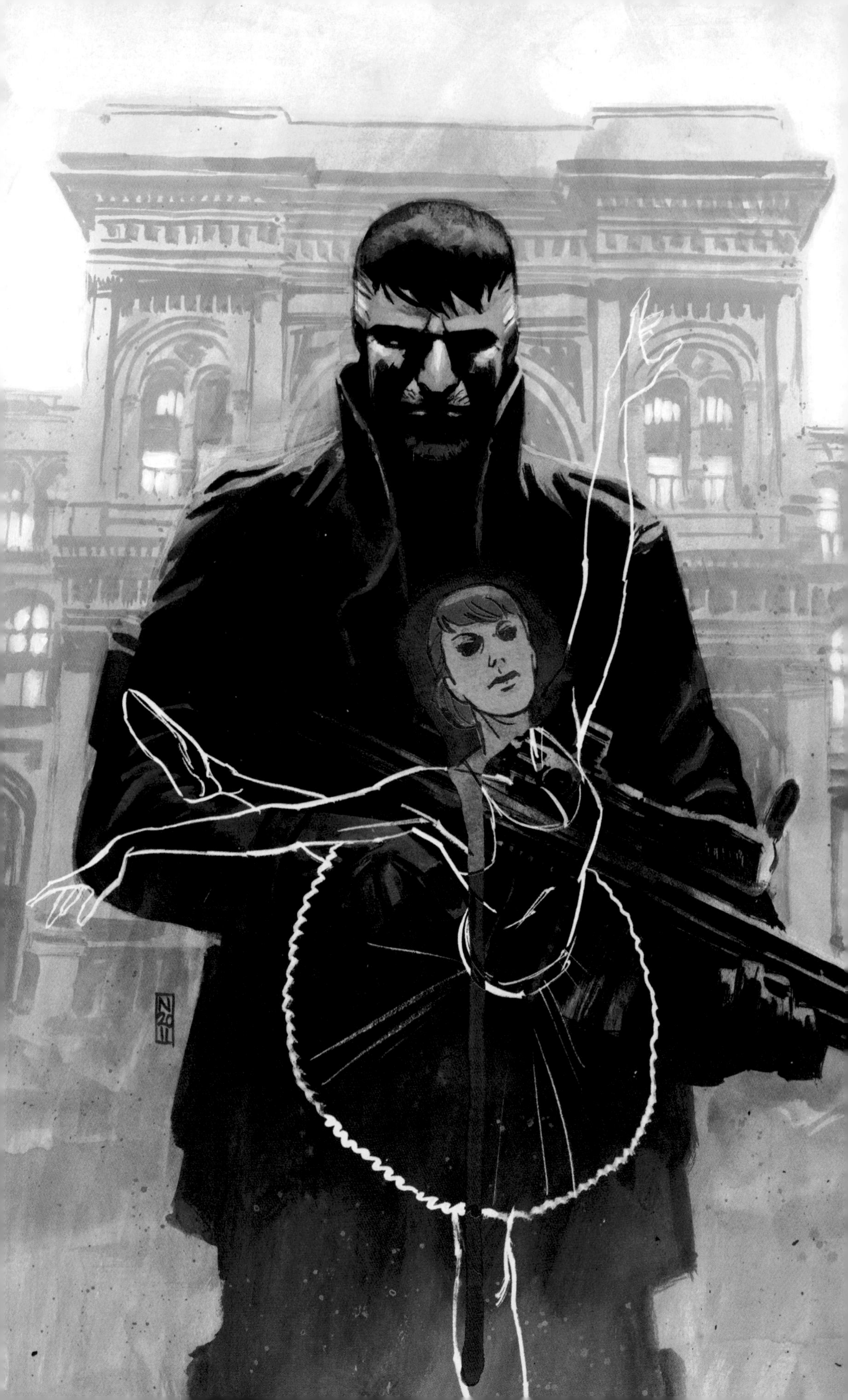

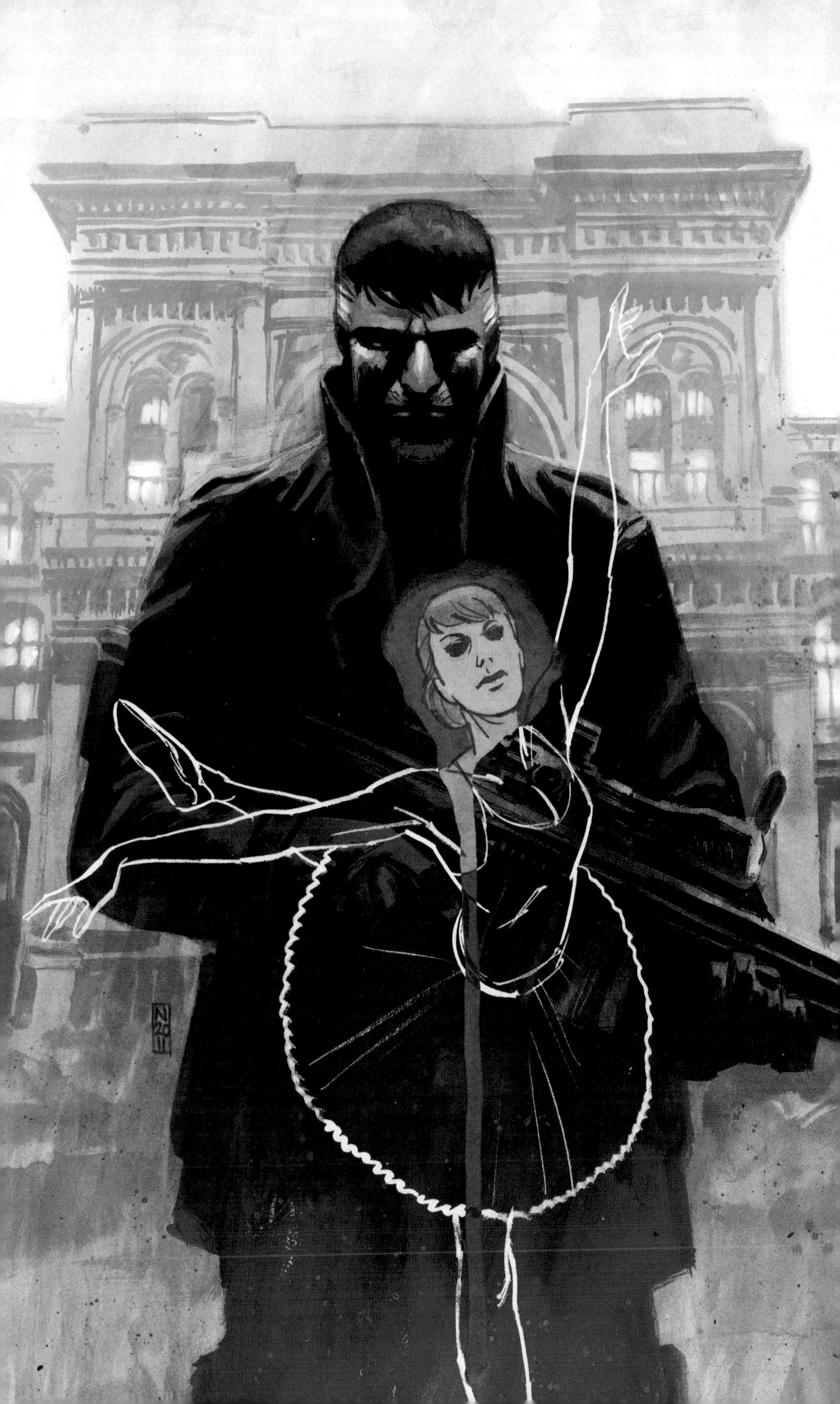

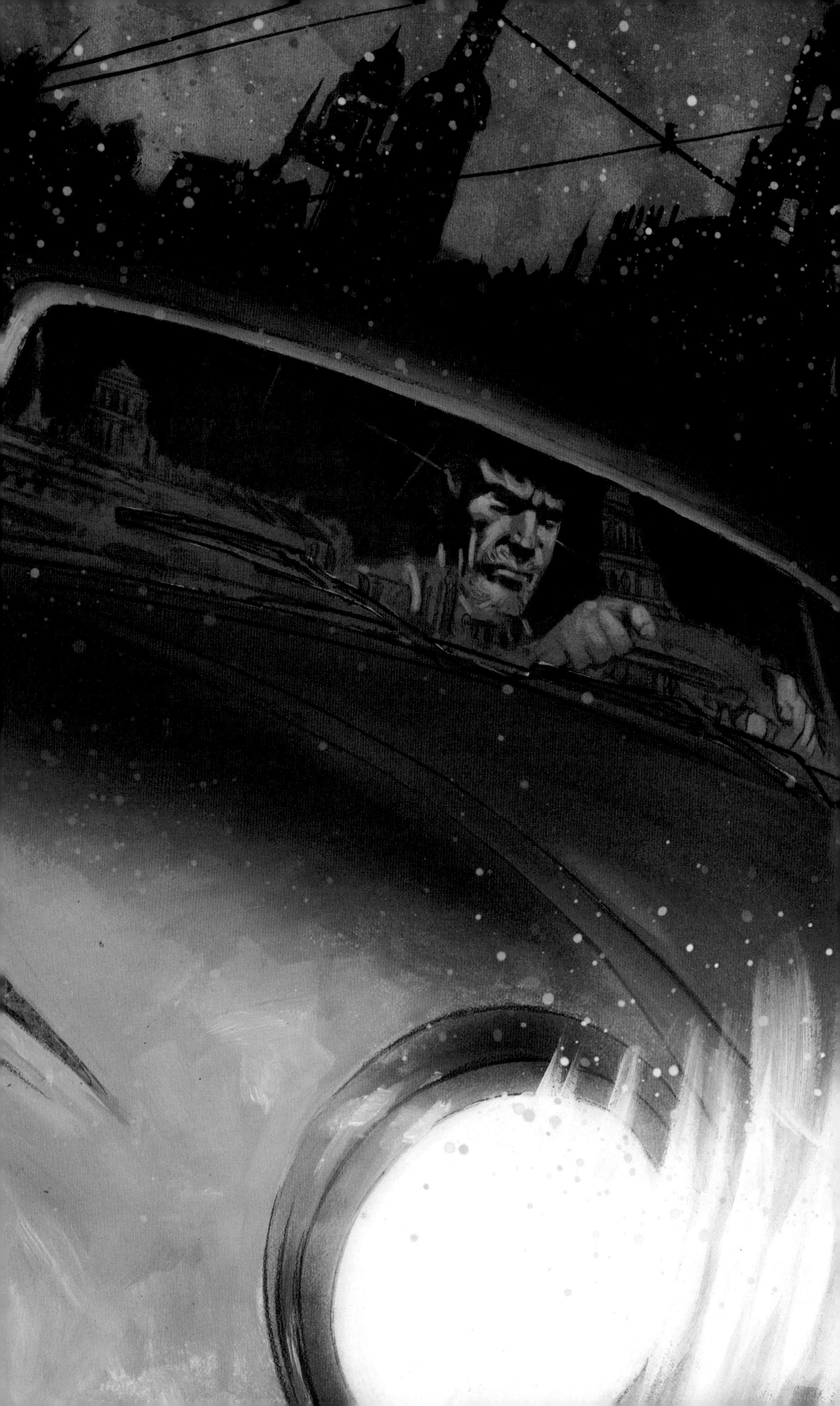

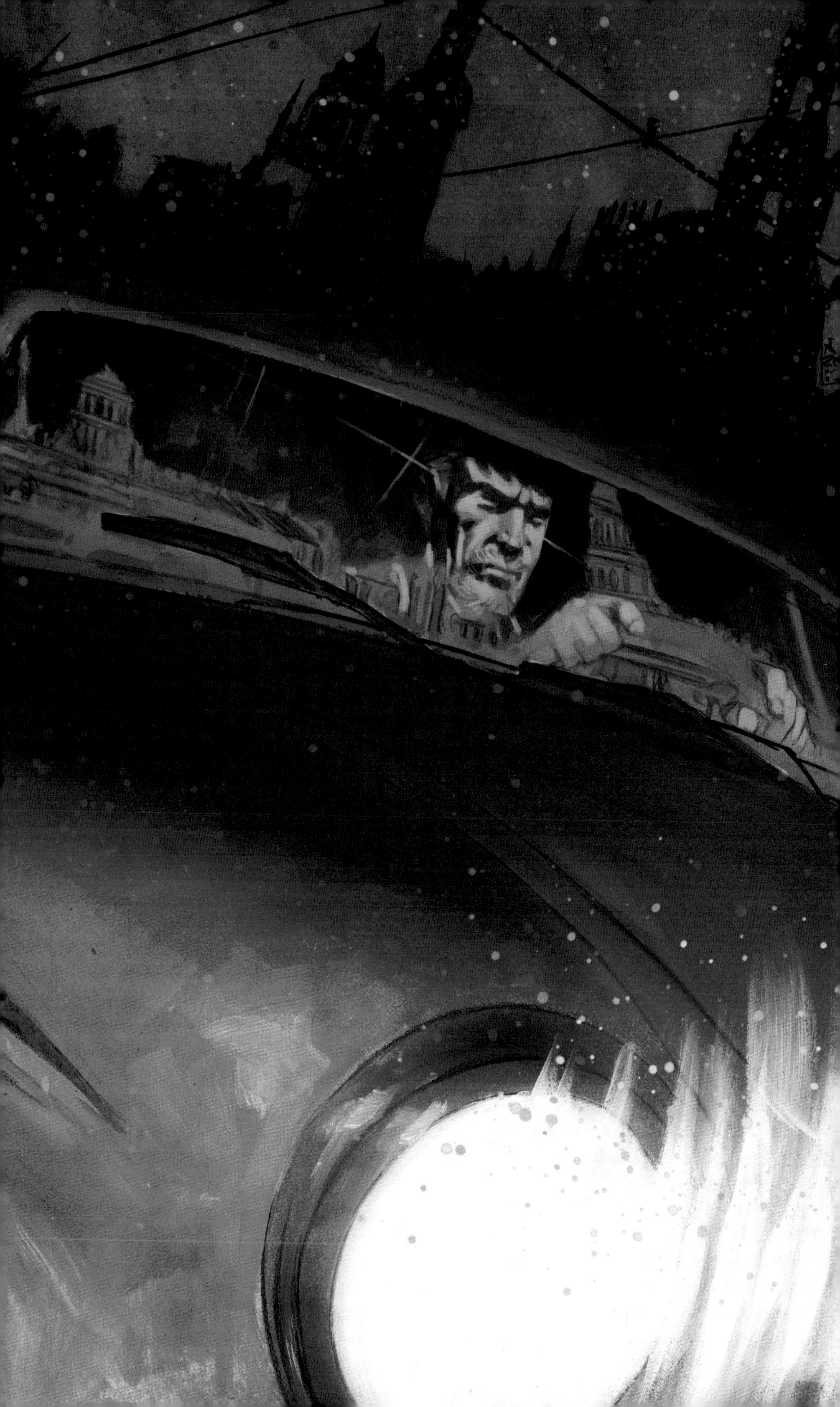

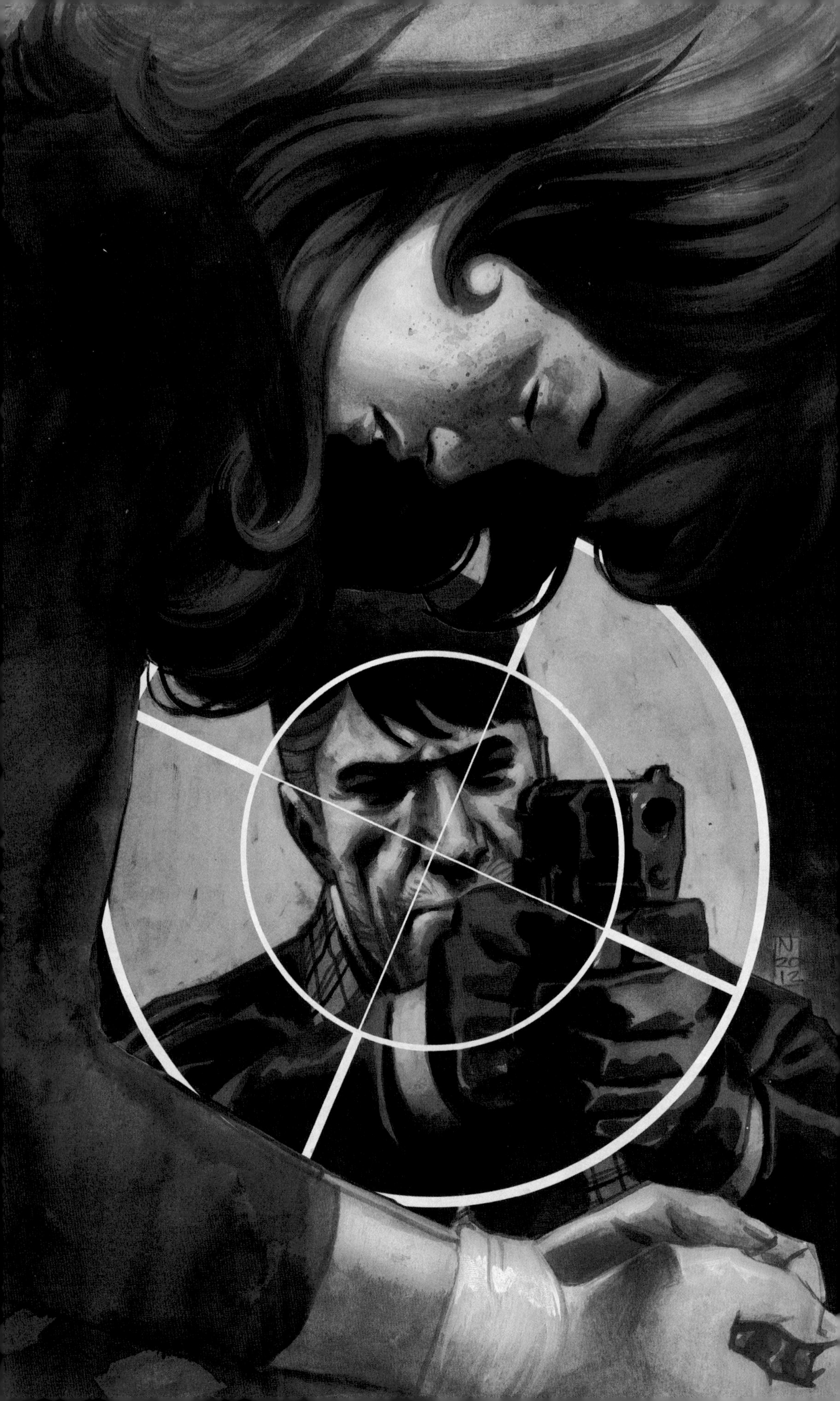

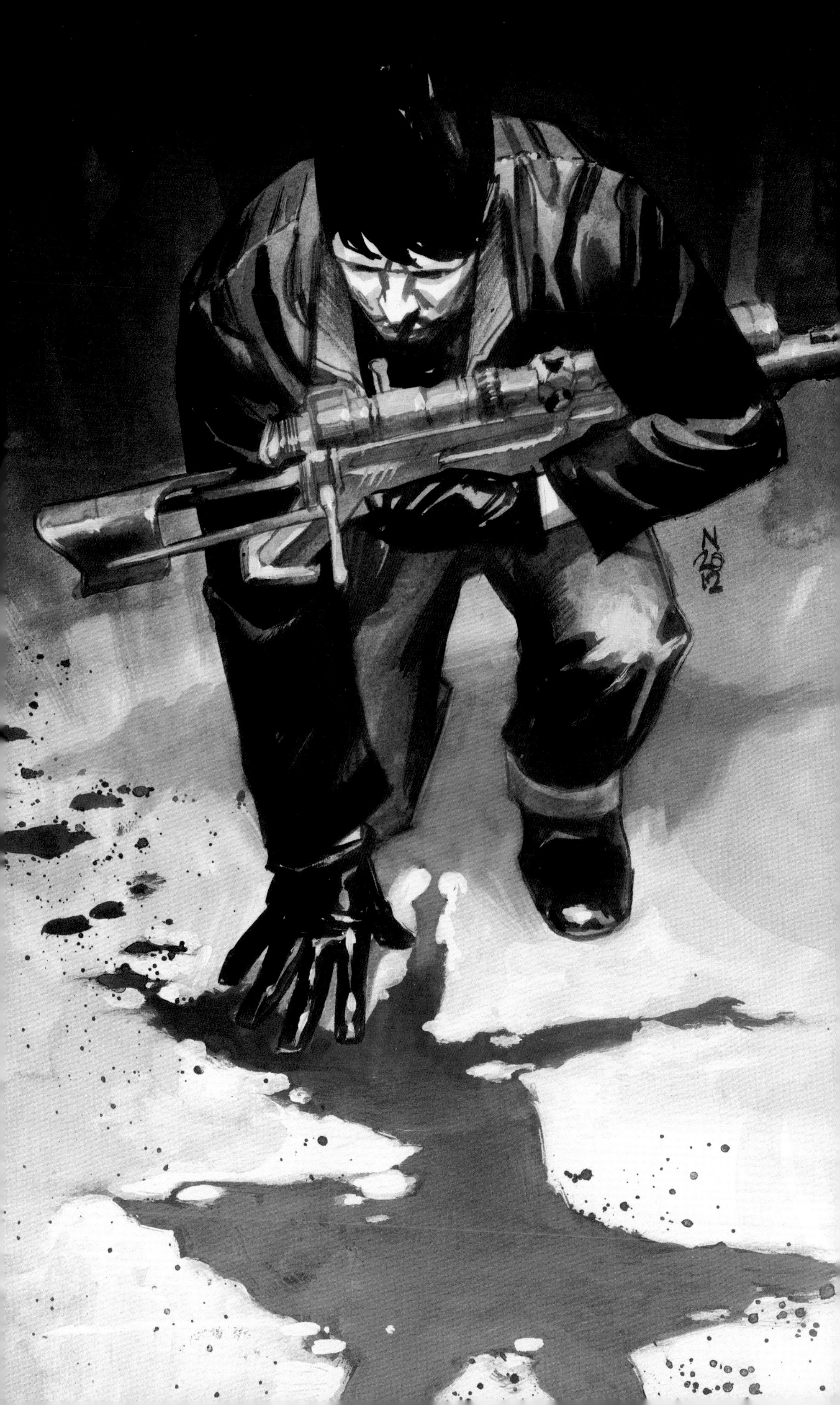

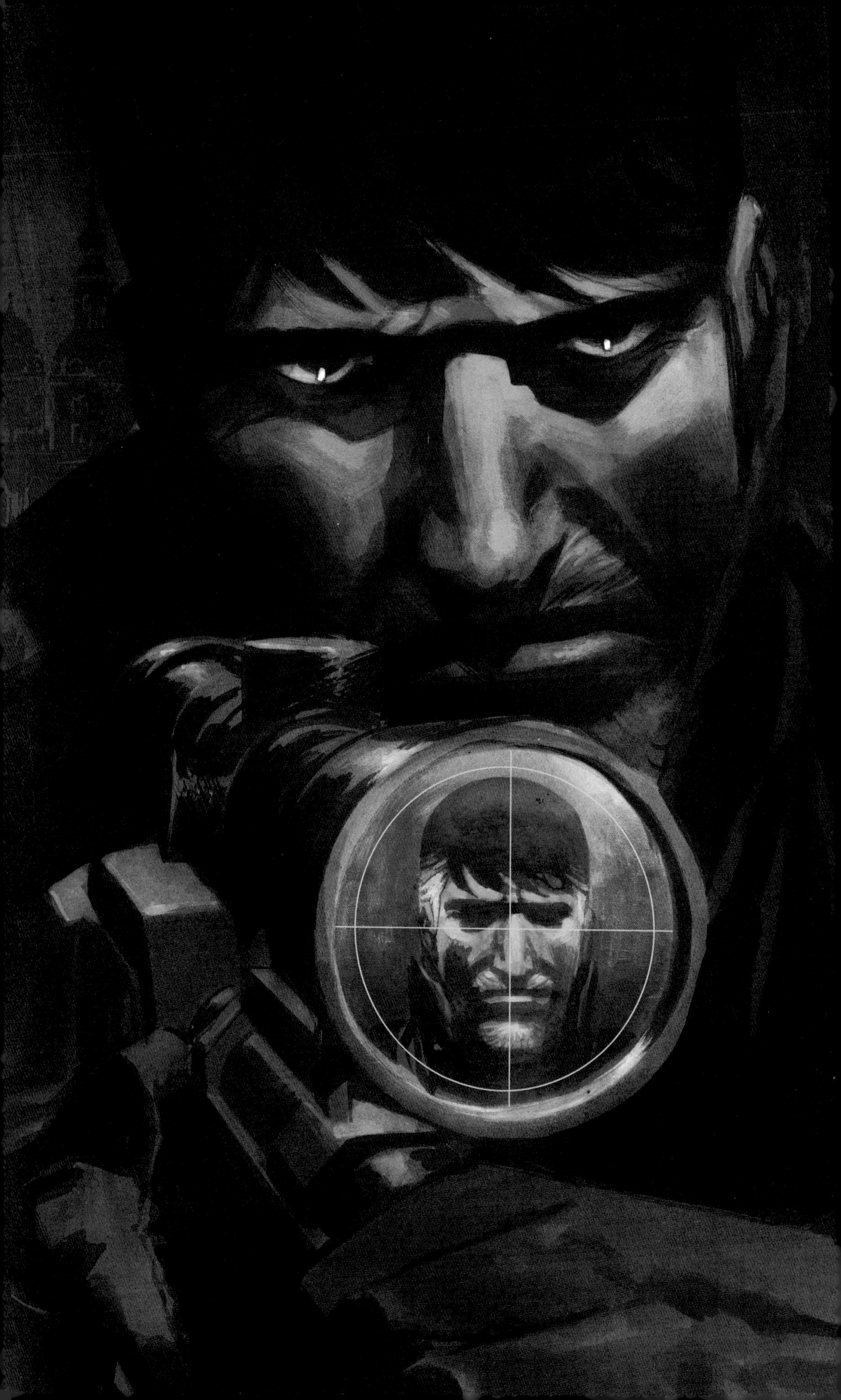

CHARACTER DESIGNS

+

OTHER MATERIAL

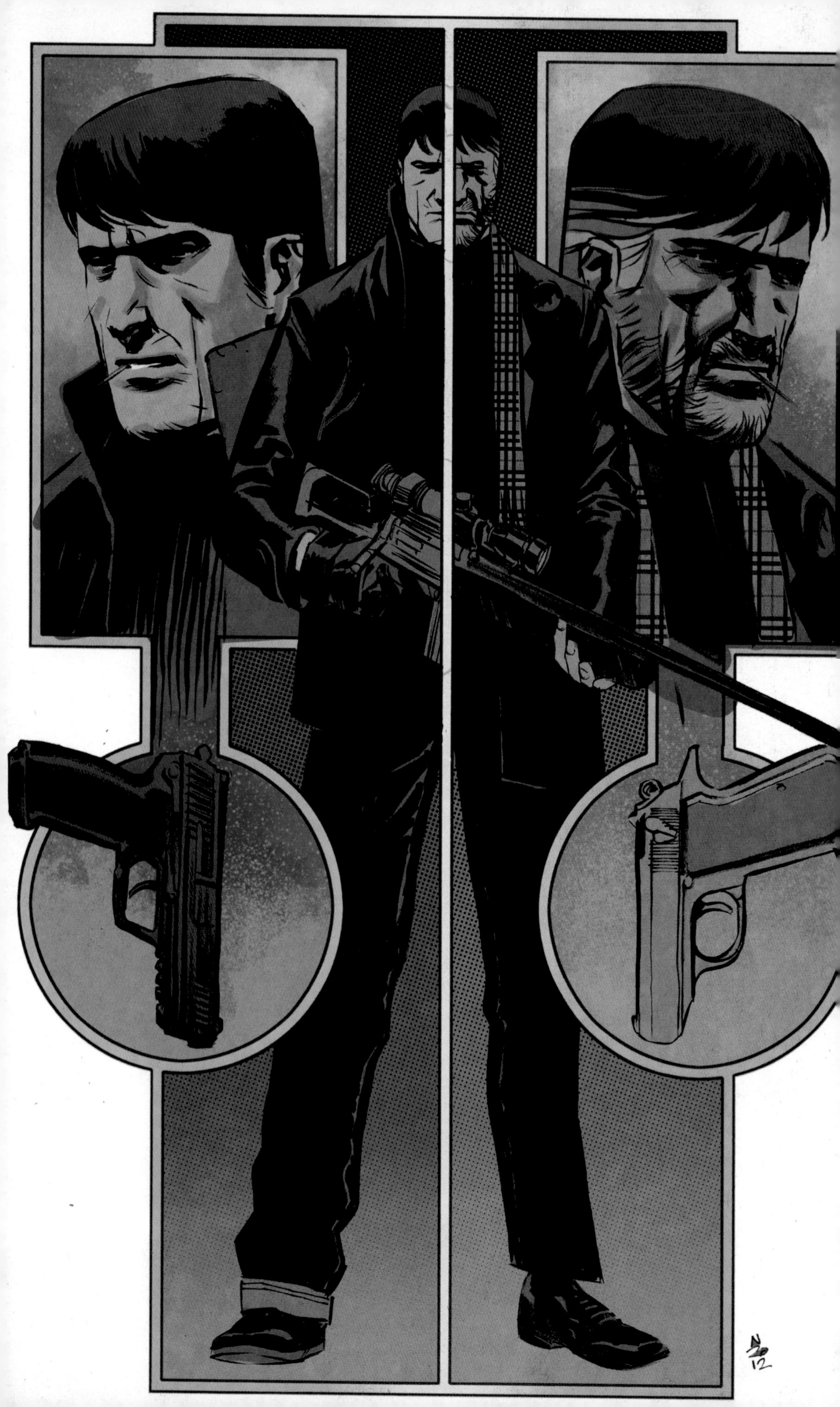

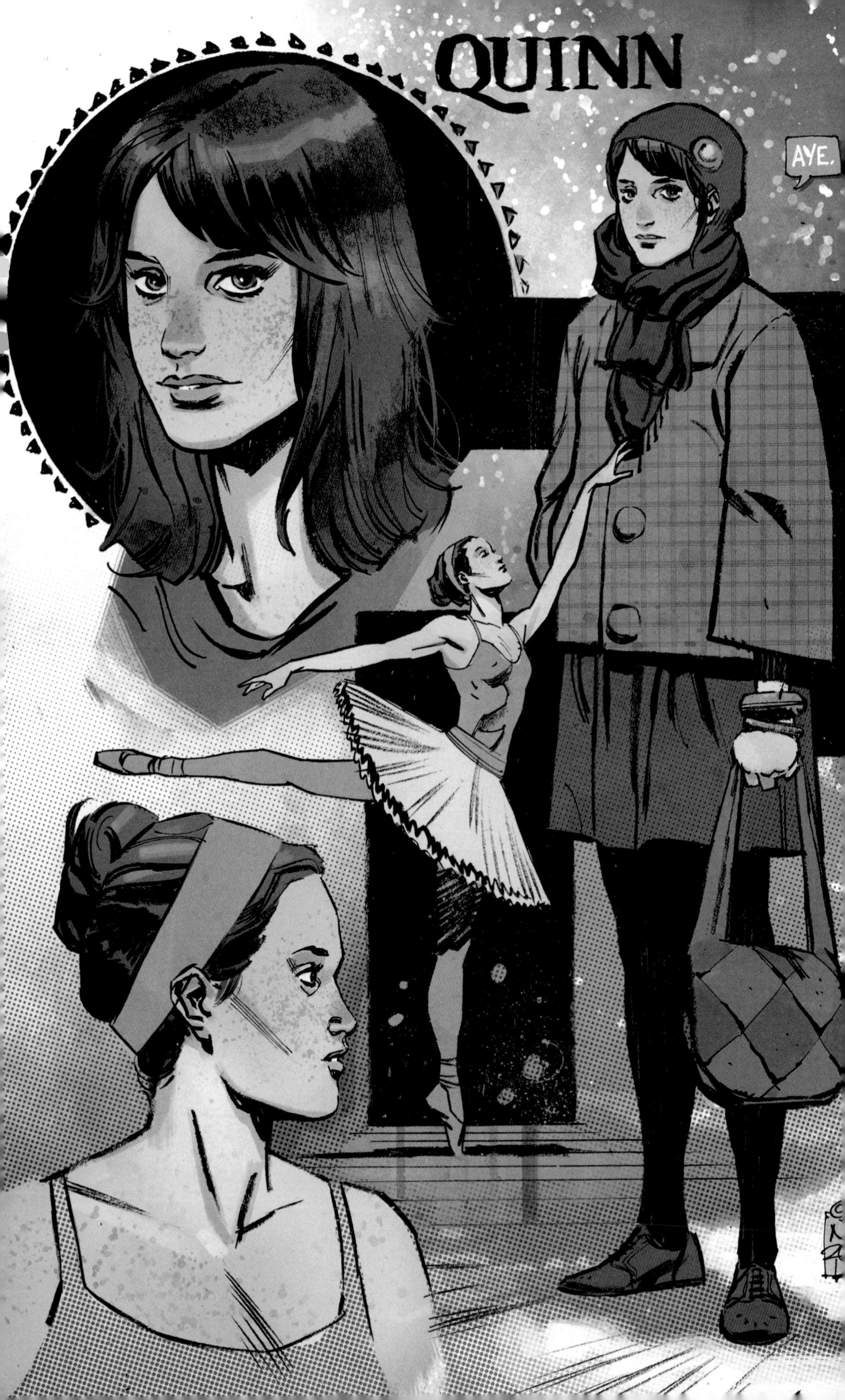
QUINN
AYE.

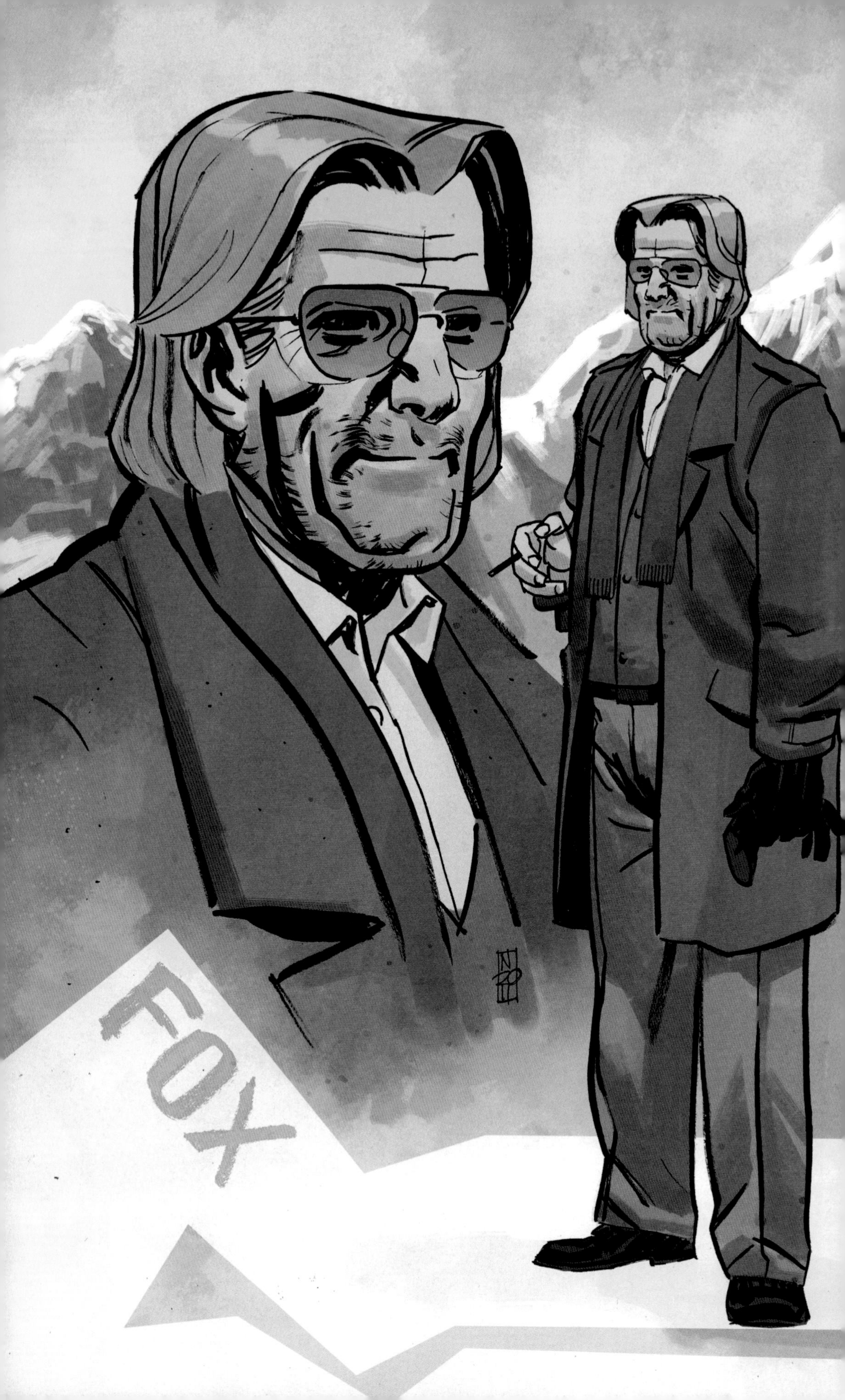
FOX

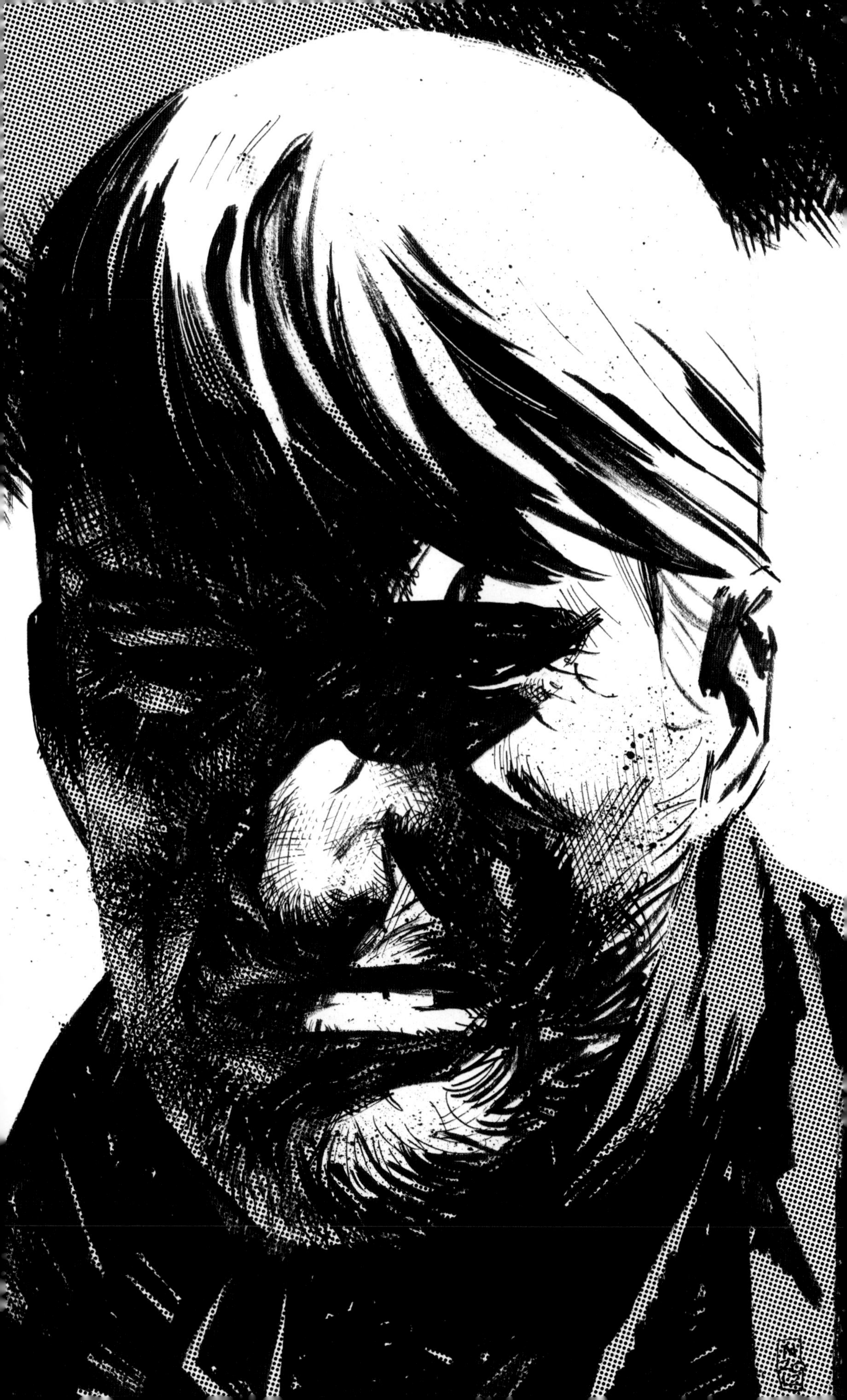

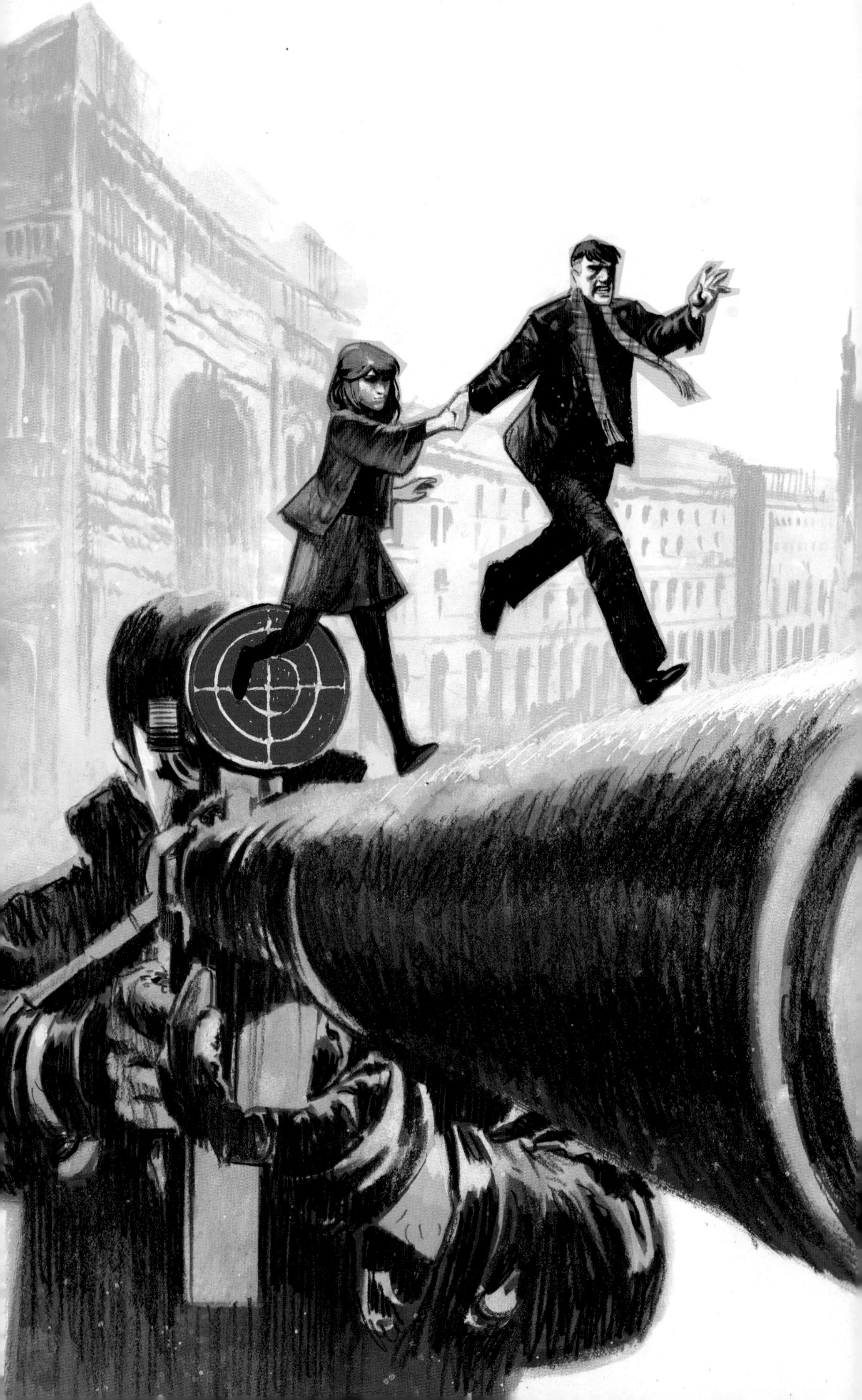

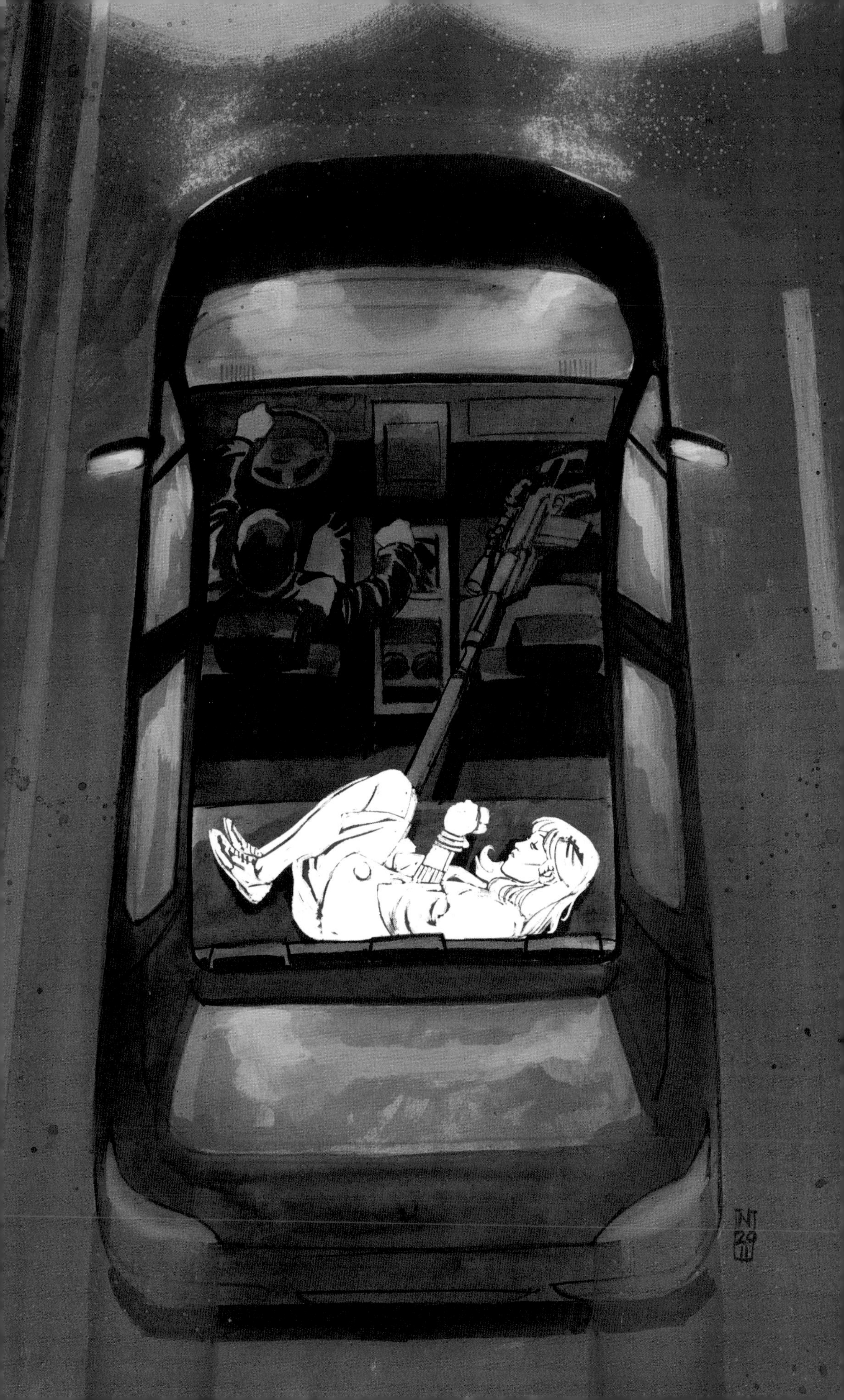

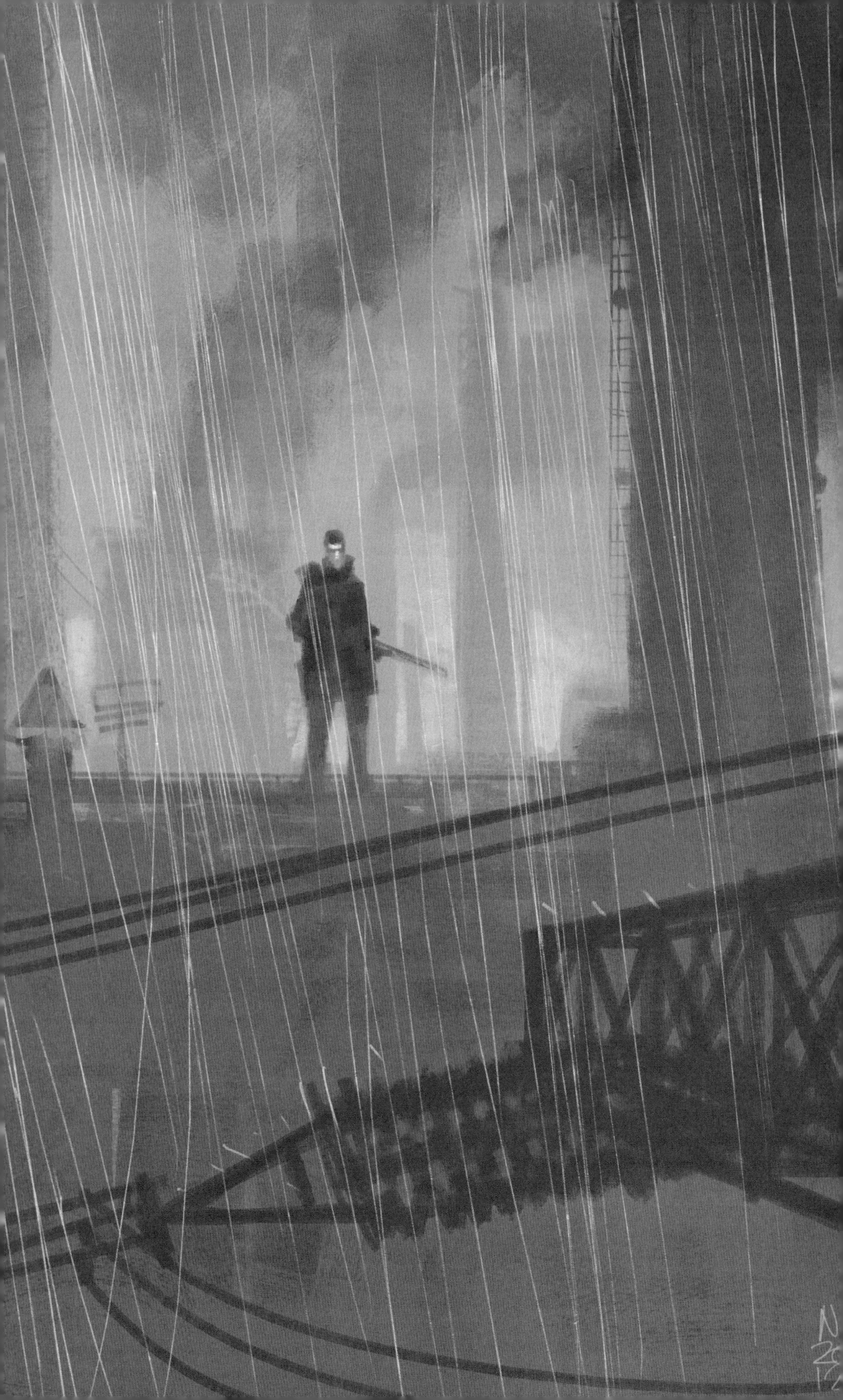

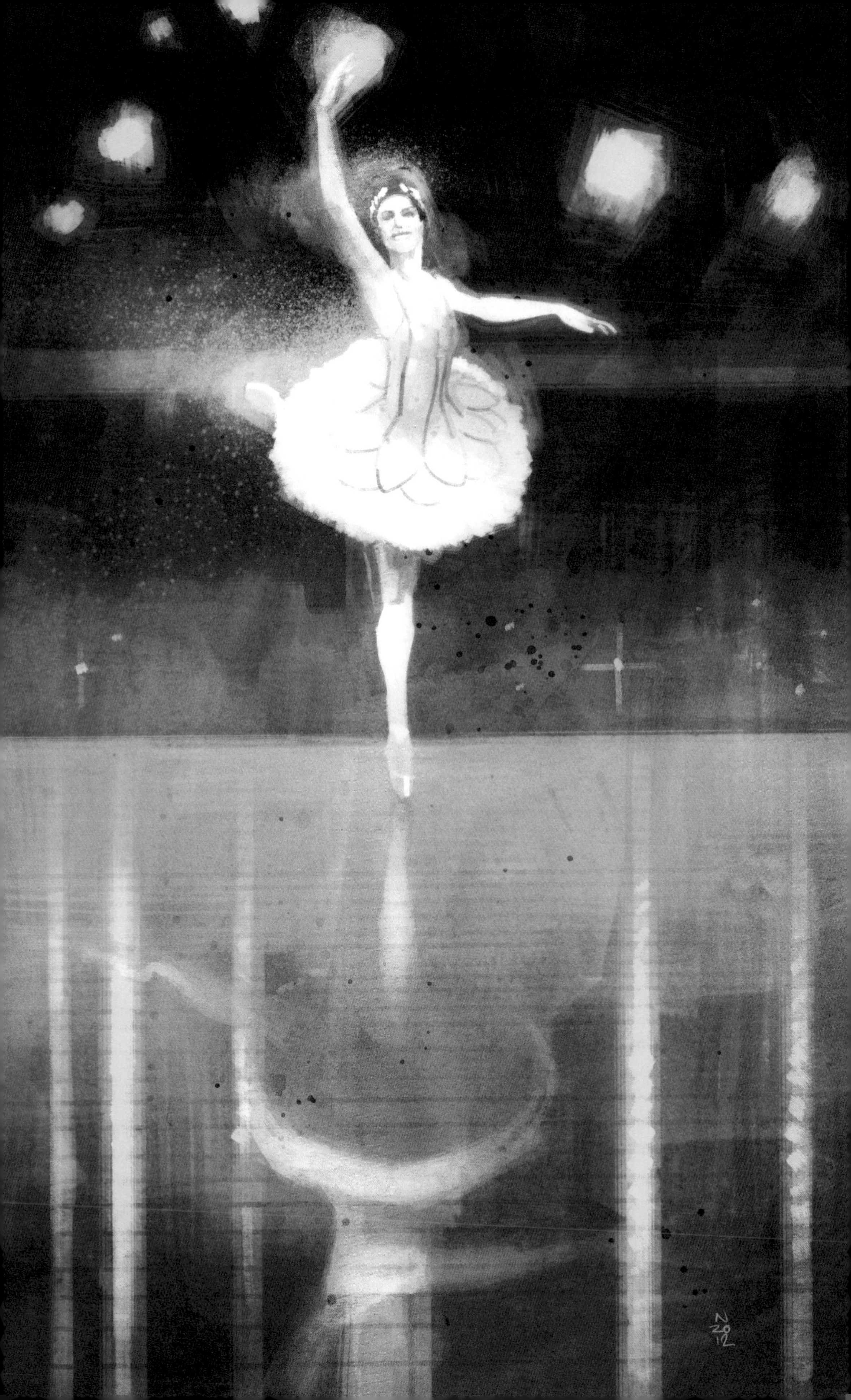

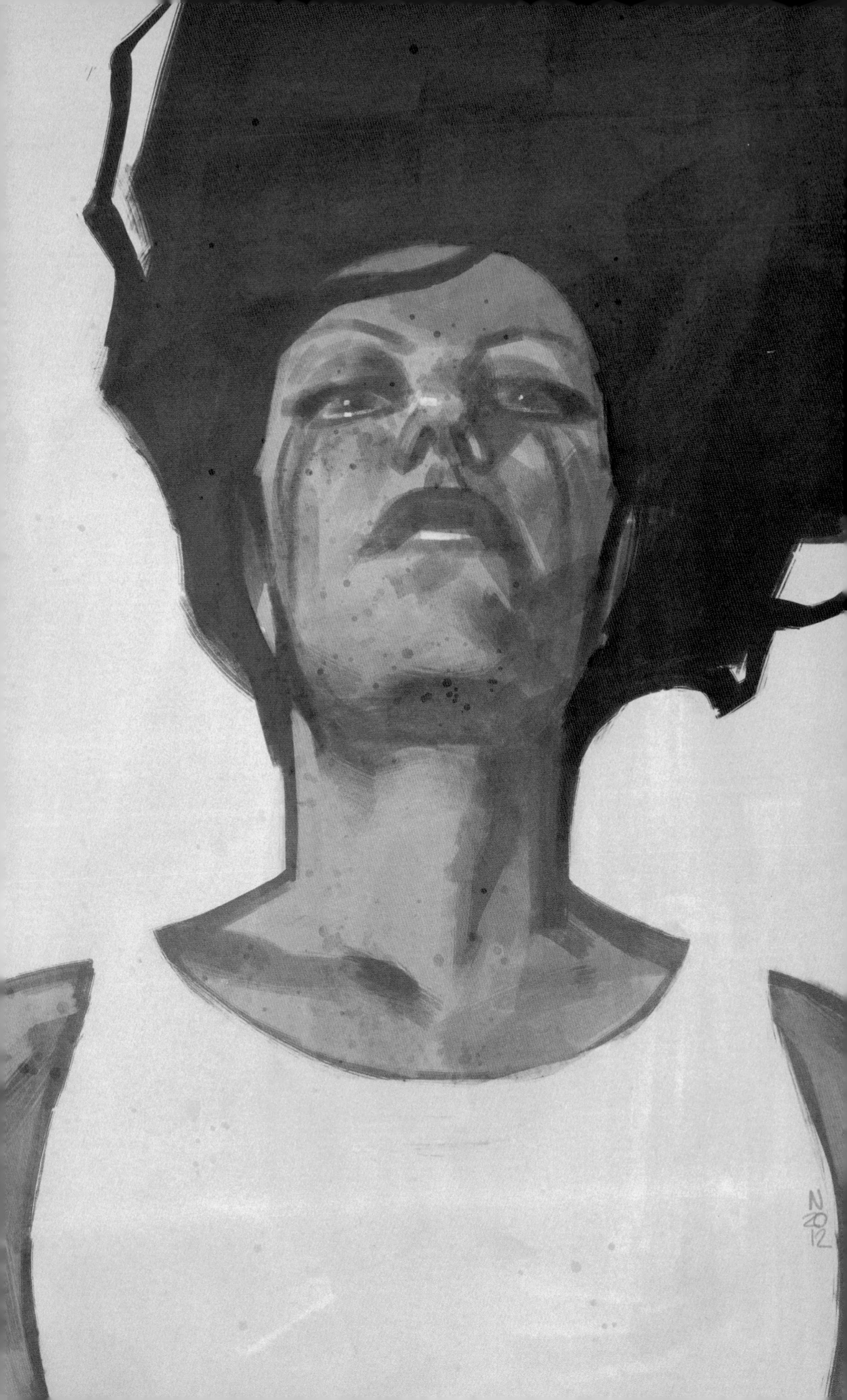
N
2012

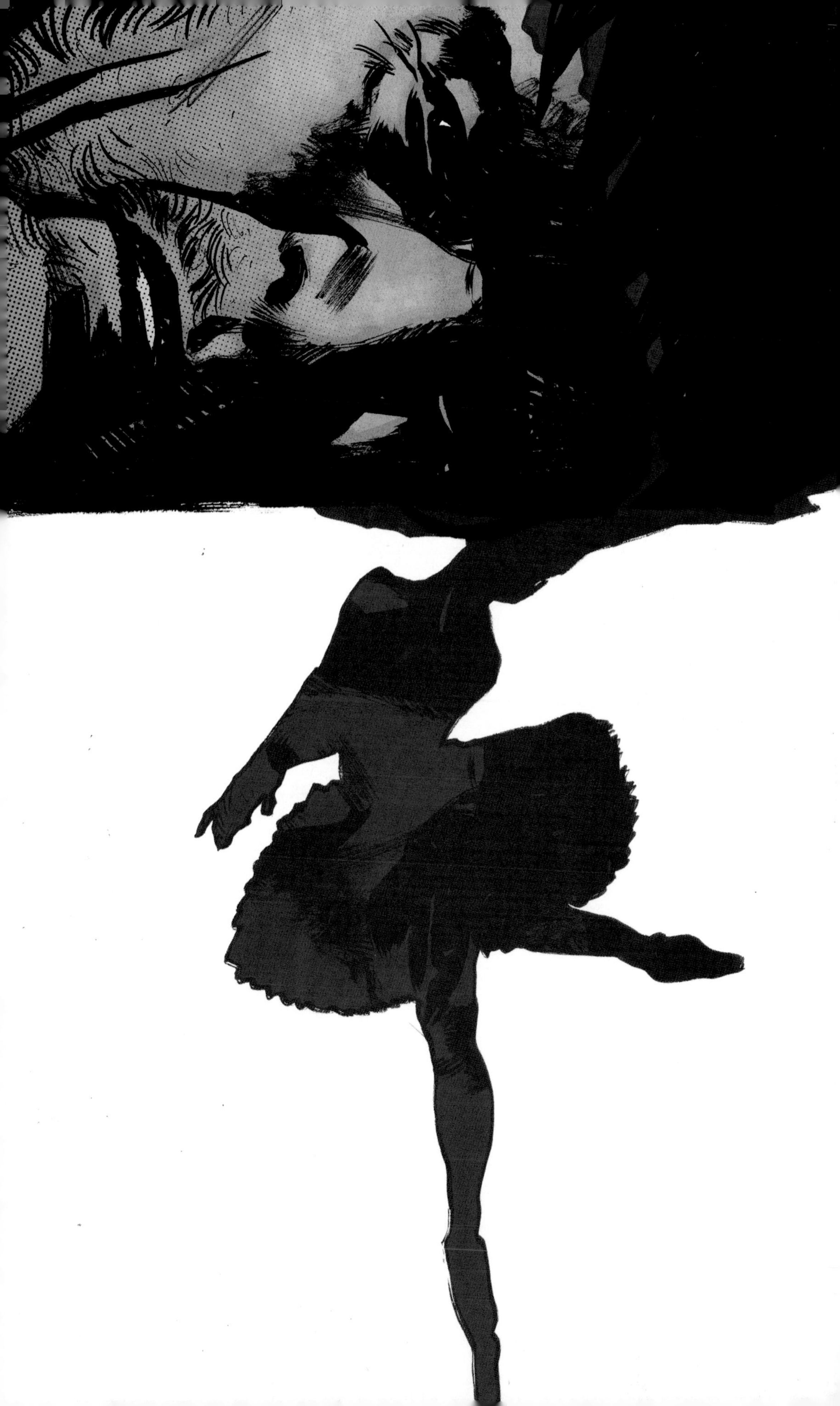

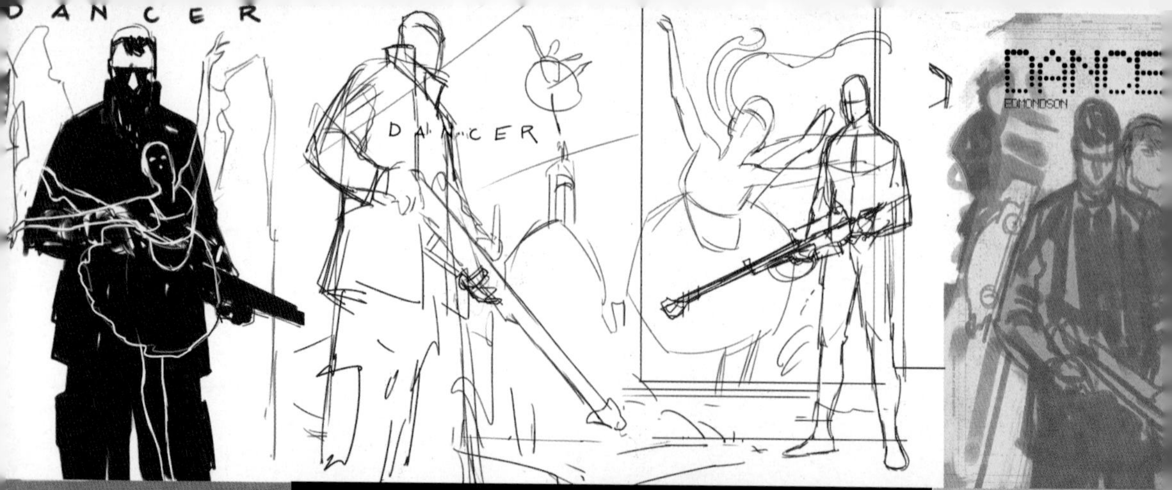
DANCER
DANCER
DANCE
EDMONDSON

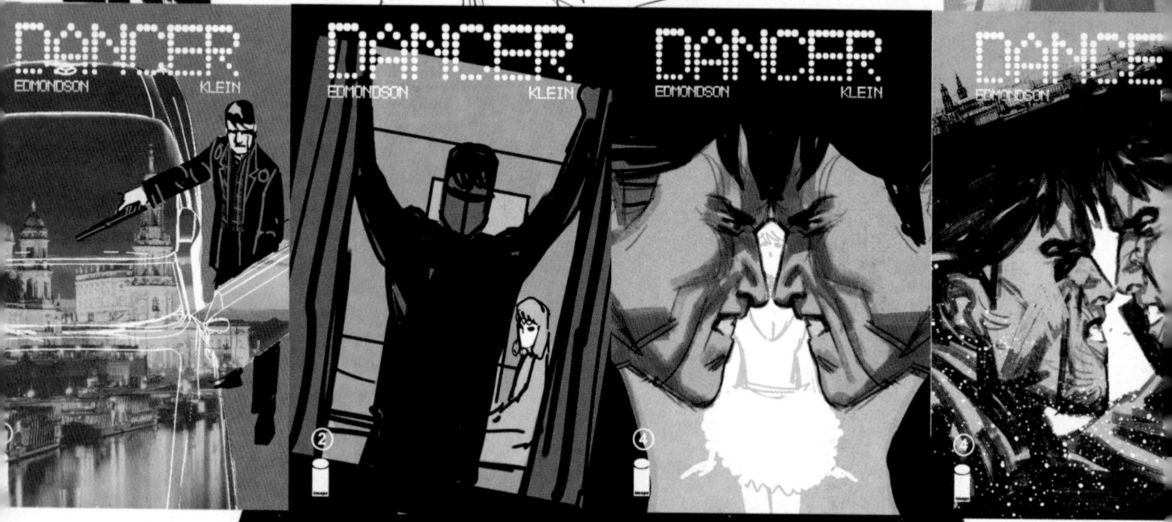
DANCER
EDMONDSON
KLEIN
DANCER
EDMONDSON
KLEIN
2
DANCER
EDMONDSON
KLEIN
4
DANCE
EDMONDSON
4

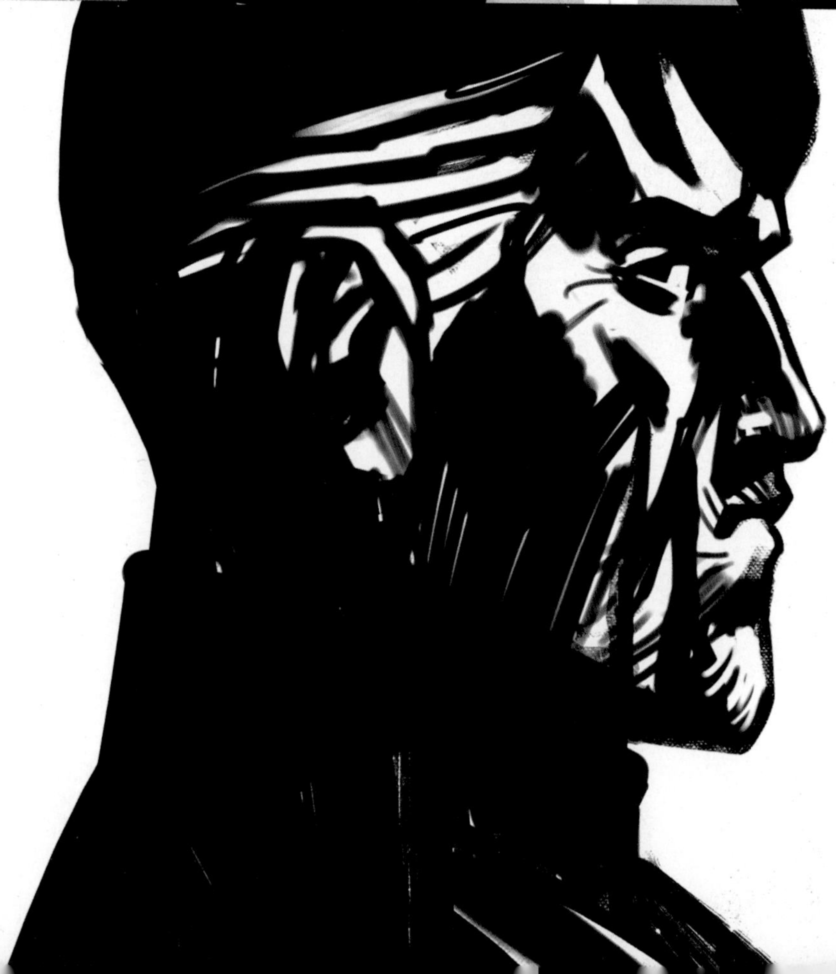

NATHAN EDMONDSON is the writer and co-creator of OLYMPUS, THE LIGHT, THE ACTIVITY and the Eisner nominated WHO IS JAKE ELLIS? He has also penned ULTIMATE IRON MAN, PUNISHER: MAX and GRIFTER. He lives in Georgia with his wife and daughter.
Find him at www.nathan-e.com

NIC KLEIN is the co-creator of VIKING and the artist for a number of different projects in and out of comics, among them WINTER SOLDIER, DOC SAVAGE and JSA.
He lives in Kassel, Germany with his fiancée Katrin.
Find him at www.nic-klein.com

JEFF POWELL can be found at negativeink.com

ENJOY THESE OTHER GREAT BOOKS BY NATHAN EDMONDSON & NIC KLEIN

WHO IS
JAKE
ELLIS?
NATHAN EDMONDSON
TONČI ZONJIĆ

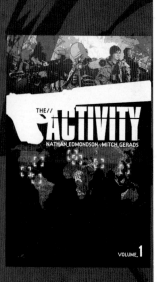

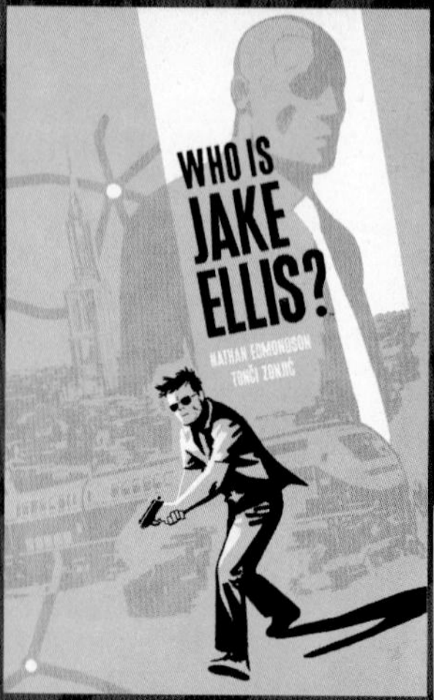

WHO IS JAKE ELLIS?

The Eisner-nominated multi-ple-sellout mini-series Newsarama calls "a modern noir package that is not to be missed" and MTV "couldn"t put down!" Jon Moore is a mercenary spy on the run across Europe, protected only by Jake Ellis, a man invisible to everyone except Jon.

...607064596
...78-

VIKING
THE LONG
COLD FIRE
IVAN BRANDON
NIC KLEIN

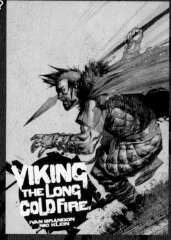

VIKING

The most violent criminal underworld in history! Finn and Egil, brothers - one bad, one worse - are trying to stab and steal their way to a seat at the table. Two men at war with the world around them. But today's the day the world fights back! From the writer of The Cross Bronx comes a crime book for the 9th Century.

ISBN-10: 1607061694
ISBN-13: 978-1607061694

$16.99

THE//
ACTIVITY
NATHAN EDMONDSON//MITCH GERADS
VOLUME 1

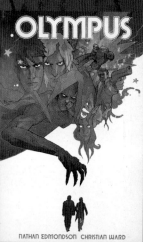

...TIVITY

...ion of global con- ...sitates the evolu- ...fare to rise and ...call. The United ...est, most ad- ...d most secret ...erations group is ...ide the INTELLI- ...UPPORT ACTIV- ...are tasked with ...ched operations, ...bleeding-edge tech, ...ing and executing ...action in the utmost ...y.

...10: 1607065614
...13: 978-1607065616

...99

NATHAN EDMONDSON
BRETT WELDELE
THE LIGHT

THE LIGHT

It is as sudden as it is deadly. Its origins are un-known. When it strikes, a father must risk all to protect his daughter and escape across the Oregon country-side - before they are infect-ed by THE LIGHT! Prepare yourself for the wildly ac-claimed horror-thriller from writer Nathan Edmondson and artist Brett Weldele. Learn to love the darkness; learn to fear THE LIGHT

ISBN-10: 160706345X
ISBN-13: 978-1607063452

$16.99

OLYMPUS
NATHAN EDMONDSON CHRISTIAN WARD

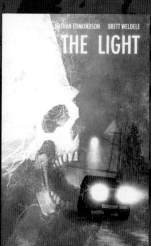

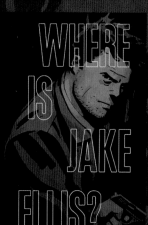

OLYMPUS

Sent to capture a messen-ger fallen from Olympus, the immortal Gemini brothers accidentally release one of the fiercest prisoners of Hades. Now Castor and Pollux must track and cap-ture this being before his rampant rage yields irrevers-ible damage to the balance between Olympus and the Earth.

ISBN-10: 1607061783
ISBN-13: 978-1607061786

$14.99

WHERE
IS
JAKE
ELLIS?

WHERE IS JAKE ELLIS?

Coming November 2012: Jon Moore is back, but this time he doesn't have Jake to help him.